REVOLUTION FROM ABOVE

Tariq Ali was born in Lahore in 1943, and educated there and at Exeter College, Oxford, where he read Politics, Philosophy and Economics. A leading radical leader of the Sixties, Ali is a member of the editorial committee of *New Left Review* and Co-Producer of Channel 4's *Bandung File*. He has several previous books to his credit, including *Street Fighting Years: An Autobiography of the Sixties*, published to great acclaim in 1987.

TARIQ ALI

Revolution From Above

WHERE IS THE SOVIET UNION GOING?

HUTCHINSON

London Sydney Auckland Johannesburg

This edition first published in 1988 by Hutchinson,
an imprint of Century Hutchinson Ltd, Brookmount House,
62–65 Chandos Place, London WC2N 4NW

Century Hutchinson Australia (Pty) Ltd
89–91 Albion Street, Surry Hills, NSW 2010

Century Hutchinson New Zealand Ltd
PO Box 40-086, Glenfield, Auckland 10, New Zealand

Century Hutchinson South Africa (Pty) Ltd
PO Box 337, Bergvlei, 2012 South Africa

Tariq, Ali, *1943–*
    Revolution from above : where is the Soviet
    Union going?
    1. Soviet Union. Political parties.
    Conferences
    I. Title
    324.247′075

ISBN 0-09-173843-1 (paper)
ISBN 0-09-174022-3

Typeset by Avocet Marketing Services, Bicester, Oxon.

Printed and bound in Great Britain by
Anchor Brendon Ltd, Tiptree, Essex

CONTENTS

For
Boris Kagarlitsy, socialist writer and activist
who helped to found the Popular Front for Perestroika
in Moscow
and
Boris Yeltsin a leading member of the
Communist Party of the Soviet Union, whose political
courage has made him an important symbol throughout the
country.

ACKNOWLEDGMENTS

In the Soviet Union I would like to thank Mariam Salganik and Robert Rozhdestvensky of the Writers' Union, whose kindness and help cannot be under-estimated. I would also like to thank the following people, who gave up valuable time to see me and talk about the events in their country: Yuri Afanasiev, Alexander Adamovich, Victor Gershfeld, Boris Kagarlitsky, Julius Kagarlitsky, Yuri Karyakin, Juan Kobo, Aider Kurkchi, Vladimir Maximenko, Pyotr Siuda, Nodari Simonia and Viktoria Tokareva. A very special thanks must go to my interpreter, Natasha Stepanova, who performed heroically in the circumstances.

The following read parts of the manuscript, and offered extremely useful advice, in some cases despite disagreements with my main argument: Robin Blackburn, Peter Gowan, Tamara Deutscher, Daniel Singer, Judith Schapiro and Susan Watkins. Judith Schapiro was also kind enough to translate the whole of Boris Yeltsin's speech from *Pravda* and the debate between Afanasiev and the editors of the paper for me. Peter Gowan, a friend and comrade for over twenty years, was decisive in ensuring that I sat down and wrote the book! Conversations I have had with him over two decades helped a great deal.

At Century Hutchinson, I would like to thank Anthony Cheetham and Richard Cohen for suggesting that I do the book in the first place. I would also like to thank Kate Mosse, my editor, whose encouragement and support was greatly appreciated. My agent, Andrew Nurnberg, who is a regular visitor to the Soviet Union, offered much useful advice. Paul Sullivan, the Librarian at Bandung Productions, ensured that I was kept well-supplied with Soviet periodicals.

For *Revolution From Above*, more than any other book, it is essential to point out that none of the people I saw and met, or those who kindly read any of the material, are *in any way* responsible for the conclusions drawn, or for my various eccentricities. They are all absolved in advance.

And lastly, thanks are due to my children, Natasha, Chengiz and Aisha. The first two maintained a heroic, Leninist self-discipline so that I could write in peace. Aisha displayed a disturbing streak of anarchism. Fortunately, it did not totally disrupt this project.

Tariq Ali
August 1988

ILLUSTRATIONS

Chapter 1
Erik Bulatov, *Perestroika*, 1988.

Chapter 2
Erik Bulatov, *Unanimously*, 1987.

Chapter 3
Arkadii Petrov, *In Chair Park, Roses are Blooming*, 1988. The title is taken from a ballad of the Stalinist era.

Chapter 4
Omitrii Zhilinskii, *The Year 1937*, 1987.

Chapter 5
Alexei Sundukov, *Station*, 1986.

Chapter 6
Alexei Sundukov, *Peaks*, 1987.

Chapter 7
Konstantin Zvezdochetov, *Perdo*, 1987.

Chapter 8
Federation of Soviet Clubs, Leningrad, 1988.

Illustrations for Chapters 1–7 are © Matthew Cullerne Bown: the work of the artists concerned is illustrated in more detail in his forthcoming book *Contemporary Russian Art*, Phaidon Press.

PREFACE

Throughout the late Sixties and Seventies a new generation in Western Europe was attracted to socialist and Marxist ideas. In a number of Northern European countries, however, the attempts by radicalised students to find a bridgehead within the working class was often met with an unfriendly response. 'Why don't you go back to Russia?' was a common refrain. In vain did one explain that socialists of our sort would probably end up in a corrective labour colony or a psychiatric ward. The argument, alas, never went beyond this initial exchange since the other party was not really interested in debate. But the 'Russian question' could not really be avoided. My own political formation had been greatly influenced by the writings of Isaac Deutscher, Leon Trotsky and Ernest Mandel (in that order) and it was through their mediation that I began to understand the real meaning of the classics of socialist thought: the writings of Marx, Engels, Lenin, Luxemburg and others. This tradition helped in both observing and denouncing the crimes of Stalin, or of Khrushchev (invasion of Hungary) or Brezhnev (invasion of Czechoslovakia, intervention in Afghanistan) or the many atrocities and injustices that were perpetrated within the borders of the USSR. These were not 'socialist' crimes, but crimes against socialism. One could say that from the vantage point of an independent and critical Marxist tradition. It was not necessary, to put it mildly, to go over to the other side and become a professional anti-communist. However, the very fact that the Soviet Union existed—despite the subjective intentions of its leaders—was of enormous importance in understanding the relationship of forces in the world.

When I first visited the USSR in the summer of 1965 there was a depression in the air. In both Moscow and Leningrad the party liberals had gone underground. Very few people were prepared to talk. I remember asking numerous Soviet communists why Khrushchev had been toppled and receiving a glum look in response. I travelled through the Soviet Union again in 1970 and 1972 when Brezhnev was settling down to a long reign. There was greater prosperity, but on the political front Soviet society appeared static. At least on the surface there was very little movement.

Then in 1979 came the invasion of Afghanistan. I was horrified. This reaction had little to do with pacifism. I thought—and still do—that the Vietnamese entry into Kampuchea to get rid of Pol Pot was necessary, albeit unfortunate. I think that the Cuban decision to go to the defence of Angola against South Africa was essential. Both these moves were backed by the Soviet Union. Even if the motives were impure and based on the needs of real-politik (USSR/USA relations had reached their nadir with the victory of Reagan) they happened to coincide with the demands of a popular and progressive cause. In Afghanistan this was not the case. As Editor of a small socialist weekly at the time, *Socialist Challenge*, I drafted and published an editorial comment under the headline: 'SOVIET TROOPS OUT OF AFGHANISTAN'. This virtually isolated me on the international Left, especially in the Indian subcontinent where the Soviet intervention received near-universal support and was welcomed as a blow against imperialism. I recall arguing with Pakistani socialists who were convinced that Afghanistan would now be 'saved' and virtually integrated into the USSR. This was seen as both desirable and possible. For me it was neither.

Even in Western Europe the Left was slow to understand the dynamics of Afghan society and the likely consequences of the intervention. I had written that the right of the Afghan people to self-determination could not be ignored simply because it was a backward society. On a number of occasions I questioned the description of the Leftwing coup as a 'revolution'. I even predicted that sooner or later the Soviet Union would need the help of the deposed monarch to restore order. It was true that the various groups fighting against the Russians and the warring factions in power were light years removed from anything vaguely progressive. It was equally true that the United States, utilising the military regime in Pakistan as a conduit, was killing Soviet soldiers by proxy: but none of this could justify the Soviet presence. In fact it became clear that the presence of Soviet troops in Afghanistan removed the question of a popular progressive government in that country from the agenda for a long, long time.

I write this because when I visited Tashkent, the capital of Uzbekistan, in April 1985 to speak at a United Nations conference on 'Peace and Security in Asia', I was not prepared for what I heard. The Soviet delegation consisted of a couple of people who had played some part in the discussion on Afghanistan. Both were senior members of the delegation. Given the sharp critiques I had made of

Soviet policy in Afghanistan, I expected an onslaught in return.
Instead I was amazed to find a great deal of agreement. In private,
one of the Soviet delegates even told me that he agreed with me
completely—that the whole invasion had been based on false
premises, that Brezhnev had used Afghanistan to show the
Americans what he could do, that there had been a division on the
Politburo and that the only solution was to create the conditions for
a rapid withdrawal. Gorbachev had only been in power for a few
weeks, but one could sense the relief. This conversation in Tashkent
made me think very seriously about the inner dynamics of Soviet
society. It was obvious that a great deal of discussion was taking
place both in the Institutes and inside the Communist Party itself.
Despite the fact that one should have been theoretically prepared for
this, practice had willed otherwise. Strong opposition to Soviet
policies in Czechoslovakia and Afghanistan as well as the creeping
Stalinisation inside the country had dominated my thoughts. Nor is
it the case that independent socialists in the West are totally immune
to the sustained cold war offensive. In Tashkent I was repeatedly
asked to come again so that we could discuss problems apart from
Afghanistan.

In 1988 I visited the Soviet Union twice—on both occasions as a
guest of the Writers Union—but I determined my own agenda and
met people whom I wanted to meet. One of the reasons for my trip
was to study the Moscow of the Twenties in connection with a novel
I am writing, but the present insisted on intruding forcefully and I
soon found my thoughts concentrating on what was taking place
now. What I saw was a country at the beginning of a major
transformation, which few had predicted or foreseen. Despite the
regular reportage in some Western papers it was only when I was in
Moscow itself that I understood the scale of what is being attempted.
I renewed old acquaintances and made new friends. The shared
excitement of a new political movement creates new friendships and
rapidly. I met people who shared the same aspirations and spoke a
similar political language. Suddenly I saw Moscow as the most
exciting political capital in the world. I felt really at home. This was
not the result of 'Gorby-mania'. It was simply that the first breath of
pluralism had transformed the atmosphere. Whether one spoke to
members of the Communist Party or the 'unofficial' activists, the
mood was one of hope. This was extremely refreshing, especially if
one compared the situation to the gloom-laden voices of socialists in
retreat in Western Europe and North America. By contrast Moscow

was bubbling with excitement. Everyone was talking about politics and openly discussing their hopes and fears.

It was this that made me want to write about the rebirth of hope in the Soviet Union. Only a deadened sectarian or a cynical hack could remain unaffected. Some prefer to suspend belief or interpret only the negative phenomena: wait for mistakes to be made and then shout a triumphant 'I told you so!' with a smug smile. There are, of course, many people inside and outside the Soviet Union who want Gorbachev to fail. This book is not for them. Occasionally I encounter socialists who were totally uncritical of Solidarity in Poland. I don't wish to be misunderstood. I, too, supported Solidarity and demonstrated outside the Polish Embassy. But few on the Left who backed the Polish workers' uprising were bothered by the fact that it had more powerful supporters than ourselves: Reagan, Thatcher and the Pope. It was crucial that socialists supported the great uprising of the Polish working class, but I must confess that I, for one, found the sight of Polish workers on their knees before the Bishop of Rome, clutching their crucifixes in ecstasy, a distasteful sight. Yet a number of the veterans who could stomach the crucifix and the Pope are nervous about perestroika. Why? Because it is a movement from above. They would have preferred (me too!) if the changes in the Soviet Union had been brought about by a gigantic movement of the Soviet working class and had revived the old organs of political power—the soviets—with totally new blood. That would have been very nice, but it didn't happen in that way. What has happened is a movement from above which has ignited the country. This book explores the conflicts inside and outside the party and argues that if Gorbachev succeeds the socialist project will have received a tremendous boost.

In a book of this sort, written in the process of a battle which is not yet finished and whose outcome is still uncertain, it is necessary to marry historical and political analysis with new and relevant facts as they emerge. This has necessitated repeating certain relevant facts throughout the narrative, something which reflects the very nature of the struggle inside the Soviet Union today. Since history and political theory are permanently on the frontline, many episodes reappear time after time in altered contexts.

Naturally any final judgement has to be delayed until matters are finally resolved in the Soviet Union. It is much easier to worship accomplished facts, but that is not the aim of this little book. It is, frankly, designed as a political intervention from the Left in a debate taking place inside the USSR. The Right intervenes permanently and on every level: state relations, trade, media offensives, etc. The Left, alas, has only its ideas, and therefore to either adopt a 'wait-and-see' approach or 'a plague on all the houses in the CPSU' stance, would be highly irresponsible at this particular time.

Revolution From Above argues that Gorbachev represents a progressive, reformist current within the Soviet elite, whose programme, if successful, would represent an enormous gain for socialists and democrats on a world scale. The scale of Gorbachev's operation is, in fact, reminiscent of the efforts of an American President of the nineteenth century: Abraham Lincoln. In order to preserve the Union, Lincoln had to push through a second American revolution based on the abolition of slavery. In order to preserve the Soviet Union, Gorbachev needs to complete the political revolution (which is already under way), but one based on an abolition of the whole nomenklatura* system of privileges on which the power of the Soviet bureaucracy rests. The abolition of the bureaucratic caste is as vital to Gorbachev's success as the elimination of slavery was for Lincoln's cause. If the latter had realised this earlier, a great deal of bloodshed might have been avoided. The analogy is not as far-fetched as it sounds. The emergence of nationalist tensions in various parts of the Soviet Union (Baltic states, Armenia and Aizerbaijan today and the Ukraine tomorrow?) can only be combatted by recreating, so to speak, the Communist Party as a popular and progressive force. For this pluralism is vital inside the party and state. This thread, in fact, runs throughout the book. I am not one of those who favour the break-up of the Soviet Union. That is one of Washington's craziest projects and needs to be seen in that light. But the only way to combat the regressive national tensions is to embark on a totally new political project. It is, of course, a risky enterprise, but a necessary one if the Soviet Union is to be genuinely strengthened. This book from afar is designed to aid and analyse that process. It will, I am sure, make some on the Left apoplectic, but that will be a good thing.

---

*Nomenklatura is a special Party-bureaucratic strategem, which consists of people in the highest positions in the USSR. It is a synonym for the privileged Soviet élite.

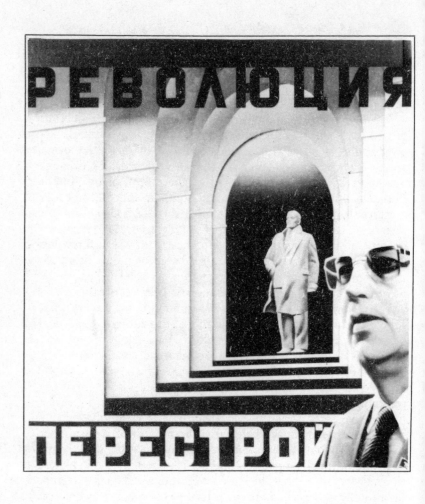

Erik Bulatov, *Perestroika,* 1988.

1. THE NEW RENAISSANCE
Politics in the Gorbachev Era

Imagine socialism
freed of everything
that upsets you
Ask yourself
Who then would be really upset
He and no other is
and remains
your real enemy

Erich Fried, *100 Poems Without A Country*

The Soviet Union is once again pregnant with possibilities. History's capacity to startle remains unimpaired. Dogmas of every variety are under threat. We are still at the beginnings of the process which has popularised two Russian words all over the world: glasnost and perestroika. Nonetheless the changes inaugurated at the Twenty-Seventh Party Congress in February 1986, mark the most decisive phase in the country's history since 1924. It is too early to predict how it will all end. There are many powerful forces inside and outside the USSR who would prefer a reversion to the old *status quo*. Enough has happened to make them realise that a great deal is at stake. In any event, the Soviet Union today has become far too important to be left to the 'experts'.

For several decades of this century—characterised by Lenin as an 'epoch of wars and revolutions'—popular attitudes to socialism have been governed by a powerful myth: that Stalinism and socialism are one and the same thing. The strong hold that this myth has exercised is explained by a simple correlation of interests: the Stalinist bureaucracy and the ruling classes in the West collaborated in fostering the notion that the only possible form of socialism was what existed in the USSR. The repetitions in China, Indochina and even Cuba, only strengthened this view. 'There is no other way!' was the unified message emanating from Washington and Moscow, Beijing and Pyongyang, Hanoi and Havana. There were, of course, regional variations, but the essential model applied had its origins in the Soviet Union of the Thirties.

The result of all this has been extremely damaging to the socialist project in the heartlands of capital. Without a clear idea of the future socialist society and with the only existing models unacceptable to workers used to collective bargaining and other freedoms, it is hardly surprising that there has been no breakthrough in the West since the Second World War. The Portuguese revolution of 1974–75 encountered these problems most graphically and foundered on the rock of the Stalinist model of socialism. The intellectual consequences too of the degeneration of the Soviet state have been extremely severe and since the untimely death of the Polish Marxist historian Isaac Deutscher in 1967, there has been very little systematic analysis of the Soviet Union from the Left.

During the first three months of 1967, Deutscher delivered the Trevelyan Lectures at Cambridge, the fiftieth anniversary year of October 1917. From his watchtower, Deutscher observed the jubilee celebrations in Moscow and commented:

> People are asked to celebrate the great anniversary, but they cannot read a single trustworthy account of the events they are celebrating. (Nor can they get hold of any history of the Civil War.) The ideological edifice of Stalinism has been exploded; but, with its foundations shattered, its roof blown off, and its walls charred and threatening to come down with a crash, the structure still stands; and the people are required to live in it.*

He spoke about the 'blessings and curses of the continuity of the Soviet regime'. It had survived. There had been no restoration of the old order as had followed the great bourgeois revolutions in England and France. The Romanovs would never return, of this Deutscher was confident. But, in polar contrast to other writers on the USSR he did not see a society without movement. However repressive the situation, however grim the conditions in the camps, the Communist Party continued to reflect some of the currents that existed below the surface. Deutscher ended his lectures with a prophecy:

> Soviet society cannot reconcile itself for much longer to remaining a mere object of history and being dependent on the whims of autocrats or the arbitrary decisions of oligarchies. It needs to regain the sense of being its own master. It needs to obtain control of its governments and to transform the State, which has so long towered above society, into an instrument of the nation's democratically expressed will and interest. It needs, in the first instance, to re-establish freedom of expression and association. This is a modest aspiration compared with the ideal of a classless and stateless society...

---

*The talks were later published as *The Unfinished Revolution: Russia 1917–67*, Oxford University Press, 1968. A special edition was translated into Russian for restricted use: it is confined to the library of the Central Committee!

These views are today shared by a very large number of people in the Soviet Union, including, some of the top leaders of the country! The revival of politics, and the flowering of culture since April 1985, has once again concentrated the attention of the world on the Soviet Union. But this time it is seen as a model for something which is not only positive, but something which holds the key to the future. For the first time since the Twenties, Moscow is seen as the capital of hope. Of course different people hope for different things. The President of the United States and big business interests in the West have never given up their plans to restore private capitalism in the USSR. They could not do it by force, but as they view the Soviet Union with greedy eyes they wonder whether they will now be able to do it peacefully. The late E.H. Carr, one of the most widely respected non-Marxist experts on Soviet history, once remarked that everyone—both Right and Left—tends to project their own concerns on to the USSR. As events in the Soviet Union transform public opinion in the West, Reagan buries 'the evil empire'; Mrs Thatcher praises Gorbachev on a special BBC Russian Service 'phone-in'; film-maker David Puttnam tells an audience of film students in Brighton that Gorbachev reminds him of Kennedy; Britain's most effective socialist pamphleteer, Paul Foot, writes that Gorbachev is the Soviet equivalent of Neil Kinnock and Martin Jacques, editor of the British Communist Party's journal, *Marxism Today*, sees him as the man who will reconcile socialism and capitalism.

The chanceries in Europe, East and West, are agog with nervous excitement. How far will he go? Tired bureaucrats in East Berlin and Prague, placed in power by Soviet tanks and sycophantic mimics of everything Russian, now begin to mutter aloud that there exist different models of socialism and they are not necessarily obliged to follow the Soviet pattern. The ironies of history are truly limitless. In Bonn and Tokyo they ask whether the new situation could mean bilateral negotiations. A great deal is at stake.

In the Soviet Union itself a storm is raging. Its tempo is varied, but whenever it intensifies there is a loud crash as doors of old cupboards fall open and the skeletons organise a mass escape. Politics, history and culture are beginning to reflect the effects of this turmoil. Frightened bureaucrats console each other in their shelters. They are waiting for the storm to subside so that they can come out again and put up the old signboard which reads: BUSINESS AS USUAL. A curious form of dual power exists in the Soviet Union today. On the face of it, it seems to be the reformers' turn, and they certainly appear to be in an incredibly powerful position. But is this really the case? Is it going to be a permanent turn this time? Few rank-and-file members would go so far as to admit this. Of course, political power is not equally divided, nor is there a carefully worked out equilibrium of forces inside the party and state. However, the fact is that the reformers are in the ascendant and by challenging the old ideological basis of the party they have seriously split the superstructure of the state.

How did things get this far? It is often assumed in the West that the long, usually boring and badly delivered speeches of CPSU leaders at Party congresses are nothing more than sterile and meaningless phraseology. But this was actually not the case during the Brezhnev period. True, the speeches were always lacklustre, but the dullness often concealed real contents. Now, under Gorbachev it has become very obvious that real politics and economics are discussed at congresses, conferences, plenums and politburos. Much of the debate is of an infinitely higher level than, for example, the average debate in the British House of Commons. One real problem for the Western reader and writer—particularly hostile ones largely ignorant of the culture of the Party—was grasping the context of the meaning, and therefore the substance of what might seem to be trite phrases and quotations from Lenin. As an example one could cite Mikhail Gorbachev's report to the Twenty-Seventh Party Congress. As usual in such reports, Gorbachev began with Lenin:

> Lenin wrote back in 1917 that Marx and Engels rightly ridiculed the 'mere memorising and repetition of formulas, that at best are capable only of marking out general tasks, which are necessarily modifiable by the *concrete* economic and political conditions of each particular *period* of the historical process'. Those are the words comrades, that every one of us must ponder and act upon.

These seemingly innocuous Marxist cliches would have been both intensely familiar and profoundly disturbing to most Congress delegates listening to the opening remarks of the new General Secretary. For Gorbachev was referring to one of the most decisive moments in the history of the Bolshevik Party, the days that followed Lenin's arrival at the Finland Station in the spring of 1917. The quotation was from Lenin's famous, brief statement to a joint meeting of the Bolshevik and Menshevik factions before the April Conference. Lenin was throwing overboard an orthodoxy that had governed the strategy and tactics of Russian Bolshevism throughout its history. The view that what was at stake in Tsarist Russia was *not* a pure, proletarian upheaval but a hybrid characterised as the 'Democratic Dictatorship of the Proletariat and Peasantry'. This concept was backed by the entire party leadership when the February Revolution erupted that year. With Lenin in exile and Trotsky still not in the Bolshevik Party, the party's leadership decided in accordance with their theory to give critical support to the Provisional Government. If that line had continued there would have been no October Revolution in the Tsarist Empire. At the April 1917 Conference where Lenin had presented his famous 'theses' he therefore had to overcome the opposition of the entire leadership in favour of a line that had been argued by Trotsky and his comrades in the Inter-District Committee (an influential, but small group) which put forward the view that the democratic revolution (February) was growing into a socialist revolution (October). It was after Lenin's theses were accepted that Trotsky and his group asked to join—and were admitted into the ranks of—the Bolshevik Party. Lenin now had a powerful ally.

These facts were not written about in the Soviet Union, in the decades that followed Lenin's death in 1924, but they were talked about a great deal. So Gorbachev's listeners in February 1986 would have understood (and many did, especially his opponents) that the use of this particular reference to Lenin implied that what was at stake was nothing less than an assault on the entire tradition of the present CPSU (a tradition, it should be pointed out, that dates back to the Thirties). Gorbachev was calling into question the entire programmatic orientation of the Party and *this* was what he was demanding 'that every one of us must ponder and act upon'. Gorbachev followed the quotation from Lenin with the following words:

> In these days, many things, in fact everything, will depend upon how effectively we will succeed in using the advantages and possibilities of the socialist system ... in bringing the out of date social patterns and methods of work abreast of the changed conditions.

So we note that *everything*—the entire future of the Soviet state and of the Communist Party—is at stake in the current turn. If it fails, everything could fail. Anyone who wants to understand what is happening in the USSR has to try and understand the meaning of these words. What is being stated is that a crucial section of the Soviet leadership considers that the state and party are facing one of the most serious crises in its history. Gorbachev is arguing that the

Party is not politically prepared for confronting and overcoming this crisis.

What are the origins of this crisis and what is the nature of the forces within the Soviet hierarchy who are trying to surmount it and move forward? It is only if we can not simply pose, but also answer these questions, that it becomes possible to unravel the dynamics of Soviet politics and the possible alternatives available to the leadership currently in power.

In 1985, when Mikhail Gorbachev became General Secretary there was no indication that the USSR and even more the Soviet leadership was facing any political crisis whatsoever. There was no internal opposition of any significance, the dissident movement having been totally isolated and defeated by 1980, many of its leading voices in exile. There were no signs of any serious discontent within the working class; the intellegentsia was in a mood of utter despair and was completely cowed; the economy, it is true, was not performing well, but then this was nothing new and, at least, it was still growing, which was more than could be said for a number of capitalist states in the early Eighties. The very tricky and sensitive problem of leadership transition from the corrupt Brezhnevite gerontocracy had been handed with ruthless skill by Andropov. The partial throw-back involved in the grotesque Chernenko interlude in 1984 had been nothing more than a brief pause before the forward march was resumed. On the external front the United States had assumed a menacing posture, but the Soviet leaders were fully aware that any first strike by the 'princes of darkness' in the US administration would not lead to an American victory, but mutual obliteration. Thus the Soviet leadership did not agree with the central thesis of peace leaders in the West who argued that 'exterminism' had its own laws which transcended politics. Even where there were regional conflicts the USSR was not threatened by any massive pressure. Afghanistan was a big mess, but a defeat of the USSR in military terms was inconceivable. So where was the crisis?

It is difficult for pundits in the West to appreciate this, but the fact was that the crisis was located within the apparatus of the Soviet Communist Party itself. It was an acute crisis of political orientation and programmatic direction. A very significant section of the party élite simply did not believe that they could carry on in the same, old Brezhnevite way, neither at home nor abroad. They felt that to continue within the existing policy framework would eventually lead to catastrophe and they could sense its approach. After all, the bells had been tolling in Eastern Europe since 1953. First East Berlin, then Budapest, then Poznan, then Prague, then Gdansk, and then?

It would be completely false to assume that this perception— namely the bankruptcy of the old framework—emerged fully-formulated out of the head of one person: Mikhail Gorbachev. Some even portrayed him as a kind of mole who finally burrowed his way into the Politburo, waited and, then, when the time was ripe, discarded his moleskin and sank his 'teeth of steel'* into the plump posteriors of the bureaucrats who surrounded him. This is an entertaining vision, but belongs to the realm of fiction, for the Brezhnev period was not some 'oriental despotism' where nobody in power ever aired their real views on any subject and where nobody knew for certain what anybody else was really thinking. Only in such a set-up could somebody get the top job without anyone at least suspecting what the new leader believed or thought.

Gorbachev was one of a number of reform-minded, modern and sophisticated lower-echelon leaders from a younger generation which had grown up in the Brezhnevite stable. It is easy to forget, especially now, that there were two sides to the Brezhnev regime. There was the crushing of those on the extreme pro-Stalinist authoritarian wing (Semichastny and Shelepin) and the hardline radical democratisers (Rumyantsev, and lesser figures like Lev Karpinsky); but simultaneously there was an effort to incorporate as many as possible on both sides who were ready to accept the rules of the system, regardless of their own specific ideological beliefs. It was, therefore, perfectly possible for figures with widely varying trends of thought to survive and rise within the same apparatus, provided they were sound on procedural matters. In other words, so long as they accepted the vertical rules of politics within the apparatus.

Gorbachev was evidently 'sound' from this point of view, while remaining a proponent of modernising, democratic reforms. Perestroika, however, was not simply the child of the young, political reformers of the Brezhnev period. Even people whose styles and political methods were far removed from any notion of democracy were for liberalising the economy. In 1982 Yuri Andropov had understood better than most the importance of destroying the basis of the corrupt and parasitic mafias who had infested many pores of Soviet society during the Seventies. The people Andropov pulled to the top shared this belief, though they

*This was the phrase Gromyko used when nominating Gorbachev to his present post in April 1985.

were poles apart on many other issues. The need for a radical turn in policy was perceived by an overwhelming majority of the Soviet élite. It was not foisted upon the leadership by any particular faction. In August 1983, Andropov gave the signal that this was the case in his last speech before he disappeared from public life because of his illness.

Konstantin Chernenko, the last of the Brezhnevite dinosaurs, represented those who opposed Andropov's turn. The public expression of the political debate in the leadership was not as Aesopian as one might have thought. The dinosaurs concentrated on party ideology and Chernenko declared that the chief task was 'the further perfecting of Soviet Man'. The reformers maintained their unity by declaring that the chief ideological problem was the development of the economy. They stressed the importance of Lenin's New Economic Policy (NEP) to the problems of today. Their opponents argued that NEP was now irrelevant and had a purely tactical significance in the history of the 1920s, since it had been superceded by the achievement of socialism in the 1930s. Chernenko had by no means been the worst offender during the Brezhnev years. He was a great proponent of a real devolution of power to the localities and regions. In the early Eighties, however, that issue was not particularly relevant. The question was no longer one of how much tinkering was necessary to improve the old framework, but simply whether the political economy of Brezhnev-ism should be retained or not. The reformists had upped the stakes by making the economy the central *ideological* issue. They were saying that it was no longer a policy discussion, but a debate about the entire framework of the system. Further perfecting of Soviet *man,* to use Chernenko's phrase, was another way of saying that it was vital to retain the status quo. The debate on NEP was not a literary exercise. It put into question the entire ideological definition of Soviet 'socialism' since the Thirties. That definition had insisted that socialist development could be measured by a very simple yardstick: the degree of abolition of market forms within the Soviet economy. This was the criteria adopted to chart the progress of the economy. Thus the Thirties were better than the Twenties, and the Sixties were a step forward from the Fifties. Socialism was equated with autarchy. The bureaucratic immobilism and corruption of the Brezhnev years led to strong opposition from within the party. So, the apparatus scattered the oppositionists by despatching them as Ambassadors or sending them out to the provinces.

Andropov brought many of them back to Moscow and promoted them within the leadership. As mentioned, they were united by their agreement to transform the existing Brezhnevite framework. Who were these oppositionists? Ligachev (banished to Omsk by Brezhnev); Vorotnikov (sent to Havana), Yakovlev (despatched to Ottawa) as well as new, younger men from the Urals, like Ryzhkov and, yes, Boris Yeltsin. These were some of the people who strongly backed Gorbachev's rise to power.

The Soviet Union at the beginning of the Eighties was a predominantly industrialised society. The urban population represents an overwhelming majority: the soviet working class accounts for 61.5 percent of the population; the peasants are down to 20 percent and the 'specialists' or 'technocrats' (or, I suppose in a broad sense, 'the intelligentsia') make up the remainder. It is this latter group who, *de facto*, administer the country and are well represented in the middle and upper reaches of party and state. The social transformation of the USSR since the Second World War has thus resulted in a qualitative shift from country to town, with all that such a change entails. (This, incidentally, is a major difference between China and the USSR and could help the latter avoid or transcend most of the problems—ideological and economic—that afflict the People's Republic.) During the Brezhnevite phase there was a big improvement in the living standards of workers. Labour productivity, however, was extremely low and the slow growth rate of the Soviet population meant that it was impossible to deal with the problem by simply pouring more workers into the factories.

There was another important factor to consider. The Soviet working class was not only distinguished by its size. By the early 1980s, this was a highly educated proletariat by any standards. Workers during the three critical decades—from the late 1920s to the 1980s—had recently moved from the countryside. Stalin's collectivisation policies had wiped out every political tradition. They possessed, if anything, only a very elementary education. Today over 80 percent of the working class has been through some form of higher education. Add to this the generally higher level of culture in the Soviet Union than the West and it becomes easier to understand why even the more relcalcitrant elements within the bureaucracy were not prepared to openly oppose the programme of reforms.

Within the intelligentsia as a whole, but especially its cultural segment, the Brezhnev period marked the end of all hopes that reforms could ever come from within the Communist Party. In an excellent survey of the Soviet intelligentsia from 1917 to the present, a young Soviet intellectual, Boris Kargarlitsky, explained the near-total disillusionment which followed the Soviet invasion of Czechoslovakia in August 1968. The Khrushchev interregnum had reawakened a creative interest in politics and socialism. Perhaps, many began to feel, it had not been all in vain? Then Soviet tanks entered Prague to topple the Czech reformers and extinguish the hopes aroused by 'socialism with a human face'. According to Kagarlitsky the events of August destroyed liberal hopes in reform Communism in the USSR:

> On the morning of 21 August 1968 the entire ideology of Soviet liberalism collapsed in a few minutes, and all the hopes aroused by the Twentieth Congress fell to the ground. Whereas previously liberal intellectuals had comforted themselves with the thought that, on the whole, our society had a sound foundation, that it had not lost its socialist character, that—as Yevtushenko wrote in his *Autobiography* —the revolution was sick but not dead, the events of 1968 scattered those illusions. It was not a matter of the 'excesses of Stalinism' but of the system itself. For many, recognition of this fact meant spiritual and ideological collapse ...
> ... It was no accident that Solzhenitsyn, who after 1968 took up more frankly extreme right-wing positions, wrote: 'Those days, 21 and 22 August, were of crucial importance to me.' If until then the intelligentsia had retained some sympathy with socialism, in 1967-8 it disappeared. A frenzied quest began for new values to counterpose against the old. They wanted to burn not only what they had worshipped but also to worship what they had burned—although, in fact, what they worshipped and burned were often the same thing under different names.*

One of the dreams of the Soviet leaders had been to create, through mass education and the spread of culture (in the classical sense of the word), a gigantic new intelligentsia committed to the system. It could have been so, but history willed otherwise. The hopes of the old Leninists were brutally annulled by Stalinism. The enforced conformity, the concentration camps, the curtain of fear that enveloped the entire country during the Thirties was enough to promote cynicism and despair. Yet—and this is the amazing fact—many of those who returned from the camps in the Fifties did so with their hopes unimpaired, some looking forward to a new future. Others, however, were cynical as they observed many of

---

The Thinking Reed by Boris Kagarlitsky, Verso, 1988.

Stalin's ideological torturers now masquerading as reformists. Despair and scepticism took over completely during the Seventies. The proletarianisation of the population, coupled with its educational and technical level, provided a strong base for a total renewal of the country's social and political structures. Repression of sections of the intelligentsia actually increased, at the same time as the Soviet press relapsed into a primitivism which bore more than a few similarities with traditional Stalinism.

The existence of bureaucratic pluralism, however, safeguarded party members, and within the Institutes through the Brezhnev period discontent was often expressed in both verbal and written form. Of all the members of the Politburo during this phase, Andropov understood better than most the necessity for change. As Ambassador to Hungary in 1956 he had observed at firsthand what could happen in the absence of reforms. He had met Imry Nagy, the leader of reform Communism in Hungary, many times and the Soviet intervention had left its mark on him. It is not known whether or not Andropov expressed any reservations at the decision to execute Nagy, but what is beyond dispute is that Andropov was strongly opposed to any reversion to the *status quo ante*. Kadar, a reformer, had been his choice as party leader. Later as Head of the KGB, Andropov was in a unique position to evaluate the social and economic situation in the country. He could see far better than his peers what lay underneath the economic growth and the veneer of prosperity: purulent sores which were incurable. Andropov laid the basis for what he hoped would be a peaceful transition to far-reaching reforms in Soviet society.

Exactly one year after the Twenty-Seventh Party Congress, Gorbachev addressed the Eighteenth Congress of Soviet Trade Unions in April 1987. The people who were listening to him were the pillars of a crucial wing of the party bureaucracy, the Politburo's transmission belt in the factories throughout the country. Gorbachev disturbed the complacency of his audience by mapping out a different role for the trade unions. He insisted that workplace democracy was a vital part of perestroika and repeated an earlier criticism that had previously stung the trade-union bureaucracy. He advised them to stop 'dancing cheek to cheek with economic managers' and 'firmly pursue a line protecting the interests of the working people'. He repeated the message of the Party Congress:

We possess necessary political experience and theoretical potential to resolve the tasks facing society. One thing is clear: we should advance without fail along the path of reorganisation. If the reorganisation peters out the consequences will be far more serious for society as a whole and for every Soviet person in particular.

Once again there is an almost desperate insistence that the USSR is facing a critical test and if it fails it might not get the opportunity again. Fully aware that the democratisation plans were under heavy fire from within the bureaucracy, Gorbachev answered it directly:

I will put it bluntly: those who have doubts about the expediency of further democratisation apparently suffer from one serious drawback which is of great political significance and meaning—they do not believe in our people. They claim that democracy will be used by our people to disorganise society and undermine discipline, to undermine the strength of the system. I think we cannot agree to that.

Democracy is not the opposite of order. It is the order of a greater degree, based not on implicit obedience, mindless execution of instructions, but on fully-fledged, active participation by all the community in all society's affairs ... Democracy means self-control by society, confidence in civic maturity and awareness of social duty in Soviet people. Democracy is unity of rights and duties. The deepening of democracy is certainly no easy matter. And there is no need to fear should everything not proceed smoothly at once, should there be potholes if not gullies ... The more democracy we have, the faster we shall advance along the road to reorganisation and social renewal, and the more order and discipline we shall have in our socialist home. So it is either democracy or social inertia and conservatism. There is no third way, comrades.

Leaving aside the fact that radical language of this sort has not been heard in the Soviet Union since the Twenties, the trade unionists listening to the General Secretary must have wondered whether he was serious. Was he really suggesting that they hand over power to the workers? Their incredulity is perfectly comprehensible. Either Gorbachev was saying all this for cosmetic purposes, in which case all was well, or else he really believed in all this nonsense. There is little doubt that the overwhelming bulk of the delegates did nothing when they returned to their factories. There have been, of course, some notable exceptions but, in general, not much has moved on this front. And this is where the entire process faces its most severe problems. Unless and until the bulk of the workers, whose social weight in Soviet society is substantial, are drawn into the movement, it will not be easy to destroy the stranglehold of the bureaucracy. Here the reformers confront a dilemma. The only way they could democratise the factories is by appealing to the workers *above the heads* of the bureaucrats, since the latter are reluctant to surrender any privileges voluntarily. The 'cheek to cheek dance of managers and trade union bureaucrats' who, after all, feel that they are part of the same social layer will only be disrupted by more vigorous music and movement from below. This could only happen if the reformers were prepared for a frontal assault on the conservatives. It might come to that over the next few years, but until now caution has been the watchword. At the Central Committee plenum in February 1988, Gorbachev did not name names, but he did make it clear to the Soviet public that he was fully aware that the problems of implementation lay within the upper reaches of the party:

> To this day we encounter those who hum and haw as they watch the process of democratisation. Some people have begun to get fidgety, and they caution us: what if democracy should result in chaos? But take a closer look. What are these people worried about? Not about problems that are vitally important to society. More likely they are concerned about their own selfish interests. I won't say anything about others, but for Party members, especially those in leadership category, this is a completely unacceptable position.

The effects of glasnost take on their most visible and dramatic form in the cultural life of the country. Soviet newspapers and magazines have undergone an amazing transformation, something which has been commented upon by virtually every Western journalist based in Moscow. Hardly a day passes without the Soviet press publishing some revelation, which creates a minor sensation at home and abroad. In the realm of literature and the arts there is no official censorship today. In the field of history and politics there are limits, which are carefully observed by the journalists, who have had a long training in the art of self-censorship. Nonetheless the level of discussion and debate, particularly in the letters from readers sections of the press, is far higher and intense than anything in the West. Not only is there nothing like a Murdoch tabloid, but a comparison between, for example, the weekly supplement published by *Izvestia* and the *New York Times* would be extremely instructive. Whereas the *New York Times* gives the appearance of a staid pro-Establishment daily, the *Izvestia* supplement, *Ndelya* (the Week) has acquired the reputation of an unpredictable and radical voice for those who want to accelerate the reforms. The Soviet literary magazine, *Novy Mir* (New World), simply has no equivalent in the West and the weekly newsmagazine, *Ogonyok* is today unrecognisable, given its reportage of subjects once regarded as taboo: the old

Bolsheviks destroyed by Stalin on the one hand and sexuality on the other appear regularly in its pages. As a consequence the magazine is rarely available on the newstands. Two million copies are published but its Deputy Editor told me that were it not for the paper shortage 'we could publish five million every week'. His estimate was that each copy was read by at least ten people and this is probably an understatement. There are many other examples and their combined impact on popular consciousness can not be underestimated.

The revival of politics is not confined to the media. Since the Twenty-Seventh Party Congress there has been a general feeling that the country is poised on the verge of an earthquake. Tremors are felt every day, and everyone is discussing the political changes underway. Victor Kuzin, a non-party socialist, recently wrote in an unofficial bulletin *Tochka Zreniya* (Viewpoint):

> Nowadays one can hardly be accused of over-exaggeration in asserting that our country is living through perhaps the most crucial and decisive moment in the whole seventy-year history of its existence since October 1917. A very close similarity can be discerned between October 1917 and the present day: the depth and acuity of the social contradictions which have now come to a head, as then, demand courage of thought and radical action in the choice of course and methods for overcoming the crisis situation.
>
> April 1985, a definite landmark on a distant and difficult road, has become the familiar line from which the democratic movement, previously nourished exclusively by the energy, persistence and heroism of isolated individuals, often resulting in self-sacrifice, began to assume the character of a developing process in improving the health of society. This process, while developing sluggishly and timidly, is nevertheless gradually encroaching into more and more new areas. The democratic movement is striving to underpin socialism, its science, ideology, philosophy, economics, politics and legislation with the only acceptable foundation: the extensive and free self-management of society. Only by achieving this goal will the comparison of the process which has begun to be a revolution be transformed from an agitational slogan into a strictly scientific verification.*

These views are shared by many socialists inside and outside the Communist Party. They are anaethema to the defenders of bureaucratic privilege. The problem for them lies in the fact that the central leaders of the party and state have given their support and

*'Some problems of internal political restructuring: democratisation, glasnost, criticism and historical memory' by Victor Kuzin, *Labour Focus on Eastern Europe* Vol 10, No 1, April 1988.

strong approval to most of the measures underway. The resulting debate has made Moscow the most exciting political and cultural capital in the world today. Popular consciousness is undergoing a daily transformation. In 1987, Yuri Burtin—a distinguished Soviet literary critic who had not been published for fifteen years because of his refusal to accept either censorship, toe the line or abase himself in the presence of literary bureaucrats—produced two essays, *You of the New Generation* and *Lessons of Courage*. He startled the cultural world by his outspoken assault on time-servers of every variety. While *Lessons of Courage* was a remarkably frank survey of the Soviet Union in the Sixties (embracing Khrushchev's rise and fall, opposition forces at the time and the traumas inflicted upon the prestigious *Novy Mir*, it was the publication of *You of the New Generation* which proved to be more troublesome. Burtin explained the reasons for this in an interview with the supplement to the *Novosti* bulletin, 'Soviet Panorama' in 1988: 'I made some critical remarks there on certain contemporary literary pundits—and nine Moscow periodicals refused to publish it. That's the usual patter now. Your ideas will be welcome, however new and daring, for so long as you theorise. I don't think there are any taboo topics left anymore. But try and offend an official, however slightly! Worse even, if that official is somebody in the editorial clan for which your contribution is meant.' Burtin is currently engaged in a project on reviving Soviet democracy. He is against the one-candidate system and favours a plurality of contenders and *real* elections.

The playwright, Mikhail Shatrov, has extended the frontiers of glasnost in a remarkable fashion, disregarded the 'NO ENTRY' signs which barred access to the forbidden zones of the Soviet past. Shatrov's trilogy—*Dictatorship of Conscience* (1985), *Brest-Litovsk Peace* (1987) and *Onward! Onward! Onward!* (1988)—has had a powerful impact on the country as a whole. His plays have, to put it mildly, excited a great deal of controversy and have offended many who claim to support the reforms. The play about the Brest-Litovsk treaty created a minor sensation in 1987 because it marked the first appearance on the Soviet stage of Trotsky and Bukharin. Even though some critics wrote that Trotsky was depicted as a bit of a caricature, the play stressed that both men were close to Lenin. Official approval to the project was signalled when Gorbachev and other members of the Politburo went to see the performance. *Dictatorship of Conscience* is about the present, and in April 1988 the play was, like Gorbachev's assumption of power, celebrating its third anniversary at Moscow's Lencom Theatre. When I visited the theatre it was packed: apparently it has been like this from the beginning. The theatre goers were an interesting mix: Veterans mingled with students, factory workers and Red Army soldiers seemed just as excited as the Moscow intelligentsia.

The play itself is a frontal assault on Stalinism. 'The real strength of the state,' a Shatrovian character declaims, 'rests on the consciousness of the people.' The skeleton of the play is a mock trial of Lenin. The witnesses for the prosecution include Churchill, Hemingway and a Stalin substitute. Why a substitute? 'When I prepared the script,' Shatrov informed me in April 1988, 'it was still difficult to attack him directly in this fashion on the stage.' But the trial is constantly interrupted by everyday life. A young truck-driver saunters on to the stage. He is questioned by another actor. Why does he persist in displaying a picture of Stalin in his truck? 'Because Stalin was for law and order. People need to be disciplined!' Another actor responds: 'Ever heard of serfdom? Of slavery? That too was based on discipline... Don't you know that Stalin's terror claimed millions of innocent lives?' Truck-driver: 'We have never been taught this at school.' This remark is greeted with a massive round of applause from the audience.

In many ways, the dialogue between the actors and the audience generates even more electricity than the stage performances themselves. The applause, the sighs, the questions, the silences as the watchers respond to the performers is an indication of Shatrov's popularity. It is a sense of the historical conjuncture that unites the audience to the playwright. Everything that was once taboo is now discussed. At one point the actor playing Engels descends from the stage and, observing a row of Red Army officers, begins a discussion on Afghanistan. Are they in favour of withdrawal? They certainly are, and the audience approves. One of the high points is reached when a young woman, an idealist it seems, attempts to join the Komsomol and discovers, to her amazement, that it is a nest of corruption and vice. When she expresses her horror to a Komsomol apparatchik his only response is to rape her. Later in the play the same woman tells the audience: 'I told my great-grandmother all this, she told me that in the future there will be only one dictatorship. The dictatorship of conscience.' Loud and repeated applause greets this remark. Shatrov's message for the month is expressed through another voice on stage: 'We say we're living through a revolutionary process, but how can it be left in the hands of those who hate it?'

Mikhail Shatrov has been writing plays since 1958. Like other artists he attempted to circumvent censorship in the Brezhnev period by utilising the voice of Lenin. For over half a century Soviet history lay buried underneath a mountain of falsification. Historical truth, banished from the academy, sometimes found an outlet in the output of poets and playwrights, novelists and filmmakers. Shatrov's project is ambitious. He wants to extend the limits of glasnost to their outermost boundaries so that no return is possible. His latest play, *Onward! Onward! Onward!,* had been published in the Soviet press in January 1988, but the resulting debate meant a delay in its appearance on the stage. In this play Shatrov is determined to fill in as many of the blank spaces in Soviet history as possible. As with all his work, the play functions on several interrelated levels. The characters introduce themselves to the audience. Even this is not a linear process. The seventh character (Trotsky) to introduce himself accused the eighth (Stalin) of having ordered his execution. Stalin does not deny this but explains why Trotsky has to be killed. This is not an issue which many people, especially academics, have wanted to discuss. It is too sensitive and it involves actions outside Soviet borders. Stalin's attack on Lenin's widow, Rosa Luxemburg's strictures on democracy, Martov's criticisms of Trotsky . . . all these things are there and a great deal else. The play is yet another devastating indictment of Stalinism *as a system*, and it is this aspect of the play which created a panic atmosphere within the ranks of the reformers. Shatrov has stated openly that though his plays are historical they are always about the present. In *Onward! Onward! Onward!* Shatrov has Lenin saying: 'A gigantic fossilised army of office-holders who will introduce reforms that undermine their domination? At whom are you laughing, gentlemen? To try to carry out a revolutionary transformtion through such an apparatus is the greatest self-deception and deception of the people.'

It is hardly a surprise that the Editor of *Pravda*, Victor Afanasiev, was very upset. On January 8 1988, at a meeting of media editors with Gorbachev, he launched a sharp attack on the playwright. Evidently Gorbachev remained silent as he listened to the arguments. This silence appears to have been interpreted as approval and a couple of days later *Pravda* carried a strong criticism of the play. Since the newspaper is correctly regarded as the voice of the Politburo, the conservatives could hardly believe their eyes. A group of *status quo* historians followed up with a lengthy critique which was again published in *Pravda*. Shatrov was defended by *Moscow News* and *Sovietskaya Kultura*. Letters from readers poured into these and provincial papers. Shatrov had argued that Stalin's rise to power was not inevitable. It could have been avoided. 'There is no subjective mood in history,' stated an angry Stalinist in the pages of a Leningrad evening paper. Most of the letters, however, supported the playwright. His supporters mounted a defence in the pages of *Pravda* in February 1988 and at a subsequent meeting with leading journalists some weeks later Gorbachev ended his remarks thus:

> We have to go ahead and look ahead. The purpose of these heart to
> heart talks is for things to sink in. So there must be no slipping back,
> no retreat, on the contrary. Onward and onward we go!

This brought the anti-Shatrov campaign to a standstill. It is worth noting the remarkable fact that the Soviet Union is probably one of the few countries in the world, compared especially to the United States and Western Europe, where a play could polarise the political life of the country in such a sharp fashion. Now it could be argued that the major reason for this is the absence of any other structures through which dissent can be expressed. In my view this is only partially true. The controversy over Shatrov has arisen at a time when a great deal is being published in the Soviet media and there are wide-ranging debates within the academy. Moreover the more the system is democratised the greater will be the impact of cultural events. The effect which the publication of Shatrov's play has had is a striking manifestation of mass involvement in affairs of this sort. The political culture of the Soviet Union is *potentially* vastly superior to that of the West. This will become more and more obvious in the years that lie ahead.

In an attempt to discourage the production of a court-culture, of which socialist realism was only the most grotesque example, the present regime has restricted the award of Lenin Prizes. In 1988, for instance, only two people were honoured, one of them was Tenghiz Abuladze for his allegorical film, *Repentance*, based on the atrocoties of Stalin's henchman, Beria. In 1953, after Stalin's death, Beria ordered the release of criminals from some of the camps. This decision inspired another director, who until recently worked exclusively for television, to make his debut as a filmmaker. Alexander Proshkin's first feature film, *The Cold Summer of 1953*, is set in a bleak and remote coastal village somewhere in the North, where everyday life is a tremendous burden. Proshkin's haunting landscapes express this just as much as the anguish written on the faces of the fisherpeople. The village has been donated two political exiles by the State. But they are not real political exiles. One man is a former official from the Ministry of Trade, the other a one-time Red Army officer. Both have been falsely accused on absurd charges and sentenced first to prison camps, and then exile. The trade official is in his late fifties, the Red Army man is in his thirties. Yet, of the two, it is the older man who is resigned to his fate and joins in with the chores of the fisherfolk. The Red Army man is totally alienated from everything. He sits sullenly, watching the sea and refuses to work in any capacity. The villagers feed him, but are resentful. And then Stalin is dead and Beria has ordered the release of gangsters and hoodlums from a nearby prison camp.

The criminals have formed a guerrilla group, armed themselves and killed the two militiamen in the region. They have also captured the village and are on the rampage. The local shopkeeper is full of ambiguities. Proshkin sees him as having a dual character. He collaborates with the occupiers, but tries to warn the others. Ultimately the former Red Army man organises a resistance and after a pitched battle the criminals are defeated. Like Shatrov's plays, the film is supposedly about the past but yet also very much about the present. During the conflict the former trade official tells the ex-officer: 'It's been fourteen years. I've not heard from my family. What a waste. It must never happen again.' It is a powerful understatement and yet everyone understands perfectly. The Moscow cinema where I first saw the movie in April 1988 is on the outskirts of the city. It was an early afternoon showing, but the cinema was full. One could feel the impact it was having on the six hundred strong audience. Cinema remains an immensely powerful medium in the Soviet Union despite the spread of television.

With the abolition of censorship in this medium, a number of projects hitherto taboo will now go into production. There is talk in Moscow of two major historical films based on the lives of the old Bolshevik leader, Nikolai Bukharin and the legendary military commander, Marshal Tukachevsky. A leading script writer who specialises in the drama of everyday life (ie soap operas) complained bitterly to me of the new turn to politics and history, which meant that people like her would find it more difficult to get a script accepted. She was half-joking, but one did suggest that she might find a lot of openings in Britain. During the Brezhnev period the cruder forms of socialist realism were abandoned, but replaced by what became known as 'problem-free' films. The influence of Hollywood was clearly visible. Some of these were technically brilliant, but added up to nothing more than escapist entertainment. There was a strong protest at this 'Hollywoodisation' from critics and viewers alike, as well as many distinguished film-makers. As Boris Kagarlitsky wrote, 'the spiritual emptiness of the commercial cinema reflected the ideological crisis in society', but it also

> played a role more complex than the one assigned to it by the heads of the propaganda department. It finished off socialist realism. More precisely socialist realism was dead and buried by the Seventies as a result of the objective development of events. But the commercial art of the late Seventies drove the traditional aspen stake into its grave. That old thing would not rise again.*

The price paid by Soviet film-makers during the Stalin period is difficult to estimate. The Twenties had seen Soviet cinema leading the world. Which other country could boast an Eisenstein, a Vertov, a Dovzhenko and a Pudovkin working creatively and producing a number of cinema classics? The victory of Stalinism crippled their development, they were compelled to view the world through a distorted lens. In the case of Eisenstein this could not totally dwarf his genius, but even he was seriously affected. Shoot or be shot was not exactly the best way to encourage innovation. The Ukrainian film-maker, Alexander Dovzhenko, was denounced savagely and without any justification whatsoever as a Ukrainian nationalist during the War. His screenplay *The Ukraine in Flames*, composed literally on the battlefront, was denounced because it depicted sorrow, with Stalin—personally—leading the attack. Dovzhenko wrote in his diary:

> X read *The Ukraine in Flames* and he said to me, 'One place is unrealistic, you write there was great weeping, that is not true. No such weeping took place. They looked sad, but they didn't weep. Nobody wept, you understand?'
> You lie, I thought, you lie, you blind bureaucrat! They poured out tears over your very pathway and you looked at them through your glasses and through the windscreen of your shut-in automobile and you saw nothing, because you didn't want to see anything. Blind one! They wept, oh how they wept! No other country in the world wept like that. Even old men cried so that their eyes puffed up from tears.

*The Thinking Reed.

After the War, Dovzhenko wrote an epitaph for his entire generation in his diary on 4 July 1945. He was writing about himself and cinema, but his words could apply to every single sphere of politics and culture during those tormented times:

> I am a film director. In all my working years I have not seen a single one of my pictures in a decent theatre on a decent screen, printed on good film by qualified technicians... The very thought of seeing one of my own pictures makes me sad. The film is always worse than I conceived and made it. This has been one of the misfortunes of my life. Not once did I obtain satisfaction or even peace from seeing the reuslts of my immeasurably difficult and complex work. As time goes by I become more and more convinced that the best twenty years of my life have been wasted. What I could have done!*

The Brezhnevite bureaucrats were certainly not blind. They could observe real talent, which they either harnessed or drove into exile. The language of cinema changed as Tarkovsky was pushed towards an idiom which bordered on mysticism. His nightmarish vision in *The Stalker* was the end result. A combination of despair and some brilliant imagery represented the haunted imagination of this great film-maker, who died abroad. The Gorbachev period has already seen some amazing changes. If the process continues there can be little doubt that a new breed of film-makers, exemplified by people like Proshkin, will take Soviet cinema to new heights. They have, of course, one major advantage. The competition from the West is not so great. With rare exceptions, the medium in the West is gripped by an infantile desire to shock. With the exception of Germany, what passes for successful cinema is usually a collection of weightless iconoclasms distinguished largely by the total domination of style over content. In one of his last public lectures in 1987, the late Raymond Williams strongly berated the practitioners of these new forms:

> Can we raise again the question whether showing the exploited as degraded does not simply prolong the lease of the exploiter? Are we not obliged to distinguish these reductive and contemptuous forms, these assayers of ugliness and violence, which in the very sweep of their negations can pass as radical art...?

The problems confronted by Soviet film directors during the Terror in the Thirties also left their impact on writers. The consequences of Stalinism for Soviet culture defy quantification. Some writers were,

*Extracts published in Masters of the Soviet Cinema by Herbert Marshall, RKP, 1983.

of course, murdered, as in the case of the great poet Mandelstam. The innovative theatre director, Meyerhold, was brutally tortured by NKVD sadists before being executed: his crime, it seems, had been that he had dedicated one of his early plays to Trotsky as the founder of the Red Army. Others were terrorised and tortured in prison. The lucky ones simply had to stifle their creativity in public. Writers were in a more advantageous position than film-makers. The cinema was still a new medium and the successes of Soviet cinema could have created the foundation for something phenomenal. Instead the process was virtually halted. Moreover censorship struck at a very early phase, long before there could even be any possibility of making the film. Scenarios could always be preserved, but they rarely, if ever, convey the scale or the real quality of the finished product.

In contrast, there was a strong and vital tradition of pre-Revolutionary literature. A set of lively literary magazines had managed to function under the Tsarist censor and the works of Pushkin, Lermontov, Gogol, Dostoeyevsky, Saltykov-Shchedrin, Turgenev, Tolstoy, Chernyevsky and Ostrovsky, amongst others, were read as widely as literacy permitted. Nor did the Revolution disrupt literary continuity in the broad sense. 'A profound break in history,' Trotsky wrote in *Literature and Revolution* in 1923, 'that is, a rearrangement of classes in society shakes up individuality, establishes the perception of the fundamental problems of lyric poetry from a new angle, and so saves art from eternal repetition.' Most of the leaders of the Bolshevik revolution were highly cultured and the notion of 'proletarian art' was never State policy in the Twenties. Trotsky argued that all talk of 'proletarian literature' or art was meaningless, these terms being pernicious because 'they falsify perspectives, they violate proportions, they distort standards and they cultivate the arrogance of small circles which is most dangerous.' The migration of themes from one class or one epoch to another was hardly surprising. Trotsky polemicised strongly against a number of *avant garde* conceptions floating around at the time: 'A new class does not begin to create all of culture from the beginning, but enters into possession of the past, assorts it, touches it up, rearranges it, and builds on it further. If there were no such utilisation of the "second-hand" wardrobe of the ages, historic processes would have no progress at all.'

Soviet writers endeavouring to produce works during the Terror produced very little of real merit. Some became addicted to the allegorical form (Bulgakov), while others produced rubbish for public consumption and wrote in secret for the future. From 1928 until the Khrushchevite thaw in 1955–6, Soviet novelists were constricted by the strait-jacket of 'socialist-realism' and produced a monotone literature totally devoid of real conflicts. Despite the fact that this sort of literature was simplistic in every sense of the word it was a painful read. Mediocre morality tales had become the order of the day. Fortunately, the great classics of Russian literature were not placed on a Stalinist pyre. Some of Dostoeyevsky disappeared, but, in general the old novels were available. Unimpressed by the 'socialist-realist' mode many of the newly educated citizenry sought refuge in the works of the preceding period. In the mid-Fifties, Khrushchev opened the gates once again. This was the time when *Novy Mir* published Alexander Solzhenitsyn's first novel, *One Day in the Life of Ivan Denisovich*. But he retreated under pressure from the bureaucracy. Boris Pasternak's *Zhivago* was banned in 1958. If it had been published in *Novy Mir* it is doubtful that the author would have been lionised in the West, leave alone awarded the Nobel Prize for Literature. Solzhenitsyn's later work, *First Circle* and *Cancer Ward* were subjected to similar treatment. This general trend was reinforced by Brezhnevism. Bureaucratic controls were strictly imposed. Literature, as is usual in these cases, went underground. Books were written and either sent out of the country or circulated in *samizdat* (ie clandestinely).

Today the pre-Stalinist literary period is slowly being resurrected. The old 'enemies of the people', Pilnyak and Zamyatin have risen from the dead, as have Pasternak, Bulgakov, Platonov and Grossman. These last two writers are of special interest. Platonov's writings were regarded as so deeply subversive that they were kept in a section of the archive which was sealed off and unavailable to even specialists in the field. Platonov's three novels were written in an experiental mode clearly influenced by the whole modernist trend. *The Sea of Yuvenilnoye* was written in 1934 and published in 1986; *The Foundation Pit* was written in 1930 and published in 1987; and *Chevengur*, which was rejected by the Federatsiya Publishing House in 1929, was published in February 1988. The rejection of *Chevengur* appears to have puzzled the author and he sent his manuscript to Gorky with a note: 'They are not publishing it... saying that the book will be understood as a counter-revolutionary one. But I worked having absolutely different feelings...' Gorky understood the problem well, but could not help. *Chevengur* was written in

1928–9. Platonov observed the menace behind the collectivisation plans and felt that the methods being used were a social peril. Simultaneously he saw the total bureaucratisation of the state machine as a disaster for the revolution, feeling that this process would distort, stifle and kill any living organism. In *Chevengur* Platonov did not simply diagnose these cancerous growths. He argued that for the revolution to survive the cancer had to be removed. Chevengur is a small town. It has exactly eleven Bolsheviks, who have already established communism. They are simple souls and believe that communism will come when the bourgeoisie is abolished, except that they do not see this as the ending of privileges based on ownership of land and factories, but as a problem of individuals. Power is in their hands. Shoot the bourgeois dogs and then the half-bourgeois and then the quarter-bourgeois and then . . . ? And then the sun will on its own compel the grain to shoot out of the ground. The novel depicts in startling fashion the execution of landlords and 'half-bourgeois' as a 'slow steam came out of the head of the bourgeois, and afterwards oozed out some raw substance which looked like candle wax . . .' It is all very hard work. Platonov's Chevengurians decide 'to wash the floors in the empty houses. To make them decent for tomorrow's proletariat'. And yet, in a curious fashion, Platonov's attitude to the eleven 'Bolsheviks' is remarkably detached. They are not seen as villains or criminals. So, who and what are they? For Platonov there are no enemies in Chevengur. There are the victims of history, products of an illiteracy that is centuries old and the children of absolutism. The author describes the leader of the Chevengurian communists thus:

> The only thing which reassured and excited Chepurnoi was the fact that there is a secret place far away, somewhere near Moscow, as Prokofy found out on the map, it is called Kremlin. Lenin is sitting there with the lamp and thinking, he is not sleeping but writing. What is he writing there about? In fact, Chevengur already exists and it's time for Lenin to stop writing and to unite with the proletariat and to live . . .

Platonov's dystopia is, of course, Stalin's Russia and it is hardly surprising that this book was perceived as a grave threat to the ideology of the bureaucracy. Stalinism, the author appears to be saying, is the socialism of fools and primitives.

Vasily Grossman belongs to a later period. He was a correspondent of the Red Army newspaper *Red Star* during the War and sent despatches from the battlefronts in Stalingrad and elsewhere. He was born in 1905 in the Ukraine, studied Chemistry at Moscow University, and worked in the Donbass mines as a safety engineer. He became a protégé of Maxim Gorky when he moved to Moscow in 1933 and published a couple of novels and dozens of short stories. None of these, it has to be said, was regarded as exceptional in any way. Grossman became aware of his Jewish roots during the Holocaust which claimed his mother. He was a loyal party member, and it was Stalin's anti-semitic outbursts and the new purge of Jews which broke Grossman from orthodoxy. His masterpiece, *Life and Fate*, was completed in 1960, confiscated by the KGB a year later. Grossman then wrote a letter to the Politburo demanding the return of his manuscript. The Politburo's ideological watchdog, Suslov, informed the writer that *Life and Fate* could not be published in the Soviet Union for another two hundred years. This was, apart from everything else, an indication that Suslov had understood the importance of the work.

Life and Fate was published posthumously, first in the West in 1985 and subsequently in the Soviet Union. Grossman had died in 1964, a broken man, but he had left behind him a work which will be recognised as one of the great novels of this century. Grossman, unlike Pasternak and Solzhenitsyn, was an insider. He had seen the intimate workings of Stalinism. He knew. *Life and Fate* is a ferocious denunciation of Stalinism and Fascism. The beseiged city of Stalingrad is really a metaphor for the twentieth century. In this city the only people for whom the author reveals a real sympathy are the officers and men in one particular house who openly disregard Commissars, but fight on regardless because they possess independent minds and a fiercely critical spirit. Grossman's heroes are the former members of the oppositions destroyed by Stalin. They have not forgotten everything. The most moving sections of the book are the descriptions of women and children being marched off to the extermination camps by the Nazis. Victor's mother (like Grossman's) will die, but she manages to send him a last letter from a transit camp:

> ... But what I really want to talk to you about is something quite different. I never used to feel I was a Jew: as a child my circle of friends were all Russian; my favourite poets were Pushkin and Nekrasov; the one play which reduced me to tears, together with the whole audience—a congress of village doctors—was Stanislavsky's production of *Uncle Vanya*. And once, Vityenka, when I was fourteen, our

family was about to emigrate to South America and I said to my
father: 'I'll never leave Russia—I'd rather drown myself.' And I didn't
go ... But now, during these terrible days, my heart has become filled
with a maternal tenderness towards the Jewish people. I never knew
this love before. It reminds me of my love for you, my dearest son.

Grossman's novel was loosely modelled on Tolstoy's *War and
Peace*. Like Tolstoy, the author of *Life and Fate* intersperses his own
views on philosophy and history. Amongst the more controversial of
these are descriptions of fascism which could just as easily be
transferred to Stalinism. In a German prison camp Grossman has an
SS officer and an old Bolshevik prisoner engaged in a philosophical
discussion. The Nazi tries to convince the Bolshevik that they have
much more in common than the latter would be prepared to
acknowledge. Grossman's revulsion against Stalinism manifests
itself on virtually every level, but he especially loathes its dengeration
into a 'national-Bolshevism'. The theme of the book, fortunately, in
no way detracts from its literary style. Beautifully and movingly
written, the plot weaves its way through the suppressed passions of
everday life in the Soviet Union under Stalin. It is the imaginative
power of the book which gives it an intrinsic strength.

Grossman's other novel, *Forever Flowing*, contains one of the
most evocative and powerful narrative accounts of the effects of
collectivisation that one has ever read, but the book is really a
shadow of *Life and Fate*. A large section contains a polemic against
that master-polemicist—Lenin. It has to be said that it is not a very
convincing debate. What it does reveal is the author grappling with a
real problem. To what extent was Stalinism inherent in the entire
Leninist project? The question is totally legitimate, but as Shatrov
and others have written there is no such thing as the inevitability of
certain events in history. Grossman, alas, did not live long enough to
see *Life and Fate* serialised in the once dreadfully Stalinist literary
magazine *Octaybr* in 1988. The publication created a sensation in
literary circles in the Soviet Union and the magazine was sold out a
few hours after it appeared on the stands. In some ways this was one
of the more courageous decisions taken by the reformers.

Slowly the drawers containing the banned manuscripts will
empty. A great deal has already been published. Rybakov's *Children
of the Arbat** is a riveting piece of historical fiction which centres on
the murder of Kirov by Stalin. Its successor, *Nineteen Thirty-Five and*

---

*Hutchinson, London, 1988.

Other Years is due to be serialised in the Soviet Union in the autumn of 1988. An unpublished novel by Konstantin Simonov (his reflections on Stalin) has been published in *Znamya*. Onward and onward certainly seems to be the motto of Soviet literature today. Dudintsev's *White Clothes**, Pristavkin's *A Golden Cloudlet Passed the Night*, Bitov's *Pushkin House*, have all been published. The literary magazines, freed of the censor, compete with each other for the best writers. There is the *Novy Mir* circle, where writers remain fiercely loyal; *Yunost* tends to concentrate on writers from the Asian Republics; *Znamya*, on memoirs.

The vitality of Soviet writing, buried underground for so many years, can now be seen in all its splendour. These are truly amazing times. What will follow? I think it is safe to predict that a new generation of poets and writers is already there, waiting impatiently for the old men and women to publish and go away so that new forms can develop. One can almost hear their excited and impatient voices: 'Yes, yes,' they are saying to the ghosts of yesterday, 'we are with you. You suffered as we never can. We have learnt a great deal from your works and the conditions in which they were written. But we will write our own way and about different matters...'

*This book will be published as *White Garments*, Hutchinson, London, 1989.

Erik Bulatov, *Unanimously*, 1987.

2. WHO'S AFRAID OF BORIS YELTSIN?
The Resistance of the Bureaucracy

My concern is easy to understand, even my fear ... for myself, for the family.
Because we all feel their breath behind our backs; their watchful wolves' eyes of
those who oppose perestroika. They flock together in the evenings, sit together
late into the night, usually in the kitchen, chain-smoking and cursing all the new
ways that have come or are coming into our lives. Everyone counts any mistake we
make, even our great misfortunes, including natural disasters such as avalanches,
and earthquakes make them immensely happy: 'Look here, what perestroika and
acceleration have brought us to!' I would say more: they note down everyone of us
who wants the renovation of society, whose soul is not dead and aching, adding us
to the list and thinking: 'Our time will come again.'

Vladimir Drozd, Byelorussian writer, *Literaturnaya Gazetta*
30 September 1987

It sometimes seems that there are two parties inside the CPSU today.
Mikhail Gorbachev may insist that the party leadership is united
behind the reform programme—and, in a formal sense, he is not
wrong since the votes on the central issues have been, in the best
Stalinist tradition, unanimous—but if there is such a great deal of

agreement within the Party hierarchy, why have there been so many difficulties in implementing the reforms? The fact is that the top and middle cadres of the party are divided. This is perfectly natural since what is being proposed marks a radical break with the dominant traditions of the Party, which were laid down at Stalin's notorious 'Congress of Victors', the Seventeenth Party Congress, in 1934. For these new traditions to become deeply embedded Stalin needed to wipe out the historic memory of the old Party, and the only way this could be done was to systematically destroy the old Bolsheviks. That is what happened. As Deutscher has eloquently pointed out the purges were not an exercise in random slaughter. Each and every possible alternative to Stalinism was exterminated. Now, Gorbachev and his leading lieutenant on the Politburo, Alexander Yakovlev, are trying to leap over the Stalinist past and revive older traditions. They are not so naïve as to imagine that this could be done without encountering serious resistance from within the apparatus of the Party/state.

There are, of course, a number of similarities between Moscow today and the Prague Spring of 1968. These have been discussed a great deal, not least in Prague, but there is one important difference amongst others. The initiative for glasnost came neither from the party rank-and-file, nor the intelligentsia, but from the leadership of the Party.* For this reason the initial reaction to the reforms from most quarters inside and outside the USSR was one of suspicion. The symbol of the reforms was not a dissident or a distinguished playwright or a minor party leader in an obscure region. It was the General Secretary of the Party. This fact disorients many people on both the Right and Left in the West and with good reason. What is being proposed in terms of institutional changes is without real precedents. It is not simply an exercise in rhetoric. Gorbachev in the past three years has challenged bureaucratic certainties and there are many inside the centres of power who are unhappy, not for any reasons of real principle, but because their political monopoly and material privileges are under threat.

Now it is perfectly true, as Kagarlitsky has pointed out that without Khrushchev and the Twentieth Party Congress there would have been no Gorbachev.† One could add that without the

---

*Though it should be pointed out that sections of the Intelligentsia, especially the Cinema Workers' Union, play an important part in the reform movement.
†The Twentieth Party Congress in 1956 saw the first real attack on Stalin. Khrushchev's speech began to expose the lies and murders. The event stunned the international communist movement.

bureaucratic pluralism of the Brezhnev period there also would have been no Gorbachev. Clearly Khrushchev's audacity is worthy of admiration. It was far more difficult to denounce Stalin in the Fifties than it is today; the risks were far greater too, as was pointed out to Khrushchev many times by his colleagues. Unfortunately his memoirs *Khrushchev Remembers*, which are extremely revealing and paint a totally believable picture of the Stalin period, do not provide us with an account of the exact circumstances of his fall. However it is now known that Khrushchev was toppled on the eve of his plans to totally reorganise the leading bodies of the Party. He was planning a clean sweep. Alexander Shelepin, a time-server of the worst sort and his protégé Semichastny, then boss of the KGB, were responsible for the concrete planning of the operation. Khrushchev's private safe was raided by the KGB, the plans uncovered, messengers despatched with the details to members of the plenum who convened rapidly to save their own skins and get rid of the turbulent Ukrainian. He was away on holiday and all contact with him was cut off, thus preventing his supporters in Moscow from warning him of what was being prepared.

The overthrow of Khrushchev was, essentially, a police operation carried out in secret. He was, of course, guilty of many errors on both the economic and political fronts. Nor could he see that, without a total political revolution, it would be impossible to qualitatively alter the conditions of everyday life in the USSR. But we should not be in any doubt that Khrushchev was not removed from office because of his vices, but because of his virtues. The main lessons that Gorbachev seems to have learned from Khrushchev's experience are to avoid abrupt or premature divisions within the leadership and to lay a strong and solid institutional foundation for the reforms, so that a return to the old corruption becomes impossible.

Although Gorbachev's speech to the Twenty-Seventh Party Congress did, as I suggested earlier, mark a turning point, the basic structures of political rule were not altered then. In fact a new power structure was constructed by the leadership so as to keep the most energetic reformer, Mikhail Gorbachev, on a very tight leash. The majority of the old central committee stayed in place and, as we have seen since the Congress, it has not exactly been a rubber-stamp for every new radical initiative. In addition, Yegor Ligachev, a senior Politburo member and self-announced kingmaker, was assigned the task of Chief Guardian of party ideology, something which Suslov had done for Khrushchev and Brezhnev. Ligachev was to be the guarantor of stability against anything which threatened to escape the control of the leading bodies of the Party, a disinterested protector of the collective interests of the party. Ligachev is not opposed to economic reforms on the Hungarian model (in that sense he reminds one of the late Kosygin, whose economic reforms were scuttled by the Brezhnevites), but he is not in favour of democracy or, according to Boris Yeltsin, 'social justice'.

At the same time Ryzhkov, the country's Prime Minister, was designated as the man responsible for the implementation of policy. The Twenty-Seventh Congress accepted Gorbachev, but the bureaucracy made sure that the braking mechanisms were firmly in place. What has happened since the Congress is, as stated earlier, the operation of dual power within the apparatus. In order to establish a real momentum, Gorbachev had to go beyond the framework of the policy compromise agreed at the Congress and launch a distinctive campaign of his own. This produced serious tensions between his own hardline supporters and important sections of the new leadership which exist to this day. He strengthened his position on the Politburo and got agreement for the convocation of a new Party Conference for June 1988. The only purpose in holding a new Conference of the Party is to establish a new set of guidelines which supersede the decisions at the Twenty-Seventh Party Congress. Gorbachev and his supporters were clearly unhappy at the balance of power and the tactics agreed at the time of the Congress. They wanted a total revival of cultural and intellectual life in the country as a whole and within the Soviet Academy in particular, and did not want to have to wait another five years for them. Alexander Yakovlev, in particular, is in favour of debate and dissent being channeled through the political system rather than prisons or psychiatric hospitals. What this entails is a new ideological framework for the Party and this is what party traditionalists oppose. Yegor Ligachev is neither an old-fashioned Stalinist nor a Brezhnevite apologist. He realises full well that the system needs economic reforms and some political readjustments, but he is clearly unhappy at the direction in which things are moving. Why? Because all the indications are that political life for the mass of the country is about to revive in a very big way. The material conditions for socialist democracy, socialist pluralism, elections to real Soviets, a free press far more imaginative than that in the West, and so forth, are much more favourable than they were immediately after the Revolution, as we will see in Chapter 6. The mere possibility of all this makes the bureaucracy quake in its limousines. What will be decisive, of course, is the ability of the reformers to transform the economy as is discussed in the following chapter. But the political offensive has already begun to bear fruit. A tiny example is the refusal of Dr Sakharov to settle in Virginia or Vermont or to be used by the cold war machine in the West.

The Soviet leader's tactics and style are of some interest. There is a careful populist display, reminiscent of Khrushchev—although much more sophisticated—which he utilises to throw new ideas at the people and gather support from below in order to strengthen his leverage at the top. Simultaneously he has adamantly refused to draw political dividing lines within the party. He presents his task as carrying the entire party with him, but whether he actually believes that this is possible remains an open question. The result of this is that opposition within the party is defined exclusively in psychological rather than political terms, a not entirely foolish tactic in the short-term, but already creating problems for the reformers. Gorbachev is undoubtedly the real leader of all those in favour of democratisation, but at the same time he wants to avoid a head-on clash within the party. His aim is to politically disarm his opponents by presenting them with a *fait accompli*, which is irreversible.

It is this which has created a number of problems. Gorbachev has not succeeded in reassuring the Soviet élite. In some quarters, there is a great deal of nervousness and hostility to his tactics and, indeed, his entire style and approach. His opponents think that he is moving too far, too fast, and this, they believe, is destabilising the system and putting everything at risk. Every public manifestation of discontent —mass demonstrations in Armenia and Latvia; small gatherings in Moscow; Shatrov's latest play; Yuri Afanasiev's (Rector of the Moscow Institute of Historical Archives) most recent pronounce-ment—is seen as an excess, and blamed on perestroika.

Stalin had conceived the post of General Secretary somewhat in the manner of a man steering a troika: a generous use of the whip to keep the three horses under control and on the same road. This was the way to contain the working class, the peasantry and the intelligentsia. Gorbachev and Yakovlev challenge this entire method of domination and their supporters denounce it as both illegitimate and barbaric. The new General Secretary is a man with a mission. Moreover he is hell-bent on achieving his aims. The upper echelons of the élite are wondering whether they have, after all, made a terrible mistake. True that Gromyko, while nominating Gorbachev, had reminded the Party that the new leader's smiles could be deceptive, hiding his steel teeth. Everyone had laughed a great deal at the time. But surely these teeth were not meant to be used against them? The time had clearly come to fire a few warning shots, but would he necessarily heed them? He was popular at both home and abroad. His position was becoming virtually unshakeable, it was clearly time to put the reformers on the defensive and use bureaucratic strength to draw in Gorbachev's reins. One can speculate as to how this might have been done, but in the event something happened which gave the conservatives their first big opportunity to go on the counter-offensive—the dramatic explosion of Boris Yeltsin at a meeting of the Central Committee, which was preparing the celebrations for the Seventieth Anniversary of the Revolution.

When Boris Yeltsin was appointed First Secretary of the Moscow party it was seen as one of Gorbachev's more imaginative appointments. One reason was that Yeltsin was widely regarded as an extremely honest and straightforward politician. In his home base of Sverdlovsk he had made a big impression on the workers as a leader who was totally approachable. At the Twenty-Seventh Party Congress, Yeltsin had spoken out in very radical language in favour of the reform programme. There was another reason, in fact a far more important one, which also helps to explain the general relief which greeted Yeltsin's appointment.

The man who was being replaced was Victor Grishin, the epitome of Brezhnevite corruption. Grishin had ruled Moscow in league with a mafia, which dominated the distribution of food. During Andropov's brief period in office Grishin was already under threat. Andropov ordered an offensive against corruption in the capital. The head of Gastronom Two, a large food shop, was arrested and charged with becoming a millionaire at the expense of the population at large: still a capital offence in the USSR. It was public knowledge that Grishin was heavily implicated. It is hardly a secret that a mafia composed of what are officially known as 'economic criminals' exists in a number of Soviet cities. These people have strong allies within the bureaucracy, and Andropov's belligerence had worried the mafiocracy.* Before Grishin could be replaced,

*In April 1988, I was told by a senior academic in Moscow that there had been two serious attempts on Andropov's life. This was in the context of a discussion as to whether Gorbachev's opponents might resort to the 'Kennedy solution'. The mafiocracy came close on one occasion and a machinegun nest was uncovered.

Andropov was dead. Grishin thrived during the Chernenko interregnum, and even made it clear that he wanted to succeed the gerontocrat. There was a grotesque scene on Soviet TV on the occasion of elections to the Soviets when Chernenko, literally on his last legs, was seen casting his vote in Grishin's office. The latter displayed a smirk, indicating his strong interest in his own political future. This display of political necrophilia had the opposite effect to the one hoped for. Grishin lost his place on the Politburo and was replaced by Yeltsin in Moscow. Whoever had replaced Grishin would have been welcomed by the long-suffering citizens of Moscow. The fact that it was Yeltsin seemed like an additional bonus.

The new leader of the Moscow Party did not waste much time. He began to break the rules and traditions of the bureaucracy from his very first day in office. He spoke directly to workers and consumers. He established at an early stage that the appalling waste of both time and resources was a scandal which could not be solved without a frontal assault on the privileges of the nomenklatura. Like Haroun al Rashid*, the legendary ruler of ancient Baghdad, Yeltsin began to make surprise appearances in places rarely visited by leading bureaucrats. Word of his adventures swept the town and it did not take him long to become one of the most popular leaders of the Moscow Party since the Twenties. Two episodes in particular deserve to be recounted in full. Observing a large queue outside a state-owned shop one day, Yeltsin had his car stopped, got out and went and spoke to various people in the queue. Then he addressed them collectively on the street and denounced the system which forced them to spend hours simply to get goods for everyday use. He then held out his party card and told them: 'With this I could go to a special shop a few minutes' walk from here and buy whatever I want! It's this inequality that perestroika wants to finish.' Loud applause and departure of Yeltsin.

The second event was more explosive. A queue mainly composed of women was waiting patiently to buy meat inside a state-owned food emporium. In the middle of the queue was Yeltsin, unrecognised, silently reading a paper. When it was his turn to be served he demanded a couple of pounds of veal. The woman at the counter stared at him as if he were crazy. The old women behind him

*Was well known for disguising himself and walking in the streets hearing the views of ordinary people.

in the queue began to mutter abuse. Who was this idiot asking for veal? It was unheard of in this shop. But Yeltsin smiled and insisted till finally he sent for the manager. The latter was about to throw him out when he showed his card. 'I know for a fact,' Yeltsin roared, 'that a big truck delivered a big amount of veal to you this morning at six am. Where is it?' The manager quaked and Yeltsin pointed out to the amazed women that there had been veal, but it had been stolen. The manager clearly was a very small cog in the large wheel of corruption. Grishin had been removed but lower-case Brezhnevites were still in place. Yeltsin's popularity soared, but with the 'wrong' people. Within the hierarchy he had become a disreputable figure. Numerous similar incidents began to enrage those under attack. A number of wives of leading officials wrote letters to the press warning Yeltsin to desist and defending their privileges. Gorbachev received many complaints, but during the early period these were ignored. One can imagine the outcry in certain quarters as a collective cry was heard: 'Who will rid us of this turbulent provincial?'

A serious campaign was mounted by the conservative faction to discredit Yeltsin. At one stage it was almost as if Moscow was being blockaded to cause further shortages and thus decrease Yeltsin's standing by showing him to be a talker who could not deliver the goods. Yeltsin responded by beginning to close down the special shops, reducing the number of official cars and cracking down on other privileges. His arguments were simple. Leaving aside the question of 'social justice' which he raised continuously, he argued that unless the hierarchy experienced the deprivations which were the daily lot of ordinary working people they would never understand the need for perestroika. Unlike every other Moscow Party leader from 1934 onwards, Yeltsin was throughout his tenure confronted with an unpalatable political fact. He was not a member of the Politburo, but merely a candidate member. Ligachev had effectively blocked Yeltsin's elevation to full membership at the January 1987 plenum and Gorbachev had accepted the compromise. Six months later Ligachev had again refused to budge on this not unimportant issue. Clearly some horse-trading had taken place. Yakovlev, a staunchly radical and innovative reformer was made a full member instead. Ligachev knew exactly what he was doing and it was a clever ploy: Yeltsin is a powerful politician who undoubtedly has a strong rapport with the workers; Yakovlev is politically on the same wave-length, but is essentially an academic intellectual. By accepting Yakovlev, the conservatives were, in effect, telling Gorbachev that they were not hostile to perestroika as such, but that Yeltsin's style was unacceptable.

Yeltsin had good reason to be angry. He had been placed in an untenable position. The appartachiks working under him realised full well that their boss did not have real power. This soon became obvious on other fronts. When Yeltsin tried moving twenty factories outside the Moscow area because they were violating the agreed pollution limits, the decision was blocked by Ligachev. Many other departments in the capital appealed to Ligachev over Yeltsin's head and had the latter's decisions overruled. The situation became explosive when Mikhail Gorbachev went on study leave to write his book, *Perestroika*. Ligachev was left in charge and he took open delight in preventing Yeltsin from doing anything substantial. Yeltsin complained bitterly about all this to Gorbachev in a letter, which Gorbachev later revealed after Yeltsin's fall:

> While on vacation, I received a letter from him, asking that the issue concerning his stay both in the Politburo and in the post of first secretary of the Moscow City Party Committee should be resolved. After returning from vacation, I talked with comrade Yeltsin and we agreed that the time was not appropriate for discussing this issue and that we would meet and talk it over after the October holiday.
>
> Nevertheless, comrade Yeltsin, in breach of party and purely human ethics, raised the issue directly at the plenum, in circumvention of the Politburo. As far as the reason given by comrade Yeltsin for his resignation—lack of support on the part of the central committee secretariat—is concerned, it should be said without mincing words that this statement is utterly absurd and contradicts reality.*

The breach of bureaucratic norms Gorbachev refers to had occured at the 21 October plenum convened to discuss the seventieth anniversary of the Revolution. Yeltsin unleashed a blistering attack on Ligachev and the people obstructing reforms. He offered to resign and, according to reports of the speech, made some angry remarks about the state of the nation. Yeltsin's speech has never been published, but as he was later to admit, he was very angry and threw all tactical considerations to the wind. He said he did not regret a single word, but admitted the timing had been wrong.

It is an open question whether the relationship of forces within the Politburo would have permitted Gorbachev to do anything else, but

*Speech at Nineteenth Party Conference in June 1988.

his desire to maintain unity meant that Yeltsin had to be sacrificed. Here Gorbachev, normally very open and straightforward, was compelled to resort to what can best be described as an untruth. The difficulties confronting Yeltsin were the talk of Moscow, and within the ranks of the reformers there was real hatred against Ligachev precisely because of the obstruction of Yeltsin's policies. If Gorbachev had remained silent on the matter it would have been bad enough. But for him to deny its existence was, to put it mildly, a political misjudgement. In his private conversations with Yeltsin he had obviously stressed the necessity for patience. If he had told Yeltsin in their private talks that Yeltsin was a fantasist who was imagining everything, it is obvious that a resignation would have been on the table the very next morning.

A few weeks after Yeltsin's outburst he was removed as Moscow party chief at a meeting which was certainly reminiscent of Stalin's kangaroo courts *prior* to the trials, purges and mass killings. Yeltsin was attacked by people who had not opened their mouths when he had been the party boss of Moscow. Listen, for instance, to the speech made by a Mr Kosarov Dal and reported in *Pravda*:

> It was no mistake on Yeltsin's part [a reference to his speech at the 21 October plenum], it was a calculated stab in the back of the Politburo and the Central Committee, with the purpose of gaining ambitious political dividends. He is guilty of treachery to the cause of perestroika. Yeltsin was after authority at any price, using political adventurism and elements of Bonapartism.

And who is Mr Kosarov Dal? The head of Mosagroprom, the Food Board of Moscow! Dal's last sentence is taken verbatim from scores of Stalinist denunciations of Trotsky during the Twenties. It is said in Moscow that Ligachev, in fact, did remind Yeltsin of another politician who had behaved in a similar fashion in the Twenties: Trotsky. Yeltsin's earlier speech or what he said at his trial were not reported in the glasnost press. Given that Yeltsin was in hospital under sedation when he was taken to the meeting it is perfectly possible that he was not fully coherent. There were reports that he collapsed after the trial and the only person to rush to him was Gorbachev, but rumours spread very rapidly when the press does not report details.

But before going on to the effects of Yeltsin's fall on the morale of the Gorbachev camp it is essential to unravel this entire episode. We have already indicated the problems confronted by Yeltsin on a general level, but what was the actual chain of events leading up to his removal and what does it reveal as far as the nature of big city politics is concerned? The Western media, with rare exceptions, has hitherto resorted to extremely superficial and psychological explanations of the Yeltsin affair. Self-appointed pundits have preferred to leave everything to the First Secretary and simply accept his version of the events. Yet such an attitude goes against the grain of glasnost. The most authoritative account to date was published in an Italian newspaper in May 1988. Mikhail Poltoranin, a senior Soviet journalist, in one of the most remarkable interviews published in this period, described why Yeltsin was axed. Poltoranin is currently Chairman of the Moscow City branch of the Journalists' Union. He was a writer on *Pravda*, but was persuaded by Yeltsin to leave the paper and become Editor-in-Chief of the *Moscow Pravda*, a paper responsible to the Moscow City Party. Poltoranin was reluctant, 'but Yeltsin was embarking on a struggle against the "mafia" and corruption. He was looking for like-minded comrades. He needed me. And so I gave up everything else to take on what I knew would be a difficult task.'

Poltoranin described the Moscow City Party as a nest of corruption. All the leading government ministers belonged to the Moscow party. As a result the special shops were kept well supplied. Nobody asked too many questions, there was a total lack of motivation on the part of the workers who knew better than most what was happening and thus scrounging became a regular pattern of existence. Yeltsin and the reformers were attempting to confront the problem frontally. They failed, according to Poltoranin, because:

The Moscow Party holds very backward positions. Its thirty-three raion committees are real bastions of conservatism. When [Viktor] Grishin was Moscow Party secretary, the officials only pretended to work; but things functioned, because bribes and corruption flourished everywhere. The Moscow mafia could give a lot of pointers to your Sicilian original. Yeltsin tried to bring order into this mess—to stop the feuds and intrigues and to cut through the network of mafia-like corruption. As a result, the whole apparatus went into opposition, as I know to my cost.

We had hardly started to denounce the Moscow mafia when Valerii Saikin, chairman of the Moscow Soviet, the city council, telephoned me and, in an irritated tone, said: 'What are you trying to do? Yeltsin is here today, but tomorrow he'll be gone. And you'll still have to work with us.' That was the climate we had to work in. Another incident concerned a high-ranking official, Yurii Karabasov, who had organised an investigation in a fraudulent way. When we tried to write up the story, Karabasov himself told us peremptorily 'not to dig too deeply.' Naturally, we went ahead and wrote all we knew.*

Yeltsin's refusal to retreat and cave in to the mafiocracy resulted in all those whose 'livelihoods' were at risk uniting. They hatched a plan to destroy Yeltsin. According to Poltoranin by summer 1987 (ie before Yeltsin's angry outburst at the October plenum) matters were already extremely tense. While Yeltsin was holidaying on the Black Sea coast, Poltoranin received many friendly warnings that he was closely identified with Yeltsin and that 'adversaries could organise something against me'. Then one day a large limousine arrived outside his dacha to take him to Yuri Belyakov, the second secretary of the Moscow Party organisation. This man was supposed to be a lieutenant of Yeltsin. Belyakov came straight to the point when Poltoranin was ushered into his presence: 'He told me clearly that I had to choose which side I was on'. Poltoranin did so in no uncertain terms and realised that the apparatus was determined to get rid of the Moscow Party leader. When I was in Moscow in April 1988 I heard many stories about the sabotage carried out to discredit Yeltsin. All of them sounded credible, but it was difficult to obtain concrete evidence. Poltoranin described the bureaucratic resistance in graphic fashion:

> It was hidden, but effective. They tried to block any kind of initiative and tried to show that what the city secretary was saying did not correspond to the facts. We had lots of farm and garden produce brought in to fill the city's stores, but those responsible then kept it to rot in warehouses instead of distributing it. There were also trainloads of foodstuffs that came from the Caucasus and were sent back without being unloaded. When we published these stories in *Moskovskaya Pravda*, Saikin and Alla Nisovtseva, who was responsible for distribution, made new threats against us. Our editorial office was an island under siege, as was Yeltsin's office.

He did not stop there, but explained how the intrigues and manoeuvres on the Moscow City level could not have succeeded without support from the top cadres of the Politburo. Poltoranin spelt out the reasons behind the conflict between Ligachev and Yeltsin:

> Their relationship reached a crisis point on the question of social justice. In Moscow, Yeltsin had begun to close down the special stores

Corriera della Serra, 18 May 1988.

for officials and to abolish other special privileges for the nomenklatura. He tried, for example, to re-establish order in the special schools reserved for the children of high officials. He had begun to do what the people wanted. Ligachev says that this is 'social demagogy'. According to him one should not touch existing privileges but merely improve conditions for those who do not enjoy certain opportunities.

Ligachev, it should be pointed out, was doing no more than defending the 'stability of cadres'. What enraged him was Yeltsin's refusal to confine the discussion of these matters to the Politburo, (where, of course, Yeltsin had no vote and hence no authority!). Far more explosive than his outburst at the plenum was Yeltsin's decision to convene a meeting of Moscow Party activists, which included many rank-and-file members (workers and intellectuals) during the summer of 1987. At the meeting, Yeltsin described his differences with Ligachev in a very straightforward fashion. In my opinion this act more than any other single event sealed the fate of this incredible politician. An open appeal to the ordinary members of the party? This was unheard of since the bad old days of the Twenties, the very thought of which sent a shiver down the collective spinal chord of the bureaucracy. Poltoranin provides us with a real insight as to the extent of Yeltsin's radicalism:

> The fact is that Ligachev is the guardian of this apparatus. He thinks that it can constitute the driving force of perestroika. Yeltsin, on the other hand, thinks that the party apparatus—and not just in Moscow—is too greatly compromised: he holds that it has to be cleared away, as one does with the upper layer of soil contaminated by radiation. On this point there were fairly serious clashes. During the meeting with the activists in Moscow, Yeltsin openly accused Ligachev of not concerning himself enough with the overall situation as the number two leader should do, and of trying instead to take control over Party matters everywhere, at all levels.

The mafiocracy noted this division and flooded the Politburo with totally distorted reports designed to harm Yeltsin. This led to a number of ministries cutting off the capital's funds to further discredit the Moscow leader. By September Poltoranin had got a clear feeling that Yeltsin was being prevented from replacing the leaders of the district committees:

> When he realised that the decisions being taken were not being implemented, he tried to replace those responsible but was 'advised not to'. I remember one meeting, at which I was present, when there was a discussion of the 'meat and milk mafia'. At one point a woman

called Rimma Zukova, first secretary of the Zhdanov Raion, in which this group of *mafiosi* was at work, rose and said: 'If you want to finish them off, you'll have to settle with me too.' Afterwards I asked Yeltsin why he had not dismissed the woman, who was evidently hand in glove with the mafia. He replied: 'I can't—my hands are tied.'

In that fateful summer, Poltoranin was approached by a Central Committee official. This man asked him to sign a statement admitting that the articles attacking corruption which he had published in the *Moscow Pravda* 'had been imposed on us by Yeltsin.' Poltoranin refused and informed Yeltsin, who commented: 'I know that they are digging my grave.' It was in this atmosphere that Yeltsin spoke harshly to the October Plenum of the Central Committee. Poltoranin did not reveal the exact contents of the speech, but speculated that Yeltsin must only have repeated what he told everyone, namely, that 'the primary enemy of perestroika was the apparatus itself, and the need was to struggle against its omnipotence and its dictatorship, because, if it were up to the apparatus to decide its own fate, it was only too clear what the outcome would be.'

The Soviet journalist described Yeltsin's successor, Lev Zaikov as a man who 'had aligned himself with the Moscow apparatus': he and Ligachev were 'like Siamese twins'. The mafiocracy had fought Gorbachev and won!

Poltoranin, reflecting Yeltsin's own views, felt that the Nineteenth Party Conference in June 1988 should limit membership of the leading bodies to two terms since this was not only just, but would also be a politically correct way to remove over half the Central Committee and make way for new people. And what if the apparatus refused to accept this decision? Poltoranin struck a note of warning:

> The Party leadership must take account of the possibility that Gorbachev may appeal directly to the whole Party. It would be an unprecedented event. And the Party, like the people, would support Gorbachev. The nomenklatura amounts to between 15 percent and 20 percent of the Party; 80 percent are workers, peasants and intellectuals, and they are with him.

Poltoranin's interview coupled with Yeltsin's appearance on Western television during the Summit, which marked a high point of that spectacle, were clearly designed to appeal to Party members in the run up to the Nineteenth Party conference. In that sense the decision to go public was a correct tactic which succeeded in arming public opinion inside the Soviet Union.

Gorbachev's supporters rallied behind him, realising that the downfall of Yeltsin was a serious blow to the reform movement. A few weeks before his speech at the plenum, Yeltsin had received an anonymous letter what he thought could only be from the wife of a senior official:

> Do not try to castigate us. Do you not see that it is futile? We are the élite and you will not arrest society's stratification. You do not have enough strength. We shall rip apart the feeble wings of your perestroika. You will not reach your destination, so restrain your ardour.

It is obvious to anyone who has visisted Moscow since Gorbachev's rise to power that Yeltsin was very popular. Why? Because he talked about things as they are and pointed the finger at those who were preventing change. Gorbachev's position within the leadership was undoubtedly affected after the 21 October plenum. The speech he delivered on the seventieth anniversary was lacklustre and designed to appease Ligachev's men. When I remarked on this to various party members in Moscow, I was told: 'You should have seen the first draft of that speech. It was different and better.' The original draft had been distributed, but was later withdrawn and the common sense in the capital was that, after securing Yeltsin's scalp, the conservatives went on the offensive. Everything seemed to slow down.

The removal of Yeltsin demoralised rank-and-file reform communists everywhere. In Moscow itself there were student demonstrations in favour of Yeltsin and a large meeting called by the party organisation at the Moscow Polytechnic to explain its version was taken over by the students and transformed into a pro-Yeltsin manifestation. In Sverdlovsk there was a workers' strike in Yeltsin's favour and the disgraced leader began to receive hundreds of letters of support from his old town, until the swamped local post office had to put up a notice: 'No more letters for B. Yeltsin will be accepted.' There is no doubt that Yeltsin's departure was received with sadness by ordinary people. Some of Gorbachev's supporters within the apparatus, however, defended the wolves. Abel Agenbegyan, a leading exponent of economic reform, told a press conference in London:

> One must judge politicians not by their words, but by their deeds. Yeltsin did not pass this test, and therefore had to give way to others ... people like Yeltsin can be very dangerous because they talk

very beautifully in revolutionary terms. They raise expectations. But then they don't translate them into deeds. It is good that he has been dismissed.

When Agenbegyan was asked why, if this was the case, had he been an important post, the Professor was taken by surprise and now described Yeltsin as 'an honest man who had been effective till he lost his way in Moscow'.

Another example of doublespeak on the Yeltsin affair came as the reult of an interview I had with Vladimir Nikolaev, Deputy Editor-in-Chief of the influential weekly *Ogonyok* in April 1988. He was a staunch supporter of the new line and his views were, in general, positive. I asked about the Yeltsin affair, pointing out that those of us in the West who were closely monitoring the changes and were supportive of the whole process had, nonetheless, found the entire Yeltsin episode distasteful and disturbing: there were unfortunate shadows here from the past which the reformers were denouncing. Nikolaev replied:

Despite the efforts of those who are ardent supporters of perestroika the past cannot be got rid of overnight. You have given me your views on Yeltsin as an outsider. Fair enough. If you're interested I will give you my personal views. I don't know whether you're aware that Yeltsin used to report at his office at eight every morning and stay there till eleven each night. This meant lots of other people had to work long hours. When I learnt about that it set me against Yeltsin. I don't want a Russian version of the Ayotollah Khomeini in my country and Yeltsin had that streak in him ... I have lived in Moscow for sixty years, minus five which I spent in the army, so I know every shortcoming and every setback to daily life in Moscow. During Yeltsin's rule I didn't see a single evil removed or rectified.

TA: But why? Yeltsin says he was obstructed, hampered and that Moscow was like a beseiged city. Under seige by the bureaucracy?

VN: OK. So he's been obstructed. That means he was unable to have his way. Let me tell you that during the first two years he had unlimited powers. I am Gorbachev's admirer. I prefer his style. Do you know who I was reminded of by Yeltsin's style? Stalin! He used to sit up nights and keep our ministers up ...

TA: This is absurd nonsense. Your explanation is somehow too glib. Yeltsin, we note, is now out of power ... In any case surely the people who should have made the decision are the ordinary Party members of Moscow. Surely under perestroika the Party's functioning has to be changed. Everything shouldn't happen from the top. There should have been a Moscow party congress, with delegates elected by members and Yeltsin's opponents should have presented their arguments. Yeltsin's supporters should have been permitted a defence. Delegates could have spoken and then voted one way or another. The delegates should have decided.

VN: Here I agree with you one hundred percent.

In contrast to Agenbegyan, Nikolaev and many others, the Chief Editor of *Moscow News*, Yegor Yakovlev, described the Yeltsin confrontation as 'sad, tragic and complex. It is a very serious event that reflects the various phenomena in the country.' Boris Kagarlitsky told me that 'while Yeltsin was not an angel, he was undoubtedly the most popular leader of the reform movement after Gorbachev. What made him unique was that he lacked Gorbachev's caution and occasionally went for the jugular. That is why so many students and workers were saddened and angry about his dismissal and the disgraceful fashion in which it was carried out...' A young academic looked to the future: 'I don't think that we should regard Boris Yeltsin's political biography as having been completed!'

If we accept that there is a form of dual power within the party apparatus then the removal of Yeltsin was a clear blow against the reformers and weakened them for a period. Gorbachev and Yakovlev, however, were determined not to permit this setback to seriously affect the reform process. The exact form their counter-offensive might have taken is debatable, but again unforgivable circumstances played into their hands with the sudden arrival of an obscure chemistry teacher from Leningrad, Nina Andreyeva, on the scene.

In the spring of 1988, Gorbachev was about to leave on an important state visit to Yugoslavia; Yakovlev, at this stage, was in Outer Mongolia. Valentin Chikin, the Editor-in-Chief of *Sovietskaya Russia*, the journal of the Russian Communist Party, took a calculated gamble. Chikin is regarded in Moscow as a somewhat unscrupulous careerist and adventurer, whose political approach tends towards neanderthalism. On 13 March, Chikin published a letter from a reader which took up an entire page. Entitled 'Why I cannot betray my Principles', the letter was an open defence of Stalin and Stalinism. It attacked the 'disciples of Trotsky and Yagoda' and unleashed a savage attack on those who were denouncing the past. On its own this letter, despite its unusual length, would not have excited too much comment. Letters similar in content, but moderate in tone, have appeared in many newspapers and magazines. What gave this particular 'letter' its surplus value was that it was reprinted by newspapers throughout the country. Instructions had been sent from above and only a Byelorussian youth magazine, *Znamya Yunosti*, refused to publish it. How had this happened? Nina Andreyeva and her husband are in the habit of writing letters to lots of newspapers. A version of this letter, too, was sent to *Ogonyok* and other journals. Chikin decided to enlarge the scope of the original and sent a journalist to help in composing what was finally published. The question is whether Chikin acted alone or cleared it with Ligachev.* Certainly no instruction could have been sent for republishing of this text without clearance from Ligachev. When one adds to this that this 'letter' was read out at factories and schools, then it becomes clear that an underhand ideological counter-offensive was under way. The most revealing aspect of this whole affair was the failure of supposedly pro-reform editors to act before the return of Yakovlev and Gorbachev to Moscow, demonstrating that they were frightened to flout a decision made by a senior party leader even though this went against decisions reached at two successive plenums of the party.

Three weeks after the Andreyeva letter was published, *Pravda* published two contributions replying to the *Sovietskaya Rossiya* broadside: one was from several intellectual groups and the other was signed by thirty-eight writers, including people not renowned for their courage such as the President of the Writers' Union, Markov. What had changed? Why this three week delay before responding? An unsigned article had appeared in *Pravda* on 5 April, which had provided the cue for the fightback. This article, drafted by Yakovlev and approved by Gorbachev (and, one presumes, endorsed by the Politburo), was a sharp and authoritative broadside against Stalinism and its by-products. Chikin's initiative had proved to be totally counter-productive. *Pravda* went on to the offensive:

> It is obvious there are people who do not realise the gravity of the situation in our country in April 1985—people who believe that command and administration can provide the best solutions to all problems. The simplicity and effectiveness of those methods are mere illusion. Why is it that socialism needs to be 'saved' today? Does this mean that the old authoritarian and stereotyped methods and practices need to be protected, that the old order, in which bureaucracy, lack of control, corruption, extortion and petty-bourgeois degeneration flourished, need to be saved? Or does it mean

---

*In an important article in *Pravda* on 26 July 1988, Yuri Afanasiev revealed that 30 party executives at district level had authorised distribution of the article.

going back to true Leninist principles, real democracy, social justice and respect for the individual?

Life is the best teacher of perestroika and life is dialectical in its nature. Engels said that in dialectics nothing was established forever; there were no sacred, unconditionally accepted things. So, everything, including nature, society, the way of thinking, can be questioned. This is the cardinal principle of the new movement, too... We need more light, more initiative, more responsibility, more glasnost, more democracy and more socialism. The revolutionary principles of perestroika are firmly based upon the concepts of Marxism and Leninism. We shall stick to them.

If Chikin's aim had been to halt the growing tide of demands for democratisation, then his effort can only be categorised as a miserable failure. 'Thank heaven for Andreyeva', Mikhail Shatrov said to me in April 1985. 'She enabled our side to go on the offensive. They miscalculated badly!' After the *Pravda* response an anti-Stalinist storm swept the Soviet media. Every day some magazine, newspaper or journal disclosed the atrocities of the Stalin period. To detail every example would be impossible, but the following selections convey a sense of the new mood which gripped the reform movement:

* Forced collectivisation was branded a crime against the Soviet people and the economy. It was stated that it cost the lives of 10 million peasants and a convict's badge was pinned firmly on the lapel of Josef Stalin. (*Argumenty i Fakty*, 4 April 1988)

* Stalin was accused of clearing the way for the victory of fascism in Germany through the policies dictated by the Comintern at the time. (*Moscow News*, 10 April 1988)

* The criminal purges of the Party claimed one million innocent communists. The purge victims who confessed did so under torture. These atrocities were personally ordered by Stalin. (Published in dozens of provincial and national papers, April/May 1988)

* Stalin ordered the 1937 purge of the Red Army because he was opposed to Tukachevsky's project for the rapid mechanisation of the army which entailed the abolition of the cavalry and its replacement by armoured decisions in order to facilitate mobile defence operations in the event of imperialist aggression (*Moscow News*, 3 April 1988)

* By decapitating the Red Army, by imprisoning the innovators of Soviet aviation. Stalin delayed the modernistation of the army for

several years. His regime, therefore, bears a crushing responsiblity for the defeats suffered by the USSR in 1941-2 at the hands of the fascist armies. (*Izvestia*, 3 May 1988)

* The military defeats were aggravated by the blind faith demonstrated by Stalin and Molotov in the capacity of the German fascists to respect the Hitler-Stalin Pact in order to avoid a war on two fronts. (*Moskovskaya Pravda*, 18 May 1988)

* Stalin's penal system was inhuman and a crime against humanity. It was directed against political opponents and the poor. The word 'gulag' is often used and a case has been cited of a 12-year old boy sentenced to five years' hard labour in 1943 for robbing a canteen to get food for his young brother and his little sisters (their father was on the front and their mother had abandoned them). He was released in 1945, but re-arrested in 1947 for stealing a fish. He was awarded ten years' hard labour. (*Moscow News*, 1 May 1988)

* A monument should be erected to honour Stalin's victims. Aleksandr Waisberg, a laboratory worker wrote:

> Collecting signatures for a request to the Supreme Soviet to create a monument for the victims of Stalinist repression is one of the activities of the Memorial Group. In our opinion, such a memorial should include not just an architectural and sculptural monument but also a museum, a library, archives and a scientific research centre—everything that could held to immunise social consciousness against Stalinism.

Ten thousand signatures were collected within the space of a few days and the figure now stands at 100,000. (*Moscow News*, 1 May 1988)

* Power belonged to the Soviet state, but—in accordance with the distorting practice—in reality it was exercised by the administrative apparatus. (*Moscow News*, 15 May 1988).

The same newspaper had commented in the preceding month that 'The Stalin and Brezhnev versions of socialism suited the reactionary forces in the West ... Socialism was compromised.... Socialism and Stalinism are two incompatible ideas. Where there is Stalinism, there is no socialism.'

The assault on Stalinism goes way beyond what was achieved at the Twentieth and Twenty-Second Congresses of the Soviet Communist Party. And the process is continuing every day. When I suggested to a Soviet architect, Ayder Kurkchi, that the Architects

Institute should, along the lines of Tatlin in the Twenties, prepare a model for a proposed monument to the victims of Stalinism, he assured me that this was already under discussion and many similar ideas were being discussed.

Yet the conservatives did not simply go underground. *Moscow News* reported that it had received an eight-page letter from the 'Ignatov Group' which was an anti-glasnost platform and defended Stalinist positions; *Molodaya Gvardia*, a bastion of conservatism has published numerous articles attacking glasnost and defending the military interventions in Hungary and Czechoslovakia. The social base of the opposition lies at the very heart of the apparatus. Nikolai Shmelev wrote in *Novy Mir* in April 1988:

> One comes reluctantly to the idea that a conspiracy of silence is developing, or has already developed, in the country against perestroika, in which there is an increasing convergence between the interests of local leaders and a whole series of central bodies.

It was precisely this layer that was frightened by Boris Yeltsin. Khrushchev had been toppled because he threatened the sacrosanct stability of cadres. Yeltsin denounced this stability as the basis for social inequality and large-scale corruption. He too was removed. Gorbachev is now proposing a form of democratising the party that would, in effect, make the party a self-governing institution. This would be a permanent threat to the stability of cadres. Stalin's way of removing troublesome cadres was to either imprison them or despatch them to the next world. Brezhnev gave their lives back to the bureaucrats. Under him they had truly never had it so good. Gorbachev has made it clear that he wants to restrict service at the top to two terms (ten years) on the level of both the party and the state. It was in this overall context that the preparations for the Nineteenth Party Conference took place throughout the country. Expectations were high. The letters that poured in to the national and provincial press were the first major indication that the entire country would be observing the process.

Soon the correspondence columns began to reflect the growing anger and irritation at the way in which delegates were being selected. In one week alone *Izvestia* published dozens of letters protesting the lack of democracy inside the party and complaining at the automatic selection of party bureaucrats as delegates

* 'Bah! All the faces are familiar. They're the same comrades you see at all the Moscow forums.' (V. Severgin, Prokopyevsk)

* 'First secretary, first secretary, first secretary—are they delegates by virtue of their position?' (A. Konova, Sverdlovsk)

* 'The bureau of the province party committee narrowed down our 70 candidates to 48 for the plenary session. There were 48 slots—so they voted for 48. What sort of election is that?' (P. Pyanov, Chief Engineer, Odessa)

* 'The system of giving preference to Party committees is, unfortunately, often at variance with public opinion.' (N. Joffe-Goncharuk, Moscow)

* 'If the delegates didn't see any violation of democratic principles in the procedure by which they were elected, will they be able to defend these principles at the conference itself?' (A. Kirilov, P. Chichagov and 23 other signatories, staff members of the USSR Academy of Sciences' Institute of Applied Physics, Gorky).

What these and similar complaints revealed was that most of the delegates elected were the result of a Stalinist-type 'selection' ritual. It was the fact that these methods were so blatantly in variance with the known views of Gorbachev and the reformers which produced a series of minor explosions in a number of provincial towns. The bureaucrats in these towns had developed a cynical motto to curb any radical instincts within the Party. 'Moscow,' they used to say with a sneer, 'is far away.' In Moscow itself there was outrage when the mafiocracy prevented the election of leading reformers such as Yuri Afanasiev, Mikhail Shatrov, Tatiana Zaslavskaya, Yegor Yakovlev (the Editor of *Moscow News*) and others. This was the Moscow Party Chief Lev Zaikov's way of thanking his patron and protector. Students at Afanasiev's Institute protested at the way their Rector had been treated. Afanasiev was summoned to the Moscow Party Executive and subjected to a condescending and humiliating form of questioning which showed the mafiocracy's contempt for his political views as well as for the reform process. Ultimately there was a high-powered intervention to ensure that Afanasiev and Yakovlev got on to the Moscow slate, but the whole way in which the bureaucrats operated was extremely revealing. All this indicates the necessity of a radical revision of party rules concerning the election of delegates.

There was a mass outcry in the Siberian town of Omsk during the first week of June. For the first time in the city's history a big rally was organised without orders from the top. The initiative was taken

by the Komsomol* leaders who brought student and worker
representatives on to the organising committee. The declared
purpose of the rally was to discuss the obstruction to perestroika and
name the guilty parties. The meeting took place at the Dynamo
Stadium and was attended by 15,000 people. The speakers were
allotted five minutes each, but demand was so great that people were
encouraged to write comments which would be published. Five
hundred people handed in such comments just at the rally itself. The
local party bureaucrats had no option but to attend the meeting,
since it was no ordinary gathering. What was happening in Omsk
was a revolt from below: the party and non-party masses were
determined to speak their minds. The reason for the upsurge was
once again centred on the method by which delegates to the party
conference were elected. It had all been done behind closed doors.
Old habits, alas, die hard. When the list of candidates was published
in the *Omsk Pravda* it took everybody by surprise including the
secretaries of the primary party organisations from which the
delegates were selected. It was all constitutional, but raised points as
to the character of the Party's organisational norms. The party
leaders who addressed the rally were severely heckled and speaker
after speaker took the opportunity to denounce the deficiencies in
the social and cultural amenities in the town as well as the alarming
ecological situation. The delegates were told to develop a
programme of action and fight for it in factories and report back on
its implementation. The meeting ended by establishing permanent
discussion clubs and a 'centre for studying public opinion'.

In Omsk they had demonstrated their anger and mandated the
delegates, but had been unable to change the composition of the
delegation. In Yaroslavl, a few days later, there was a similar
occurence. The initiative here was taken by a small group of thirty
people, all 'unofficials' and members of a local 'Club for Social
Initiatives'. They had plastered the city with home-made posters and
banners calling on the citizens of the town to come to a rally to
discuss perestroika on the following day. Several thousand people
gathered on the banks of the Volga below the monument to
Nekrasov. The rally was given official permission by the executive of
the local Soviet and Yaroslavl party leaders attended the event. They
too spoke for the first time to a crowd that had not been stage-
managed and found it difficult to convince it that the Party was, as

*Young Communist League.

usual, correct. The cause of dissent was the same as in Omsk, except that the Yaroslavl activists concentrated on the particular selection of F.I. Loshchenkov, a former First Secretary in the area and a corrupt and totally discredited Brezhnevite. The fun began when the carefully selected delegates began to escape the control of the apparatus. A metal-worker, V. Kozmenkov, an official delegate, got up to speak. At first the response was sullen. Then Kozmenkov declaimed: 'I understand that my election as a delegate shows great trust on the part of the city's residents, and it remains for me to justify it. I'll admit that the elections left me with a bad taste in the mouth. The whole campaign followed the old rules. The principles of glasnost and democracy were violated.' The crowd cheered. When a delegate, a teacher, G. Lyadova took the microphone her message was short, but sweet: 'Here today before you I am defining my civic and party position. I'll come to the point immediately.' (The heckling stopped.) 'The main thing I want to say is that I wholeheartedly support your demands, comrades!' This was, unsurprisingly, greeted by a storm of applause, but the real surprise was to come in the days that followed. Several thousand people had signed a public petition as they left the rally which protested at the violations of glasnost in the election of delegates: it was agreed that these would be forwarded to the credentials committee of the Nineteenth Party Conference.

The provincial party executive in Yarsolavl decided to convene an emergency meeting a week after this meeting. There was only one item on the agenda: the case of F.I. Loshchenkov and the letters and petitions demanding his removal from the list of delegates. This meeting was of crucial importance since it revealed the divisions within the provincial hierarchy. These might have been present from the very beginning, but there was little doubt that it was the mass movement which brought them to the surface. Loshchenkov defended himself vigorously and received some strong support from the apparatus. The secretary of a collective farm committee, N. Zhukova, defended the former chief bureaucrat by claiming that he was a victim of slanders. She was answered by the local chief of police, A. Razzhivin, who defended the mass movement and stated:

> The people care who will be going to the conference. This is why protests have been lodged against Loshchenkov's election as a delegate. And in doing so the masses have exhibited keen political awareness and ardent support for restructuring. The restructuring is under way, but you, Fyodor Ivanovich, haven't changed at all. The

people refuse to put their faith in you. I voted against you at the last plenary session and I'm going to vote against you today.

Then B. Smirnov, recotor of the Agricultural Academy spoke to defend Loshchenkov:

I see it differently. Fyodor Ivanovich Loshchenkov is a victim of restructuring and of the democracy we are putting into place [loud laughter in the hall]. Some people might think it's funny, but he deserves to be a delegate.*

The former party chief was asked if he wanted to withdraw voluntarily, but he refused and the plenum moved to a secret ballot on the question. The resolution was simple: 'That F.I. Loshchenkov be removed as a delegate from the Yaroslavl Region to the Nineteenth Party Conference of the CPSU.' 87 members of the Party committee voted in favour and 13 against. A new delegate was elected after the vote.

In Sakhalin, the capital of the Kurile islands, a very similar pattern emerged. Here the initiative was taken by an 'unofficial' group. On 28 May 1988 there was a spontaneous gathering of a few hundred people to discuss the lack of democracy in the period leading up to the conference. A working group was elected from the meeting to draft resolutions to send to the Politburo in Moscow and to organise a further meeting. Half the members of the organising committee were active members of the Communist Party. On 18 June 1988 the Democratic Movement for Perestroika was legally registered as an organisation and its first meeting drew over a thousand people. Svetlana Shorenko, a young computer-systems analyst, who was a member of the new grouping gave me this information. It was agreed to plan a second meeting. 'Given the enthusiasm,' she told me, 'we were convinced that we would draw anything between thirty and forty thousand people.' But then the party apparatus intervened.

They put pressure on the party members on our committee and persuaded them to go on local television and declare that the meeting was cancelled. We were very angry and distributed leaflets saying that the meeting would still take place. It did. Five thousand people came! Everything was discussed in public. The party members now admit that they made a very big mistake and have joined our new organisation.

Perhaps the most sensational developments took place in the

*_Izvestia_, 10 June 1988.

Urals. There was a great deal of speculation as to whether or not Boris Yeltsin would be a delegate. His removal in Moscow had not detracted from his popularity. A young party member, Misha Malyutin, who is also a central figure in the Moscow Popular Front for Perestroika told me that the Yeltsin affair had created widespread anger and despondency:

> The whole method used was awful. It was the first whiff of Stalinism since Gorbachev's victory. It really did smell of the Thirties. Yeltsin represented the first centre of opposition within the Central Committee since Bukharin. Their first response: stamp it out!

There were many requests from Sverdlovsk that Yeltsin return to his old town, but these were refused by the Central Committee. Then, in early June, the giant Uralmash plant which produces tanks witnessed an amazing working class mobilisation. The factory committee proposed to the provincial party executive that their delegate for the Conference should be Boris Yeltsin. The party refused to accept this decision. The workers were livid and went on strike, something which would have been unheard of even in the late Twenties: then the conditions of war and famine had crushed the working class. Workers had realised that the Oppositions were making correct criticisms, but had wanted to be left alone. This was not the situation in 1988. A self-confident working class was not prepared to tolerate chicanery especially when Gorbachev talked endlessly about democracy. The strike of the Ural machine workers was a political strike which struck fear at the heart of the bureaucracy, and it lasted for a whole week. Moscow intervened by accepting the decision, but with a proviso: Yeltsin would be a delegate, but not from the factory which had elected him. That, you see, might create an unhealthy precedent. He was made a delegate from Karelia near the Finnish border.

The lesson to be drawn from these related events is very simple. The revolution from above begins to be really implemented only when there is a massive show of support from below. If what happened in the Ural machine factory, Sakhalin, Yaroslavl, Omsk, and parts of Moscow had been repeated throughout the country the complexion of delegates elected—even under the existing rules— would have been very different. If a decision was made to grant the party masses the sovereignty which should belong to them by right, then we can have no doubts whatsoever that at least half the members of the Politburo would not have been elected. Ligachev might have needed to travel to Aizerbaijan to win support. More importantly the Conference would have been able to elect a leadership that reflected the moods and aspirations of the party masses throughout the Soviet Union. That this did not happen can only be seen as a setback to the reformers.

There are basically two ways of looking at the Nineteenth Party Conference which took place in Moscow 25–29 June 1988. On the one hand, the apparatus was undoubtedly nervous and angry, but it managed to hold the line in terms of preventing any changes from being implemented at the Conference itself. On the other, the mainstream reformers proclaimed that the very fact that all the resolutions were passed should be treated as a historic victory since the road is now clear to move onward and onward. This is a tempting view, but should be rejected. In effect the Conference—for all its positive features—represented a political stalemate and a compromise. The decision to offer party secretaries the virtual right to become heads of the local Soviets, the failure to elect a new Central Committee or tackle the mafiocracy whose tentacles extend into the heart of the apparatus of the Central Committee, the refusal to denounce the methods used to remove Yeltsin, and so on: all this must be seen as a negative outcome, even though more changes are likely to be pushed through successive plenums.

On the positive side, however, the mood was well-expressed by Yegor Yakovlev in a column in *Moscow News*. Entitled 'Four Days that Shook the World', Yakovlev captured the mood of the conference, though the analogy with John Reed's *Ten Days That Shook the World* was somewhat far-fetched:

It was well after 10 pm when Mikhail Gorbachev made his final remarks. At 11 pm the delegates sang the 'Internationale'.

Together with all the rest I repeated the familiar words and, together with them, something that had been read long before, something half-forgotten, came back to me. Only when I left the Kremlin and walked off into the dark blue of the summer night did I understand that I was recollecting John Reed. At home I got his *Ten Days That Shook the World* from the bookshelf. John Reed was telling about the Second Congress of Soviets, about the birth of the worker-peasant power, about how the 'Internationale', bursting through the lighted windows of the Smoiny Institute, swept over night-bound Petrograd. For the sake of these minutes, he wrote, 'thousands and tens of thousands had died in the prisons, in exile, in Siberian mines. It had not come as they expected it would come, nor as the intelligentsia desired it; but it had come—rough, strong, impatient of formulas, contemptuous of sentimentalism; *real. . . .*'.

I felt like rereading the familiar lines of this famous book after the

four days of iron-hot debate, tempestuous expression of different
viewpoints, the hands sore with applause 'for' and applause 'against';
the four days of trying hard to understand others and to be thoroughly
sincere with yourself, four days of unprecedentedly frank political
passions. And you understand that this is a life that has been denied
your Party, and hence you, for so many decades. And yet it had
come—rough, strong, impatient of formulas, real... Could the
thousands and tens of thousands who had overtly or in the depths of
their souls resisted Stalin's one-man rule and who died in the prisons,
in exile, in Siberian mines... could they have imagined how it was
going to be? The delegates to the Conference decided to do what had
long needed to be done: a monument to the victims of lawlessness and
repressions will be erected in Moscow.

I apologise for having taken so long to arrive at the obvious: a moral
revolution has been accomplished in the country. Indeed, no end of
work still lies ahead, we are merely at the first stages of perestroika, but
the moral revolution has occurred. Fear, docility, demagogy, life with
eyes shut in a cat-and-mouse game—people have started to discard all
this. Man is changing his skin.

The poet Robert Rozhdestvensky described the Conference to me
as 'temperamental as a Soviet train'. He described the joy of hearing
real debates, which spilled over into the foyers and corridors. 'Much
of the *real* discussion between the two sides took place outside where
passions were strong.' Inside the conference hall, too, there were
amazing scenes.

Any public parading of statistics and sycophancy was treated harshly
by the delegates. These people were unused to this behaviour. The
Second Secretary of the Moscow Committee didn't initially
understand the slow handclap and mistook it for applause. Finally he
realised it was a show of contempt. This trivial episode was traumatic
for the apparatus. You know a lot of useless collective labour goes into
the preparation of a speech. An entire party apparatus of a region can
be involved. For a bureaucrat a prepared speech is like a life-belt.
Without it there is only the open sea. The rostrum was elevated, of
course, but it couldn't save you this time. And I must say the best
speeches were from workers and farmers. The conference laid the
foundations for the birth of a democratic culture. The chosen few can
no longer dominate everything.

Rozhdestvensky described how once years ago, while he was
reading a poem aloud, Khrushchev had muttered loudly from the
front row: 'I can't understand a word,' and the refrain had been
taken up by timeservers in the audience. When he finished
Khrushchev had shouted to him: 'Come and join us underneath the
red banner, comrade Rozhdestvensky!' This had puzzled him since

he felt he was already 'under the banner.' How did he compare Gorbachev to Khrushchev? 'Gorbachev belongs to my generation,' he replied.

> He has entered life on the crest of the storm which has shaped our century. Khrushchev was head of the Moscow party in the year 1937 and then in the Ukraine. He was part of the old Stalin Politburo. That formed him and though he was an audacious man as we saw at the Twentieth Party Congress, he could never transcend his formative years. Gorbachev has lived through the period when the wave was being rolled back. He is an emotional and passionate man, but with an amazing degree of self-control. Some people tell you: 'How do I know what I'm going to say till I've said it.' Gorbachev is not like that. One big reason for his popularity is the peace plank. You can tell with him it's not an act. He believes in it deeply and this unites him to our people. The danger of a nuclear war obsesses many of our citizens. I remember once during the Cuban crisis a car tyre burst with a loud bang on Gorky Street. For a minute everything stood still. The whole street was traumatised. Gorbachev wants to make the world safe.*

Everyone was agreed that it was the public show of dissent that made the Conference a truly historic event. Moreover all the speeches were reported in the press the next day and every day there were special conference editions on television. It was in this atmosphere that Boris Yeltsin polarised the conference with a sharp attack on the conservatives and a demand for his political rehabilitation. This latter proposal has been deliberately misunderstood by some commentators, but all the unofficial groups and many party delegates saw it for what it was: to rid the party of Stalinist-style methods.

Yeltsin's speech to the Conference† was not universally popular, but Yegor Yakovlev in *Moscow News* described him as receiving a 'never-ending ovation'. Why? Yeltsin is not a great public speaker. It was the contents of his speech. These reflected the concerns of the party masses. Yeltsin stated bluntly (a) that the election procedure for delegates was undemocratic; (b) it was necessary to institutionalise popular power to guard permanently against any throwback to the past and (c) he had strong differences with Ligachev on the question of 'social justice' and the entire question of implementing perestroika:

Moscow News, 6 July 1988.
†See Appendix I.

The proposal of the report on the combining of functions of the first secretary of the party committee and the organs of soviet power turned out to be so unexpected for the delegates that a worker speaking here stated: 'To me it is still not comprehensible.' As a minister I say: me too! Time is needed to think over this proposal. It is a very complex question. And so I, for example, would suggest a popular referendum on this question [Applause]...

Some proposals on elections. They must be general, direct and secret, including secretaries, General Secretary of the Central Committee, etc. From top to bottom the staff of the bureau in the oblasts or the Politburo should be elected in the same way by all communists (as if to have two rounds of elections). This must also extend to the Supreme Soviet, the trades unions and the Komsomol...

In the ranks of the country there is an estabished rule: a leader goes, a leadership goes. We are accustomed to blaming the dead for everything. You can't get a comeback. Now it turns out that during the stagnation only Brezhnev was guilty. And where were those who for ten, fifteen, twenty years then as now were in the Politburo? Each time they voted for a different programme. Why were they silent when the apparat of the CC was deciding the fate of the party, the country, of socialism...

Yeltsin then raised the issue of corruption:

Comrades! Our conference must take historically important decisions. Some demand the elaboration of the CPSU Rules and the Constitution of the USSR. They function. We don't think that it is necesary to set about solving this question only when the 'ugly duckling' grows into a beautiful swan as was proposed on the whole by some speaking here. Why was the ailing Chernenko put forward? Because the Party Control Commission was afraid of calling for a smallish deviation from the norms of party life and is now afraid to attract the leaders of the major republics away from their bribes, their millions lost to the state and other things? And probably knowing something from them. It is necessary to say that this liberalism on the part of comrade Solementsev [Head of Party Control Commission] towards the millionaire-bribetakers calls for some sort of unease.

I consider that some members of the Politburo, guilty as members of a collective organ, invested with the confidence of the CC and the party, must answer: why has the country and party been brought to such a condition? And after that to draw the conclusion—to remove them from the make-up of the Politburo. [Applause] This is a more humane step than criticising them posthumously and then burying them again!

Yeltsin was attacked principally by apparatchiks from the Moscow party and elsewhere, but the star turn in this debate was when Ligachev, the principal defender of the apparat against the 'excesses' of glasnost and perestroika, took the floor. Ligachev's over-familiar reference to Yeltsin as 'Boris' and 'tu' did not go down well. Those who attended the conference told the author that it was a classic bureaucrat's speech. Ligachev was surprised when he paused, but did not get the applause. He attacked 'that ersatz newspaper *Moscow News*' and defended the Politburo. A Siberian delegate, S. Melnikov, had attacked the Politburo and demanded the removal of Gromyko, Solementsev, Ryzhkov and others. Ligachev now told the conference that the Politburo members under attack had voted for Mikhail Gorbachev at a critical moment. The implication here was that the king-makers should be immune to democratisation. Ligachev taunted Yeltsin with the fact that the latter had introduced rationing in Sverdlovsk whereas he, Ligachev, had managed Omsk without such measures. The bulk of Ligachev's speech was an attack on Yeltsin, thus confirming—if confirmation is still needed—that the apparatus saw him as a dangerous figure who threatened all their privileges. Ligachev said that many people had asked what he had been doing at particular times. 'I was building socialism,' he answered but met with little response.*

The first reply to Ligachev came from V.A. Volkov, secretary of the Party committee at a Sverdlovsk machinebuilding factory:

> I would not be the only person here whose spirit would be heavy if everything remained as it was after the speech of comrade Ligachev on Boris Yeltsin. Yes, Yeltsin is a difficult man with a strong character. He is a hard, even a harsh man. But this leader, working in Sverdlovsk oblast party organisation did a great deal for the authority of the party worker in the party. He was a man whose deeds did not diverge from his words. Therefore his authority still remains high among ordinary people. It is my view that the Central Committee of the party injured its own authority by not publishing the materials of the October plenum [applause]. I don't agree with the declaration of comrade Ligachev as regards rationing. The situation as it was with products under Yeltsin unfortunately doesn't exist today.... Therefore I want to say and I think the Sverdlovsk delegation support me that Yeltsin did a great deal for the Sverdlovsk oblast where his prestige remains high with ordinary people [applause].

The point being made about rationing is an important one. Yeltsin made sure that everybody was entitled to the same amount of

---

*The week after the Party conference this phrase was immortalised on the Moscow stage. 'Where have you been all this time?' a wife asks of her husband. 'Don't you know?' comes the reply. 'I was building socialism.' Wild applause from audience.

food and closed the special shops. This was popular with the population, but unpopular with the nomenklatura. Gorbachev's summing up referred to Yeltsin in a totally different tone, but was critical of his inability to get Moscow under control. In particular Gorbachev referred to the fact that Yeltsin dismissed three different layers of officials and still did not get anywhere. We could give Gorbachev the benefit of the doubt here even though to do so would be an insult to his enormous intelligence. Leaving aside the odd tactical mistake it is now indisputable that Yeltsin was, from the very beginning, a target of the mafiocracy. Any sober investigation of the situation in Moscow would reveal that Grishin's apparatus is still in place and the mafia criminals still have a hotline to the Moscow City Executive. Yet the First Secretary did not deal with any of this at the Conference.

In fact the whole issue of corruption is a time-bomb underneath the apparatus. The big Uzbekistan scandal revealed the existence of corruption on a gigantic scale at the very top of the Party. When I was in Tashkent in April 1985 the long-lasting First Secretary, Rashidov, had died in mysterious circumstances. It was widely believed to be suicide. Then in 1987 one of his leading lieutenants, Adilov, was arrested. He ran a private torture chamber and had amassed a private fortune in gold. Adilov told the Uzbek police who arrested him to get out of the region since he would soon be back in power and they and their families would be executed. This threat was made from a prison cell. A high-powered investigation team was sent from the Moscow police. Out of the team of six, three had nervous break-downs, as it became clear that they were uncovering a major scandal which involved top party and government leaders in the region. The money was rapidly hidden and lodged in houses all over the district. In June 1988, I. Kosymbetov, Minister for Education in the Kara-Kalpak Autonomous Republic was arrested. He was a custodian of the money. He voluntarily handed over 100,000 rubles to the state treasury. This money alone, as a local journalist wrote, would be suffiicent to improve the 'badly-needed water main in Nukus, capital of Kara-Kalpakia or a hospital or a kindergarten...' In April 1988, the chief investigator Gdlyan had organised a press conference at the office of the Procurater. His statement was reported in *Ndelya*, the weekly supplement to *Izvestia*. The investigator announced that a total of eight million rubles had been confiscated in Uzbekistan, but that it was wrong to refer to the scandal as an 'Uzbek case' since all the threads could be traced to

Moscow. He complained that very high officials were obstructing the course of justice. The general feeling after this was published was that the finger was pointing firmly at the apparatus of the Central Committee. A month passed without a response. Then, two days before the conference the same material, dressed in sharper language, was published in *Ogonyok* and casually titled: 'Confrontation'. The implications were clear: the top leaders of the party were protecting the miscreants. The investigators gave Vitaly Korotich four names of senior party figures who were implicated. Korotich did not publish the names, but when he was attacked by an apparatchik at the Party conference for spreading malicious rumours he created a sensation by saying that he had handed the four names to the Presidium of the conference. It was announced that the CC would investigate the matter. The legal position in the USSR is that a member of the CPSU can not be brought to trial or arrested until s/he has been expelled from the Party! Who are the gang of four? I was informed in Moscow that the four men were working directly under Solementsev, the man who as head of the Control Commission investigates all complaints of misconduct! Very few people would be surprised if this were true and many party members would be delighted if this led to the removal of Solomentsev from the leading bodies. *Ogonyok* in one passage in particular seemed to have cast a wider net: 'Of course there are honest people in the apparatus who believe that they've had enough and they defend these corrupt people.' The reference here is unmistakeable: the person the magazine has in mind is Yegor Ligachev, widely regarded as an ascetic and honest man, but who is now opposed to the thorough cleaning of the Central Committee stables. The reason for this is clear. It threatens the 'stability of cadres'. It weakens the apparatus and that is intolerable for the old guard.

Gorbachev himself was not totally euphoric as to the results of the Conference. He revealed this in a discussion with the President of India, and the joint communiqué stated that the Soviet leader had admitted the strong presence of conservatism at the Conference which he regarded as one of its weaknesses. The real problem, of course, is that the balance of forces on the leadership still reflects the situation of the Twenty-Seventh Party Congress and the preceding period rather than what exists now. When I asked Yuri Afanasiev what was to prevent the apparatus from getting rid of Gorbachev and Yakovlev when the moment was ripe, his reply was somewhat sober:

> Everything is possible because I believe that today we have no
> guarantees. Such guarantees can only exist when we have functioning
> social and political institutions. So far we have drawn an outline. Now
> it has to be filled in. We have to revive soviet democracy. Gorbachev
> and Yakovlev possess very great qualities, but on their own these are
> not sufficient guarantees of success.

Yuri Karyakin, a well-known Soviet writer, who together with
Yegor Yakovlev and Lev Karpinsky served on the Central
Committee apparatus during the Khrushchev era and was sent into
exile, expressed his anger at the apparatus. He had started off by
denouncing the way in which Stalinism and the Western Left had
transformed the thought of Marx and Lenin into a religion. I
expressed agreement, although it soon became clear that the dogmas
of the Brezhnev period had made Karyakin deeply cynical about
socialism. He spoke angrily about the corrupt apparatchiks, but
nonetheless like many others his hopes were rekindled by
Gorbachev. His judgement on the Conference was clearcut: 'It was
Yeltsin who fought Ligachev all the way. He's totally honest and he
has polarised politics. For me he's worth more than almost all of
them put together.'

The resolutions passed at the Conference represented an
important advance, but unless there are some concrete results the
rise in political consciousness could begin to falter. The spectre
which haunts the party masses who back the reforms is of their
leader as a prisoner of the apparatus. A number of people referred to
this possibility, of political consciousness starting to fall back,
although it is far more likely that if the obstruction continues
Gorbachev will indeed either appeal over the heads of the
bureaucracy and win, or lose and resign. The verdict on the
Nineteenth Party conference, perhaps, could be expressed in a
simple formula: one step forward, two steps sideways.

This was the view of many participants, as well as the mood of
many workers listening to report-backs from the Conference. At the
Slava Factory in Moscow, which has a workforce of over 12,000, the
factory delegate was cheered as he reported Yeltsin's speech. The
delegate from Sverdlovsk, Volkov, had been reprimanded by the
Party Secretary for his speech defending Yeltsin. When Volkov
returned to Sverdlovsk he was treated as a local hero, and given a
prime time half-hour slot on the local television station where he
further elaborated on his speech. When he reported back to his

factory he was greeted by a standing ovation. The workers were extremely angry at the action of the local party secretary who reprimanded him, and that same night dozens of them went to the offices of the Party secretary: in thick black paint on the road outside they left behind an extremely rude message. The next morning the slogan was the talk of the town. Since the workers had used a very special paint it was not possible to remove it by normal methods. At mid-day the patch of road outside the Secretary's office was given a fresh coating of tar and re-surfaced to the great amusement of the passers by. The secretary in question was subsequently transferred to the Diplomatic Service!

The unofficial groups immediately began a signature campaign on the streets in support of Yeltsin and demanding his return to the Politburo. In Sverdlovsk, Sakhalin, Omsk, thousands of signatures were collected. In Moscow, Andrei Babushkin, a young student from Moscow University and an activist of the Popular Front went out into the streets. He was beginning to collect hundreds of signatures when the militia arrested him. He was kept in prison for five days. When I met him at a Popular front press conference in July 1988 he was totally unrepentant. He had not been mistreated at all. The food in prison was just like that in the Young Pioneer camps and 'in the prison van I talked to the militia members about Yeltsin. They saw the petition and most of them said they agreed with me. They, too, were on the side of Boris Nicolaevich.' Babushkin and his young Komsomol friends were planning on returning to the streets again. His shirt was adorned with two badges: one was an image of Che Guevara, the other was a badge in Russian which bore the inscription: 'ALL POWER TO THE SOVIETS!'

Arkadii Petrov, *In Chair Park, Roses are Blooming,* 1988. The title is taken from a
ballard of the Stalinist era.

3. SOCIALISM IN ONE COUNTRY?
The Crisis of Autarchic Planning

In the long struggle between two irreconcilably hostile social systems—capitalism and socialism—the outcome will be determined in the last analysis by the relative productivity of labour under each system. And this, under market conditions, will be measured by the relation between our domestic prices and world prices. It was this fundamental fact that Lenin had in mind when in one of his last speeches he warned the party of the coming '"test" to be applied by the Russian market and the international market, to which we are subordinated, with which we are bound up, and from which we cannot break loose'. For that reason the idea of Bukharin that we can go along at any pace, even a 'snail's pace', towards socialism is mere petty-bourgeois trifling. We cannot hide from the capitalist environment under cover of a nationally exclusive economy...

The Platform of the Left Opposition, Moscow, 1927

Seventy years after the October Revolution the model of autarchic state planning is in a crisis. A country which sent the first Sputnik into space and which regularly orbits its space-people in the stratosphere is incapable of providing toothpaste in sufficient quantity to its citizens. An economy which can produce high-grade weaponry has to import its grain for livestock. A state which provides massive aid to Cuba and Nicaragua suffers a permanent shortage of sugar and coffee. The crisis of consumer goods has, of course, a long pedigree in the USSR, but almost five decades since the Second World War the problem remains unresolved. The fact that this is now publicly admitted has made possible an open debate on the changes needed to increase labour productivity and introduce a mechanism which reflects consumer needs outside the rigid constraints of 'the plan'.

It was in 1982–3, when Andropov was General Secretary, that a qualitative shift in the orientation of the top Soviet leadership took place. It was decided to break with the existing system of social relations that prevailed in the USSR and with the political system designed to service them. This decision was necessitated by *quantitative* difficulties. The economy had not only not been growing fast enough, but as Abel Agenbegyan informs us* during the 1981–5 plan period, the economy was plunging towards zero

*The Challenge: Economics of Perestroika, Hutchinson, London, 1987.

growth and eventual regression. This quantitative crisis provided a dramatic backcloth to the discussions within the Politburo, but it did not, of itself, produce a consensus for a qualitative break with the old system. It could have been argued that a limited economic reform, based on a new breed of dynamic managers, could replace the moribund gerontocracy of the Brezhnev period and move things forward again. Nor was it the case that Andropov's accession to the General Secretaryship involved the victory of a new political faction within the CPSU apparatus, a faction moreover that had already formulated an anti-Brezhnevite programme and seized power on Brezhnev's death. There was no such faction. In fact a number of thoroughly disparate groups and networks from an earlier period seem to have combined around a common idea which involved a fundamental rethinking of Soviet political economy based on the victory of Stalinism in the late Twenties and early Thirties. Simultaneously the top leaders of the Party had no clear idea on the way forward. This heterogenity and lack of policy definition has indeed persisted right up to the present and Gorbachev himself has frequently complained about the shortage of clear-cut ideas. In other words all that happened in 1983 was a virtually unanimous realisation that the old, inherited system was qualitatively bankrupt and that new alternatives were desperately needed. Why? In order to answer this question we have to return to the quantitative aspect and define its features sharply by putting it in a coherent framework. This will give us a picture of the equations that threatened the Soviet leadership in the early 1980s and even more so today.

The gross domestic output of the Soviet economy can be divided—utilising the parameters of classical Marxism—into two main parts: the first is the necessary product for reproducing the economy at its present level; the second is the surplus product that can in turn be devoted either to extra investment in the civilian or military sectors or to boosting living standards. Throughout the Seventies there was a slowdown in the growth of the total product, which meant that the surplus was becoming relatively smaller. A larger and larger part of the necessary product was being poured into consumer subsidies (food, rents, public transport) while a larger and larger part of the statistical (as opposed to the real) necessary product consisted of undisposable stocks: goods produced but unusable. This meant that any attempt to make the economy grow more rapidly would involve the following alternatives:

(i) increasing the social surplus available for investment by *cutting the real living standards of the population* and thus reducing the size of the necessary product;

(ii) slashing the military budget thereby releasing investment funds to get the civilian economy growing again;

(iii) heavily borrowing capital from abroad, so that the investment fund could be enlarged immediately to stimulate economic growth and exports thus enabling the money to be paid from an increased social surplus (in the form of foreign currency) tomorrow.

It was the unattractiveness of all three options that pushed the Soviet leadership towards a realisation that the whole mechanism was bankrupt and a total overhaul was necessary.

Since the early Seventies, for instance, cuts in living standards had been taking place in the domain of social welfare. The leadership had permitted the share of health, education and pension rates within the total budget to fall. The result was a disastrous decay of the health service which began to reach serious proportions, and of course corruption registered a sharp increase. The Soviet leadership, unlike its Western counterparts, was irrevocably committed to steadily rising living standards, even embodied in the Brezhnev Constitution of 1977. To have flouted these commitments would have been politically explosive.

The reduction of military expenditure was an appealing solution, but posed certain problems. Brezhnev's entire foreign policy had been a dialectical one: firstly, downgrade all interest in developing popular political support in the advanced capitalist countries and thus become more popular with the ruling classes of these countries. France was the prime example in this scenario. Secondly, build up the military might and reach of the USSR, turning it into a genuine super-power which, as Brezhnev loved to say, must be drawn into the solution of any problem or crises anywhere in the world. Thirdly, and herein lay the dialectical twist, the realistic wing (another Brezhnevite concept) of the Western and especially the United States bourgeoisie, realising both how powerful *and how reasonable* the USSR had become, would sign sweeping accords on military, political and economic matters. In this view the military effort was an excellent investment with a superb rate of return: détente would permit military reductions, the entry of the USSR into stable trade and economic relations with the USA and other capitalist states, and an all-round consolidation and re-invigoration of Soviet security and the Soviet economy.

In the pursuit of these aims, Brezhnev ignored China, respected Washington's nerves by making no move towards the Japanese, by behaving 'responsibly' towards the West Germans, and sacked Podgorny for being too militant on Africa. In short Brezhnev abased himself before the Americans in the political sphere while pouring money into his military build-up.

All this boomeranged and hit the Brezhnevite leadership smack in the face in 1979 with what the *Economist* in a famous front cover of that time called 'The Fun of Rearmament'. The West re-introduced economic warfare against the USSR and embarked on a serious bid to destabilise Eastern Europe, as well as Soviet allies in the third world. By 1980 what Brezhnev had trumpeted even as early as 1978 as his greatest historic achievement—finally and irrevocably securing the USSR from any military threat—had become what Marshal Ogarkov referred to as a 'new imperialist encirclement' of the USSR, more menacing than anything the Soviet Union had faced 'since 1941'.

Brezhnev could have argued that the unrealistic sections of the bourgeoisie had taken over in Washington and that he was the only realist, but economic statistics told a sorry tale. The Soviet share of world Gross Domestic Product stood at 14 per cent; the United States, its NATO subordinates and Japan among them shared 56 percent of GDP and, for good measure, China had been driven into the anti-Soviet camp. This was the real context in which Reagan offered the USSR a flat-out arms race. The Americans knew that if the Soviets accepted the challenge its economy would explode sky-high. If they refused, the USA would by the 1990s be able to 'prevail'. Crazy, perhaps, from the point of view of humanity, but unrealistic? Thus the early Eighties were hardly a time for slashing the military budget. The real pressures were for an increase in arms spending.

The option of borrowing from abroad was, quite simply, a non-starter given the conditions of all-out economic warfare in the early Eighties. But even if the conditions had been absent, the risks entailed in borrowing were very great. Soviet exports were dominated by raw materials, particularly by oil and gas. Manufactured and processed goods represented a small proportion, mainly, it has to be said, because of the extremely low quality of these goods. And if oil was to be the means of repayment then everything depended on world prices. In the 1980s these slumped. So large-scale borrowing on all counts was not a serious option for the planners in the Politburo.

So far we have looked at the crisis of orientation within the Soviet leadership from the viewpoint of attempting to generate new growth in the economy without qualitative changes in its structure and mode of functioning. But other critical issues must have entered the picture, especially relations with Eastern Europe. A transfer of allegiance by any Eastern European state, or a restoration of capitalism there, would represent a catastrophic blow to the political authority and, indeed, security of any Soviet leadership. Perhaps less obviously, the last thing that any Soviet leadership would ever want to repeat is having to use military force to bind any Eastern European state into the Warsaw Pact and COMECON. The entire strategy of the Soviet leaders following the invasion of Czechoslovakia in 1968 had been directed towards making the use of military force redundant. This was done partly through constitutional changes—stressing the 'leading role of the party' and the alliance with the Soviet Union in the constitutions—partly through much closer collaboration between ruling parties, involving more give and take on the part of the CPSU itself, but above all through a growing economic integration and division of labour within COMECON itself. This meant creating conditions whereby it would be in the vital economic interests of each Eastern European state to maintain good relations with the Soviet Union. This task became even more important for the states of 'Northern Triangle' (East Germany, Czechoslovakia and Poland) after the Treaties with the Bundesrepublik and the Helsinki Accords which accepted the present boundaries; thus the alliance with the USSR was made less important in terms of guaranteeing their post-War territorial integrity against any possible West German/NATO rejection of Potsdam or a revival of the territorial claims based on the 1937 frontiers of the Third Reich.*

The Soviet efforts at developing a real division of labour and economic integration were exposed as extremely vulnerable during the Polish crisis of 1980–83 and by the slump in world oil prices. During the Polish crisis serious proposals were considered by the Poles to move out of COMECON and/or for a large bulk of its productive assets to be handed over to Western capitalist creditors.

---

*These demands have, of course, been revived by the extreme right-wing elements inside the CDU/CSU and the legal status of the Treaties of the early Seventies is still a matter of constitutional debate in West Germany. But it is extremely unlikely that German revanchist claims on Poland or Czechoslovakia would receive support from the United States or the non-German NATO powers.

In such circumstances what could the Soviet Union have done? It could have scuttled any moves in this direction by a multi-billion dollar aid package, but did it have the resources to afford such a bail-out? Possibly, but it would have represented an extremely severe economic drain. As it happened, the Jaruzelski coup of 13 December 1981 ended that particular crisis, but with the collapse of world oil prices, integration of Eastern Europe with the USSR via oil was plunged into jeopardy. The Hungarians or East Germans could buy oil on the world market as cheaply as Soviet oil. Why then should they remain oriented economically to the East? This problem has worsened in the Eighties as far as the Hungarian economy is concerned; the East German economy is also much more dependent on its special relationship with West Germany and therefore less subject to purely economic reasons of state binding it to the Soviet bloc.

By the early Eighties the entire Soviet effort of the preceding decade to achieve a more 'organic' relation with Eastern Europe through economic integration was under a very serious threat. This was due to the chronic backwardness and weakness of the Soviet economy or, at any rate, its non-military branches. This fact was another source of nightmares for Andropov as he and the Politburo surveyed the horizon. It was against the combined background of all that we have listed above that the Soviet leadership evidently came to the conclusion that drastic, qualitative changes were needed. New questions arose. What qualitative politico-ideological steps could be taken that would make Soviet workers accept some belt-tightening *voluntarily*? What qualitative foreign policy moves, again involving a massive politico-ideological operation, could reduce the external threat to the USSR? And what new growth engines could be introduced into the economy? It is this last question which soon assumed a central role in a debate which has still to be resolved. Nor is it a debate limited to the Soviet Union and Eastern Europe. It has been discussed at great length by socialist and Marxist economists in the East and West,* and it is this debate that we must now address.

Socialism and the Plan
The most common explanation in the West today is a very simple one: planning does not work and you must have a market. This

---

*In the West there has been an extended debate in the pages of *New Left Review* from 1986–1988 in which Ernest Mandel, Alec Nove, W. Burus, Diane Elson, among others, have attempted to come to grips with the problems faced by the Soviet economy.

simple thesis is then given an ideological colouring: the market equals capitalism and it works; the plan equals socialism and it does not work. This is an entirely worthless argument at the level of general principles. Perfect markets would be fine and perfect planning would be fine, but neither are feasible in the present world. The neo-liberal case is based on an obvious double-standard. It compares a non-existent perfect market with the actually existing Soviet planning mechanism. As the Polish economist W. Brus has often pointed out, in the East people exaggerate the qualities of markets because they haven't experienced it. The fact is that both planning and markets possess benefits and deficiencies. What is clearly required is to practically combine the advantages of each while minimising their costs.

In the USSR, part of the cause of the crisis does undoubtedly lie with commandist planning, by which I mean that if the measure of enterprise performance is the achievement of material output targets within a narrow time-span, then clearly there is no space to encourage technological innovation and thereby increase productivity. Simultaneously a failure to assess the relationship between material inputs and outputs results in the total lack of incentives to economise on inputs. This in its turn results in a massive waste of raw materials, energy and, primarily, labour. Furthermore since output is assessed from enterprises rather than on the basis of sales to voluntary buyers, performance is not judged on the quality of the output. The consequences are a great deal of substandard and unusuable products.

There are, of course, other costs entailed in the central planning mechanism. For instance the absence of price indicators means that the planners might decide to invest in branches of production which have low rates of return instead of others with far higher capacities to generate an economic surplus. And there are the social costs of failing to provide consumers with the products they prefer. But all of these costs simply refer to the fact that planning as a technical economic mechanism for total management of the economy is far from perfect. But these should be seen as defects, not by any means as a blanket *condemnation* of centralised planning. It should not be forgotten that historically such planning has achieved remarkable results, especially in the Soviet Union itself: it was not perfect, of course, not economically optimal, but very remarkable if one compares it to economies at a similar level of development as the Soviet economy in the Twenties, Thirties, Forties and Fifties. A commandist planning structure is perfectly capable of achieving a limited set of ambitions. In the Soviet Union today the results can be seen in the fields of energy, metallurgy, armaments and space, to name the most important areas.

Nor must we forget the substantial costs of the market, whether it is capitalism proper as in the West or Mexico, Brazil, India and South Korea or 'market-socialism' on the Yugoslav model. The economic and human wastage of unemployment, the costs of inevitable social and class conflicts and the costs of transactions (advertising staffs, sales, marketing and other non-productive spending). Add to this the continuing monopolisation and cartelisation which is an integral part of all actually existing market economies. The notion that the market is 'free' is clearly a joke in bad taste. There is also the little matter of the enormous social costs of the war machine, which in the United States, France and Britain has reached formidable proportions.

The real question is this: why could centralised planning achieve such remarkable results in earlier decades yet be incapable of doing so now?

There is no doubt that central command planning using material volume targets can be applied much more easily when growth is achieved through adding new factors of production, such as extra labour, extra machinery and extra raw materials. In other words, extensive rather than intensive growth. The latter would entail gaining an increased output from the existing labour force, stock of machinery, energy, and so on.

The slowdown in Soviet economic growth in the late Seventies was partly due to the reduction and near exhaustion of reserves of labour. The pool that had existed in agriculture had dried up and soviet agriculture in the Eighties faces a serious labour shortage. The reserves of female labour are exhausted; pensioners, mobilised in their millions during the Seventies via a scheme of material incentives have also been used up. This leaves the vast reserves of Central Asia, but the labour shortages are in the main industrial regions of Russia and the Ukraine. Labour shortages can cripple any economy regardless of whether it is run on capitalist lines or is planned. The same holds true as far as sources of energy are concerned. In the Soviet Union these remain enormous—the largest reserves in the world—but the easily and cheaply attainable oil supplies began to run down by the late Seventies and the costs of developing the new supplies in Siberia will be very large and so will represent a further drag on the overall growth of the economy.

These are substantial problems, but by themselves can not explain the stagnation and incipient crisis of the economic system. Apart from anything else the formal shortage of labour is the product of very large reserves of underutilised labour within the state sector itself. The relative shortage of energy could be better described as a wastage of energy. The shortage of consumer goods is combined with a massive surplus of undisposable, poor quality stocks of consumer goods. The list could be multiplied endlessly. None of this is the result of planning *per se*, though it could be argued that it is the outcome of very bad planning. Nor is it the result (rather than the cause) of reaching the limits of extensive growth. So, we must probe a bit deeper.

The Socio-Political Origins of The Crisis Of Planning

The great professional error to which Western economists often succumb is an assumption that is largely valid for capitalist economics (though even here many professional economists tend to exaggerate): namely, that economic activity can be treated separately from the political sphere. State planning in the USSR was never a technical-economic mechanism. It was never simply a set of procedures for calculating and allocating resources for economic reproduction in advance. What central planning has always meant in the USSR has been the allocation and exchange of resources through a *continuous political process:* a process of bargaining, negotiation and exchange carried out by literally millions of people every working day. The actual Five-Year Plan document is simply a periodic summing up and overall guideline for future molecular politics and nothing more!

This real—ie political—planning process takes place through two interlinked administrative hierarchies: the state hierarchy running from plant to enterprise management to central government ministry; and the party hierarchy running from primary organisation in the plant, through *raikom* (local level) and *obkom* (district level) to the apparatus of the central committee. At each level of these parallel hierarchies, it is the party executive which has the formal authority to dominate the corresponding state body, with the former handling general policy and control, and the latter handling administrative detail.

Two basic features of this arrangement are often overlooked. The first is the fact that the quality of this planning process depends precisely upon the *ideological, moral and socio-political 'health'* of these hierarchies. Is there a legal culture embedded in them? Is there a strong public ethic within them? Is there a strong common commitment to shared socio-political goals? Are career structures that promote talented, honest, energetic people operating or not? The second feature, usually ignored in the West, is that these hierarchies do not and can not stop at the level of plant management: they extend down into the very heart of the production workers themselves. This is something completely alien to the market conditions of capitalist enterprises. For workers in Britain the spur to work is overwhelmingly negative: the threat of the sack and consequent economic hardship for one's family if one does not perform 'adequately'. In the USSR, this threat has not faced workers *who keep aloof from political conflicts* since the Fifties. They have been given very great job security, not only in law, but in practice, not least because for every plant manager there is a powerful economic incentive to hoard labour and maintain labour reserves in order to meet future plan targets. Thus the planning system—in other words the Party, Komsomol and trade unions—must *positively mobilise the workers to work*. The functioning of the plan depends very much on 'its' ability to achieve this task. So such questions arise as: do the workers respect the local party leadership? Do they trust it as acting in their interests? Do they feel that an equitable system of rewards operates? Do they have adequate material incentives to work?

When the centrality of politics in the planning mechanism is understood it then becomes easier to grasp why the system may work very differently in one country then to another, or why there may be good results in some periods and not in others in the same country. If we look at the Soviet experience of the last decades in this light it is easier to see the outlines of the picture.

In reality, an authoritarian structure is perfectly adequate to a market economy in which the logic of profit is sufficient to assure the maximum efficiency compatible with this type of system. There are many cases of this: Hitler's Germany, South Africa, Pinochet's Chile, South Korea under the Generals. When neither the market nor the logic of profit exists, as is patently the case with the Soviet economy, the absence of economic and political democracy becomes a strong brake on development and the overall advantages made possible by total planning are increasingly unable to compensate for this. If we then start at the very bottom of the dual hierarchies, it is obvious that a fundamental shift took place after the death of Stalin in 1953. After Khrushchev's victory over Beria and Malenkov, the heavily managerialist social composition of the party that Stalin had developed since the early Thirties was put into a sharp reverse. From 1953 to the present day the percentage of manual workers who were members of the Communist Party has risen steadily. Today one male worker out of nine is a member of the CPSU, and in the big plants the figure is often closer to one in five. As party members these workers are expected to provide a lead for non-party workers in production tasks. Workers who belong to the Party gain a good deal of political information and knowledge through their membership. All the surveys conducted in Eastern Europe reveal that workers who belong to the Communist Party tend to be more politically aware and more critical of general political conditions inside the country than non-party workers. Research also reveals that even in a country like Poland prior to 1981, workers belonging to the party were, in general, not treated as alien beings by non-party workers. The ties are close and in disputes the usual pattern is for party workers to side with non-party colleagues. To worker Communists it is axiomatic that in their country the working class is the ruling class. For the bureaucracy this latter is a cynical phrase, but it was, for instance, taken very seriously by workers in Poland during the Solidarity upsurge.

Another change occurred in the Fifties. Khrushchev sharply attacked the pattern of wage differentials and reduced the very large gulf between the incomes of managers and specialists on the one hand, and the incomes of manual workers on the other. Here too, Khrushchev was breaking with what had become a rigid norm under Stalinism. This policy was continued under Brezhnev. The Fifties also saw the beginning of a major effort to expand and develop the Soviet welfare state: housing, pensions, health, education, holidays and kindergartens all received a tremendous boost. There was also a strong committment to freezing prices, minimal rents and a steady, carefully calibrated rise in annual incomes. The trades unions were given new powers and were urged to strengthen the mobilisation of workers for production tasks by defending their *social rights* and improving working conditions. There is a widespread belief in the West that Soviet workers don't go on strike because they are terrified of the secret police. This is nonsense. Soviet workers undoubtedly have what we could call a 'healthy respect' for the KGB, but that has nothing to do with strikes. The basic reason why there are so few strikes for increased wages is because the problem has not been the amount of money, but the quantity of goods and services available. To acquire many of the most valued such goods, workers have had to gain them through the political process in the enterprise itself: a better house, a place in the best trade-union holiday centre, a car, other consumer durables. Nor should it be forgotten, especially by tourists to the USSR who visit Soviet food shops, that the workers in the big plants buy their domestic food supplies through the plant canteen and food shops.

As the economic crisis deepened in the USSR, the Brezhnev regime did the maximum to ensure that the workers in the big plants continued to be well-provided for, cutting into the living standards of other workers to keep the work-force in the big plants happy. Yet at the same time, workers in these big plants, especially the CPSU members amongst them, could peer into the internal organs of the planning system—into the managerial layers of the party-state machinery—and observe some extremely ugly sights. There were two important changes for the worse under Brezhnev. This was not the handling of dissidents, since they were treated harshly during the Khrushchev period as well especially if they were proclaiming a heterodox *political programme*. The two major regressions affected the functioning of the daily life of the system: first, the golden rule of the 'stability of cadres' and second, the total abandonment of any serious project regarding human emancipation or any vision of building a more just, more free, more creative world.

The much-vaunted 'stability of cadres' became, in practice, a charter for corruption, sloth and criminality within the Soviet managerial strata. The Soviet press was deluged with a flood of accounts (many of them letters from factory workers) when the *Andropovschina* against it began in 1982. There had been some brutal jabs against the most corrupt members of the Brezhnev circle while Brezhnev himself was still more or less alive. It was not a secret that Brezhnev himself was a deeply corrupt figure. This knowledge provided encouragement to the prefects of the bureaucracy elsewhere in the country. Soviet Central Asia became particularly notorious in this regard.

The important point here is that such phenomena completely destroy a social mechanism such as the Soviet-type planning systems. They do so not only through the mafia-isation of large parts of the managerial élite; but equally important is the ideological impact of all this on the working class base of the system. Why should workers exert themselves when they can see exactly what is going on? There is no shortage of evidence that worker-communists reacted to all this with a ferocious anger during the early Eighties. This anger is expressed most strongly by a political leader such as Boris Yeltsin, but even ascetic types such as Ligachev would be enraged by the scale of the corruption, while not favouring any significant moves towards democratisation.

Less direct, but in some respects even more fundamental was Brezhnev's ending of the emancipatory project. Even a cynical Labour politican like Harold Wilson managed to grasp in the Sixties that the 'Labour Party is either a crusade or it is nothing'. This is a thousand times more true of the socio-political processes that underlie centralised planning. It requires a great commitment, a belief in the future, in building a better world. Stalin generated this commitment through a permanent use of negative symbols: the Soviet Union under threat, enemies of the people everywhere, superhuman efforts needed to crush enemies. It is not that there were no enemies of the Soviet Union during the Stalin period, simply that Stalin himself had an uncanny knack of spotting them entirely among those who favoured socialism and Marxism. Khrushchev deserves enormous credit for appreciating that the Soviet people required a positive, emancipatory programme to work and live for. Khrushchev's vision had a genuinely socialist substance, although most of what he actually achieved was in dismantling the monstrous realities of the Stalinist gulag. His attempt to translate his positive vision into a full programme for full communism by 1980 was naïve and counter-productive and his practical attempts to implement his programme did involve too many hair-brained schemes. But Khrushchev was not a philistine. He understood perfectly well that socialism is ultimately about creating a new culture. For this to happen the activity of the Communist Party and its members had to be restored to a central place in society, which would require a new deal for the intelligentsia. It meant neither jail nor forced exile for writers and film-makers; it meant an attempt to seek truth through debate and discussion; it meant, above all, avoiding the casual criminality of invading a country like Czechoslovakia. Whether one likes it or not (and I certainly do not), the invasion of Hungary did not appear in the same light to Soviet communists as the entry of Soviet tanks into Prague. Kagarlitsky has described how this event marked a watershed for the Soviet intelligentsia. The philistine destructiveness of Brezhnevism had, by the early Eighties, ravaged the cultural communities inside the Soviet Union. The tragic consequence was a retreat by many intellectuals to an ultra-nationalism which was reminiscent of Black Hundred propaganda in the pre-revolutionary period or a reactionary mysticism.* The Brezhnevite mafiocracy had simply spat on any idea of progress through human emancipation. The intelligentsia was told to shut up or get out of the Soviet Union.

In these conditions workers could be forgiven for wondering what was the ultimate purpose or cultural meaning of the Five-Year Plan. Nothing whatsoever unless it be the private enrichment of the mafiocracy. The Soviet economic mechanism could not be run on this basis. Brezhnev's successors understood that quantitative measures were not enough. Talk of 'economic reforms' impressed nobody. A qualitative breakthrough was required. But of what type? This was the question that Gorbachev sought to answer in April 1985. At that time he insisted that he was taking on the job of General Secretary only on the basis of carrying out a definite programme of thoroughgoing change. It is this process that is now *beginning* and creating havoc within the ranks of the apparatus.

Socialism in One Country?

What we have argued above is that politics and economics are so closely bound together in the Soviet Union that perestroika only makes sense as a combined operation. Democratisation is vital for many reasons, but principally because it provides the only mechanism whereby working class interests can be discussed openly and defended. However if there is no quick improvement in the economy the democratic process in the Soviet Union could be seriously threatened since the General Secretary could find himself without any social/political base outside the ranks of the bureaucracy. This is a danger of which he is well aware, but it also explains why the conservatives in the party are content to raise their hands in a listless fashion for almost any reform while they sit and wait for Gorbachev to fail. And they are not alone. There are many politicians in Europe and America—not to mention far-Left sectarians of almost every hue—who also think (and, in many cases, hope) that everything will fail as it did before. For the politicians of the Right, nurtured on their own rhetoric and the writings of the experts, democracy is impossible in the Soviet Union. For the

*See chapters 6 and 8.

sectarian technicians of the revolutionary Left too much of what is happening contradicts their own dogmas. In public they say that they have seen it all before: Imry Nagy, Alexander Dubceck, Nikita Khrushchev, they never tire of reminding us, came to a sad end. But deep inside they are nervous. A little voice inside them keeps asking: 'What if Gorbachev succeeds?' The arguments on both the far Right and the extreme Left are based on a simple axiom. It has never happened before, so it can't happen now. Marx, a man remarkably free of dogmatism, explained on many occasions that history did not proceed in that fashion. In 1877, for instance, he explained in a letter to a Russian journal, *Otechestvennye Zapisky*, that:

> Events strikingly similar, but occurring in a different historical mileu, lead to compeltely dissimilar results. By studying each of these evolutions separately and then comparing them, it is easy to find the key to the understanding of this phenomenon; but it is never possible to arrive at this understanding by using the passe-partout of some historical-philosophical theory whose great virtue is to stand above history.

I have sought to explain the necessity of fundamental and far-reaching reforms in terms of the specific conditions of the political and economic structures of the Soviet Union. I have attempted to explain the rise of a politician like Gorbachev in relation to the socio-political environment which has produced him. The political and economic failures of the Brezhnev period are now referred to in official jargon as the 'years of stagnation'. This is a slight understatement. What Brezhnevism left behind was a huge, ugly boil which needed to be lanced. Gorbachev has done that and it marks a tremendous step forward. But on its own the measure is insufficient. Yeltsin, Shatrov, Yuri Afanasiev and many others in the more radical section of the reform wing of the party understand this very well, as do Gorbachev and Yakovlev. They all know that the Soviet body-politic needs to be thoroughly cleansed through new blood transfusions so that the deadly boils do not recur. This is what the real debate is about and, unsurprisingly, it centres on the changes necessary in the economy.

There is a universal and burning need in the Soviet Union today. It is felt by *everyone* except for the more privileged members of the bureaucracy. It is a desire for cheap and plentiful consumer goods. This is obvious even to a casual visitor. The perennial shortage of even the most elementary consumer goods products constitutes one of the scandals of the Soviet economy. A worker in Sao Paulo or

Seoul, Durban or Delhi, not to mention Calcutta or Mexico City, might be earning less than a Soviet car worker in Togliattigrad or a steel worker in Sverdlovsk, and in real terms this is indeed the case. Yet the working man in Calcutta or the woman selling pottery on a street stall in Mexico City have a far greater choice in what they *can* buy. One is not now referring to cars or colour television sets or refrigerators. No, nothing fancy as all that, but simple items that consumers need: razor blades, toilet paper, toothpaste, batteries, spare parts of all kinds, a variety of coloured material which could be used to make clothes. One could add the abundant supply of transistor radios which can be bought by even less well-off peasants, many of whom carry a transistor while they are ploughing the fields in India and Pakistan. Then there is the choice of food. Again, I stress, we are not talking about *haute-cuisine* restaurants, but small, family-owned eating houses or street stalls which acquire a loyal clientele in most parts of the world. The food is cheap, good and there is a great variety available. Why should Soviet citizens be deprived of these very basic choices?

It is on this level that perestroika has not worked well in the past. The fact that their everyday economic life has not changed very much makes many Soviet citizens cynical. And, incidentally, the sight of Western socialists, who have a great deal of choice on this level, warning against 'capitalist restoration' when all that is being proposed is an opening up of the economy, is somewhat grotesque. Nikolai Shmelev, an economist in the North American Institute in Moscow made a very good proposal in 1988. He suggested that the USSR sold off a part of its gold reserves in order to get foreign exchange to buy cheap consumer goods to fill all the shops in the country for a few years. This would provide a mass base for glasnost and a breathing space to build the Soviet consumer goods industry. He should have added that these goods should be bought from Brazil, India, South Korea and Hong Kong. Shmelev could have made his suggestion even more concrete by suggesting that the authorities could make a start by selling off the gold reserves of the Spanish Republic which Stalin so adroitly confiscated.*

But if the problem of the Soviet economy existed only at the level of consumer shortages it *could* be solved without too big an upheaval. However, much more than simple consumer needs is at

*Though it could be argued that the Spanish gold should be used to set up a special fund to aid the Latin American peasantry.

stake. The existing economy is no longer capable of delivering the goods. What is to be put in its place? The Novosibirsk school of thought, which is currently in favour, had begun to argue during the twilight of Brezhnevism that there was a growing chasm between the relations of production established in the Thirties and the forces of production of the Seventies and Eighties. It did not take too much for party academics to understand that the situation was nearing a point of explosion. The two best-known academics of the Novosibirsk Institute, the economist Abel Agenbegyan and the sociologist Tatiana Zaslavskaya, developed a set of theses which now influence the economic thinking of the men who exercise power. During a visit to Britain in 1988, Agenbegyan painted a grim picture of the Soviet economy. In order to reverse this process he suggested a drastic reorientation of the economy. This necessitated a fundamental shift in priorities on three different fronts. Agenbegyan pointed out that social provision in the USSR needed to be strengthened in the spheres of housing, food supplies and public health. 'Priority,' he stated, 'had in the past been given to heavy industry; social needs have received only what was left over.' According to him, perestroika meant a separate house or a flat for every family over the next decade. He spoke about the shortage of food and offered a solution that entailed an increase in agricultural output and a reform of the sturcture of retail prices by 1990:

> Retail meat and milk prices will have to be raised and compensation made to ensure that there is no fall in living standards. There is serious popular concern here and it is intended to debate publicly all price rises at least four months in advance of these planned changes.

The situation in the field of public health and education also revealed a significant regression. The reduction of the proportion of national income had led to a sharp deterioration in standards. Corruption was rife and the ordinary people suffered as a result. 'As steps to rectify matters,' Agenbegyan told his audience, 'the health care budget and capital investment in health for 1986–87 were raised by fifty percent.' In education, too, a shift of resources had been planned:

> In the 1950s education took ten percent of the National Income. When the first Sputnik was launched (1958), a Commission in the USA examined the cause of Soviet advances and decided that the secret lay in Soviet education at school level. At that time the USA spent only 4 percent of GNP on educaton compared with our 10 percent. By 1985

US spending on education had risen to 11 percent, while that of the Soviet Union had fallen to 7 percent, well below the demands of modern life. Schools are badly equipped, teachers badly paid and of low quality.

The other two areas of concern specified by the Soviet economist and his colleagues are, of course, the transition from extensive to intensive growth through the application of advanced technology and, most difficult of all, the reforms needed in the large enterprises which lie at the heart of the Soviet economy. These are referred to as 'moving away from administrative methods to economic measures.' Now there are two ways of viewing these reforms and they are the subject of a sharp debate within the USSR. However, before discussing the options open to Soviet planners it is worth restating that the one choice which is unavailable is a reversion to the *status quo ante*. The reasons for this were indicated by the Central Committee at the June 1988 Conference:

> The years of stagnation put the country on the brink of an economic crisis. An extensive, spend-away system of economic management fully exhausted itself. Its structure and requirement technical level are at variance with modern requirements. The commandist-administrat-ive methods of management became a serious brake. Production, its efficiency, and living standards of the population ceased to grow. Many social questions were neglected. The finances of the country became seriously disrupted and the sense of responsibility of personnel and labour discipline slacked.

Bureaucratic ideology had insisted over five decades that consumer goods were irrelevant; that queues, shoddy products, cramped and ugly housing, bullying manners, inculcation of servility were all part of a dedication to socialism. Changes are now on the way, but what will they be? Agenbegyan defines the core of the economic reforms thus:

> The distinctive feature of this reform is industrial democracy moving towards self-management in enterprises. The increased role of the workers in enterprises will involve them in determining the enterprise plan, the allocation of resources and the election of managers. It is a revolutionary programme. There will be much opposition, especially from management that fears the risk and dislikes change. This can only be overcome because the whole society wants to make a change. The driving force is democratisation ... Enterprises have to change in their economic management from commandism to regulation by economic means—prices, interest charges, wholesaling. This means the reform of finance and banking as well as price formation, and a

move away from centralised allocation of resources to buying and selling in the market.*

As it stands one could further explore what the last few sentences will mean in concrete terms, but utilising a realistic price mechanism is perfectly acceptable provided that the statutory right to employment is unaffected. The NEP period of the Twenties, when private enterprises were permitted to revive the economy, is often viewed with nostalgia by sections of the technocratic intelligentsia. What they forget is the shadow of one million unemployed workers which haunted the Soviet leaders of that period. If industrial democracy prevails then Agenbegyan is quite right to stress that the managerial strata will revolt, but there is another aspect of self-management/democracy which should not be underestimated. It is highly unlikely that workers will accept unemployment. They might accept redeployment, but they will need convincing as to why they should shift jobs. So, redeployment could only happen if workers are permitted not simply to elect managers, but to participate fully in the *political* life of the country. Lenin once defined politics under capitalism as being a form of concentrated economics. One could almost say that in the Soviet Union today economics is concentrated politics.

There is a layer amongst the technocrats which has argued for a full-blooded marketisation. Since the people who put this view forward are not in favour of a restoration of capitalism—or, at least they do not think that they are—the only possible way working class dissent could be contained in such circumstances would be through permanent repression. If Stalin's collectivisation plans could only be implemented by a mass butchery in the countryside which entailed the loss of millions of lives then any run-away marketisation which casts the social rights of the workers to the winds would require throwing lots of workers into the gulag. Nikolai Shmelev (who often says sensible things) is perfectly capable of an amorality which would greatly please Milton Friedman and other advisers of General Pinochet in Chile. Shmelev's motto is expressed in a simple formula: 'Everything that is effective is moral.' Leaving aside the defective philosophy which could be used to justify many things, what ideas like this reveal is a total and utter contempt for democracy. One of Shmelev's associates, the technocrat G. Lisichkin, argued in the pages of *Literaturnaya Gazeta* in 1986 that reforms meant asserting

*New Left Review, No 169, May/June 1988.

the will of an enlightened élite over the 'tyranny' of the majority. Boris Kagarlitsky has argued convincingly that despite their anti-Stalinist rhetoric, this particular layer of technocrats

> has converged more and more with the conservative-Stalinists. The brutal apparatus of political control has proved an essential element in a strategy based on frustrating the interests of society and lowering the standards of living of those at the bottom . . . It is no accident that G. KH. Povov, one of the major ideologists of the technocracy, appeared in the press with denunciations directed at Yeltsin while bluntly suggesting that, in this complicated situation, the Left might prove more dangerous than the conservatives.*

If Kagarlitsky is correct, and the conservatives have indeed decided to link up with the anti-democracy technocrats, that would leave the radical Left forces inside and outside the Party as the only defenders of working class interests. This would involve a total disruption of bureaucratic stability inside the party. The open contempt with which sections of the technocratic and cultural intelligentsia regard ordinary workers is hardly a secret. Most of them, however, seem to be out of touch with the majority of the population. For the Soviet workers today are not, in a cultural or political sense, the modern equivalents of the peasants of the Thirties. They are the products of the gains of 1917 and in their letters to newspapers and their speeches at regional and national party gatherings they display an awareness of the situation which is both more subtle and more realistic than the Soviet Reaganauts. Amongst the most interesting speeches at the Twenty-Seventh Party Congress and the Nineteenth Party Conference were those made by workers from the big plants. In a letter to *Izvestia* published on 14 April 1987 and entitled 'We Want To Live Differently' a woman worker in a ferro-concrete goods plant in Kurgan described the appalling conditions under which she and her comrades worked. She described the corrupt managers and trade-union leaders, bad housing conditions, inefficient public transport, lack of safety and health supervision and concluded thus:

> Excuse me for writing what I think. I am not able to express all at once everything that is in my heart. We have been storing up insults for too long, while remaining silent. Now life has taken a new turn. We see changes for the better. We want to believe that there will be more. Election of administrators, state product acceptance—all this is

New Left Review, 169.

correct and necessary. But I am afraid that behind the restructuring of production, the restructuring of everyday life might be forgotten. To be honest, for me the main thing is my home and my family, my children. I work for their sake. Believe me, the majority of women think the same. And if all around they are saying: 'We are restructuring', and in the homes it remains cold as before, and if you cannot squeeze into the public transport, and cannot buy anything in the stores, then for us it turns out that there are no changes. That is what we think about. In a word, we want not only to work, but also to live differently than we have until now.

The leaders of the Soviet Union are perfectly aware of this problem. Gorbachev and Yakovlev are *not* in agreement with the view that everything that functions efficiently is moral which is simply a new version of 'the trains run on time' syndrome which swept Italy in the Twenties and Thirties. Nor is it the case that the Reagan/Thatcher belief in the market, leaving aside the demagogy that surrounds it, even in economic terms proved effective, except for the rich. The large-scale unemployment and the growing misery in both the USA and Britain have been too well documented, and not just by writers on the Left, to require a further description here. Shmelev and his colleagues admire from afar or during short visits to the West the startling and colourful plumage, but they never look underneath and inspect the dying bird. Brecht once described Los Angeles as 'hell and heaven in one place'. He clearly meant that it was hell for a large majority of its citizens. Today, the American political analyst Mike Davies, has mapped in great detail the conditions of the poor in late-capitalist America.* It is clearly inadequate simply to argue that the market has not solved the real problems confronting workers in the West, since as I have already suggested, despite conditions of unemployment in Europe or the degradation suffered by blacks, non-whites and poor white workers in the United States there are still some consumer choices available. For this reason solutions which continue to stress productionist answers and treat consumer needs as irrelevant or as something which can be subsumed under an all-embracing hierarchy of elected workers councils, are beside the point. The main need which workers stress time after time is the need for consumer goods and the right to a choice. How can this be achieved? By strengthening the co-operative movement which has already begun and has become a modest success and to transform Soviet import-export policies.

Prisoners of the American Dream by Mike Davis, Verso, 1986.

There is absolutely no reason why some goods cannot be imported from the semi-industrialised countries in the 'third world', although this raises other problems such as the convertibility of the ruble, which will become essential if the reforms move ahead. A long-term solution, of course, would require a big shift in existing investment priorities, a change which would also be welcomed by the workers. If a worker is asked to move from a factory, to take an extreme example, which is producing missiles or chemical warfare weapons to another one which is going to be turning out products to satisfy human needs it is very likely that the workers would agree to change jobs. But this will depend very much on whether there is effective democracy in the country.

The Soviet economist, V. Seliunin, writing in *Sotsialisticheskaya Industriya* on 5 January 1988, sharply criticised official economic policies. He pointed out that though glasnost had been enthusiastically received the economic reforms had failed to excite any positive responses from below. He felt that what 'structural shifts are required in the economy—it is necessary to turn from work for its own sake to people and their needs.' A socially-controlled marketisation would be accepted by everyone from below, but workers refuse, quite correctly, to pay the price for decades of corrupt rule, economic mismanagement and the allocation of priorities over which they had very little control. On occasions the only way they could get rid of a corrupt or especially oppressive foreman was to stage an industrial 'accident'. A large object would suddenly fall on the victim and kill him. In the absence of real trade-union and political rights this appeared to be the only way to deal with the problem. Why, workers constantly ask, should *we* be punished for *their* crimes? Their confidence in the reform programme is not exactly strengthened when they see yesterday's oppressors now talking glibly of the need to transform society. The very people who yesterday were assiduously cleaning Brezhnev's posterior with their tongues are now praising the new General Secretary to the skies. Small wonder then that in such circumstances all the research data reveals that 70 percent of the population is nervous about the 'economic reforms'.

Those who want to remove all social provision and raise prices in the name of improving the 'country's financial health' have nil support inside the factories. Their only social base is amongst sections of the technocracy. The problem for Gorbachev and his team is to mobilise support from below. But this cannot be done without (a) rocking the party boat and (b) making sure that workers by hand and by brain experience concrete changes in their everyday existence. It is this and this alone which will transform consciousness. Social justice does *not* mean as Tatiana Zaslazskaya sometimes tends to suggest, a system of wage-differentials based exclusively on strict monitoring of productivity. It is not simply that the creation of a new breed of mercenary Stakhanovites is not an easy task in the USSR today, but the fact that workers do take their *social rights* very seriously. Only if these are strengthened further and there is a movement towards a different set of production values will the reforms have any chance of success.

No discussion of the Soviet economy could be complete without a mention of the country's foreign trade. The failure of the autarchic model based on the line of 'building socialism in one country' has *de facto* been labelled a failure. The Stalinist economy distorted social relations on every level, and produced a theorisation which pandered shamelessly to a crude Slav nationalism in the field of culture, in the realm of scientific discovery and in the sphere of research. All things foreign were bad, including many 'foreign' communists. The results of this degeneration are clearly visible today and acknowledged. A revival of the Soviet Union as a major exporter depends on massive structural reforms within the internal economy. Stalin's critics had pointed out as early as 1926–27 that the monopoly of foreign trade could defend a socialist economy

> only if it continually approaches the world economy in respect of technique, cost of production, quality and price of its products. The goal ought to be, not a shut-in, self-sufficient economy, at the price of an inevitable lowering of its level and rate of advance, but just the opposite—an all-sided increase of our relative weight in world economy... Resting our hope upon an isolated development of socialism and upon a rate of economic development independent of world economy distorts the whole outlook. It puts our planning leadership off the track, and offers no guiding threads for a correct regulation of our relations with world economy.*

Most of the signatories to the *Platform* that contained these and other demands for total democratisation were physically eliminated by the regime. Most of them have now been rehabilitated. Soon their articles and books will be published. When this happens many technocrats will be surprised to see how much the economic debates of the Twenties prefigure what is being debated today.

Platform of the Left Opposition, Moscow, 1927.

Omitrii Zhilinskii, *The Year 1937*, 1987.

4. THE CHIMES OF HISTORY
Trotsky, Bukharin and All That

The amazing confessions of Bukharin and Rykov, of Kamenev and Zinoviev, the trials of the Trotskyists, of the Right Opposition and the Left Opposition, the fate of Bubnov, Muralov and Shlyapnikov—all these things no longer seemed quite so hard to understand. The hide was being flayed off the still living body of the Revolution so that a new age could slip into it; as for the red, bloody meat, the steaming innards—they were being thrown onto the scrapheap. The new age needed only the hide of the Revolution—and this was being flayed off people who were still alive. Those who then slipped into it spoke the language of the Revolution and mimicked its gestures, but their brains, lungs, livers and eyes were utterly different.

Vasily Grossman, *Life and Fate.*

History has always played a vital part inside the Soviet Communist Party. It has always been seen as a weapon. It has been manipulated, doctored and used in a partial way from the early Twenties onwards. But the difference between the Twenties and Thirties was, however, decisive. In the first decade after the Revolution it was still possible to discuss and debate historical issues. Thus when Zinoviev, Kamenev and Stalin began an ideological offensive against Trotsky while Lenin lay dying, the former, then Commisar for War, responded with a series of articles entitled 'The Lessons Of October' which were published in *Pravda* and later as a book. With the advent of Stalinism the systematic falsifaction of history was begun, a process which reached its apogee during the late Thirties and Forties, a very formative period for the Soviet population and the international communist movement. Stalinism could not permit people to decide anything for themselves: Lenin was published only in a carefully-edited version; his widow Krupskaya's works were confined to the restricted section of the libraries and all Stalin's opponents were written out of the history of the Revolution. Since these comprised the overwhelming majority of Old Bolsheviks, a new history had to be devised. A classic of this genre was Stalin's notorious *Short Course History of the CPSU,* written on his behalf by timeservers and published in several and often changed editions from the early Thirties onwards. It was a pack of falsehoods, but it was used to train cadres and the teachers of history. 'Who will educate the educators?' Marx had once said. In the Soviet Union the answer was that the educators would 'educate' themselves. Stalinism drove history underground, where it survived in different forms. Since it was a crime to own a book written by any Old Bolshevik who had been executed by the orders of the Stalinist Politburo, the dissemination of history became part of an oral tradition in which memory played a major role. The truth could only be spoken in whispers.

Today some of the biggest resistance to glasnost has come from history teachers in schools and universities. It is easy to understand the reasons for their anger. Every day students read newspapers and magazines or watch occasional television documentaries or go and see a powerful new film or read about Shatrov's plays. Everything they read or see teaches them about a totally different history from the archaic lies that they have been—and are—taught at school or university. There have been reports of many incidents where students confronted their teachers and challenged the 'official' version of history, and in May 1988 the contradictions had become too explosive to be contained. The old textbooks had become so completely devalued that history could no longer be taught in the same old way. History examinations were postponed throughout the Soviet Union. New history books are currently under preparation. Who is writing them? There will probably be some important new works, but there is a real possibility that the new books will be written by the old authors. This time they will attempt to project the new orthodoxy. If this does happen it will be just as unconvincing, for if the style and method is the same, the new contents will not impress too many students. All the signs are that the new generation are both deeply sceptical of officially-received truths and passionately interested in history. It is a thirst for an elixir that has always been elusive.

The public discussions currently taking place in the Moscow State Institute of Historical Archives, represent the high point of glasnost in the historical domain. The Rector of the Institute, the historian Yuri Afanasiev has refused to avoid controversial subjects. The Institute, under his Rectorship, has become the meeting point for historians and all those interested in uncovering the truth. Two lectures by Yu S. Borisov drew large crowds and the second of these, on 13 April 1987, was followed by an incredible discussion. The star performer was a twenty-two year old student, D.G. Yurasov, who took the floor to provide those assembled with some information he had gathered while working in the archives of the Supreme Court and the Military Collegium:

> There is a confidential letter from Gorkin, then Chairman of the Supreme Court of the USSR, addressed to Khrushchev. It is signed by Gorkin himself and by the head of the Military Collegium of the Supreme Court, General Borisoglebskii. In this letter they report that from 1953 to 1957 inclusive about 600,000 people were rehabilitated. They are divided as follows: Military Tribunals rehabilitated about 200,000 people approximately, I don't remember the exact figures. Regional, territorial and other courts also rehabilitated about 200,000 people; the Military Collegium of the Supreme Court about 48,000; plenums of the Supreme Court, etc are also listed, a total for 1963–7 of 612,500 people, this is absolutely precise. EIDELEMAN (Chairing the meeting): Posthumously? YURASOV: Simply rehabilitated, both posthumously and still alive. The Military Collegium rehabilitated 31,000 condemned to a supreme sentence, ie. executed by shooting. From 1935–40 the Military Collegium condemned a total of 50,000 people. In 1953–7 it rehabilitated 48,000, including the 31,000 who had been executed.

Yurasov also detailed tortures by the NKVD and told the audience how the great theatre director, Meyerhold, had been forced to drink urine and how his left arm had been smashed. The official lecturer, Borisov, thanked the student by admitting that Yurasov 'knows much more than I do and, I expect, more than anyone else in the hall and I am very grateful to him.' Yurasov told the meeting that he had a personal card index of 80,000 victims of Stalinism and had been collecting information for ten years, that is, from the age of twelve onwards. After the meeting he was asked whether he was afraid of his sincerity getting him into trouble. He replied: 'Well, it will become clear whether a perestroika has really begun, or whether it's merely words again!'*

Since Stalinism was an illegitimate offspring of the Revolution, it had to erase the historical record as well as those who had made history, in order to prove its legitimacy. From 1957 until 1964, when Khrushchev was General Secretary, a very serious attempt was made to change course on this front. A great deal of research material was amassed and much of what is being published now was first discussed after the Twentieth Party Congress, but then the historians who wanted to dismantle the mountain of lies that had been constructed by Stalin over three decades were frustrated in their

---

*Recounted in 'Soviet History in the Gorbachev Revolution' by R.W. Davies, *Socialist Register*, 1988. Davies' extremely informative essay is supplemented by an interview with Yuri Afanasiev in the same issue of the journal.

efforts. Many of their colleagues had been responsible for building the artificial mountain in the first place. Too many individual historians had contributed a few shovelfuls of untruth to feel comfortable under Khrushchev. Under Brezhnev the process came to a full stop. According to Afanasiev 'the campaign to stop scientific initiatives in historical science was headed in the early Seventies by S.P. Trapeznikov, who used unlimited authority in the leadership of science to appoint to almost every post people who were dependent on him and on that basis held together by *business* connections.'

Brezhnev's time-servers had once again stopped the flow of history in a very literal sense. Fortunately the real historians were not sent off to be executed as had happened in the Stalin period, but the consequences for Soviet society were still disastrous. In his attempt to understand the victory of irrationalism in Germany, the late Hungarian Marxist philosopher, Georg Lukacs, assigned a central role to the misuse of history.

> An important ideological obstacle to the origin of democratic traditions in Germany was the ever-increasing, large-scale falsification of German history. Here again we cannot even outline the details. It was—to summarise very briefly—a matter of idealising and 'Germanizing' the retarded sides of the German development, ie. of a version of history which extolled precisely the retarded character of Germany's development as particularly glorious and in accord with 'Germany's essence'. It criticised and repudiated all the principles and products of Western bourgeois democratic and revolutionary developments as un-German and contrary to the character of the German 'national spirit. And the seeds of progressive turns in German history—the Peasants' War, Jacobinism in Mainz, specific democratic trends in the era of wars of liberation, plebeian reactions to the July Revolution in the revolution of 1848—were either totally hushed up or so falsified as to strike the reader as terrible warnings. This re-writing was not limited, however, to historical facts, their selection and treatment. It influenced in a significant way the methodology of the social and historical sciences, and indeed, far over and above them, the whole of social and historical thinking in Germany.*

Somehow I cannot believe that Lukacs was writing this just for Germany since everything here becomes, if we substitute different examples, applicable to Stalinist Russia. The slogan of 'socialism in one country' marked a retreat on every front. Nationalism of a very crude variety was encouraged. The Opposition were denounced as

*The Destruction of Reason, 1962.

'rootless cosmopolitans' (a not very coded variety of anti-Semitism) and reactionary episodes in pre-revolutionary history were glorified, especially during the Second World War. Tsarism was retrospectively defended against Napoleon and the defeat of the Japanese in 1945 was even hailed by Stalin as a revenge for the Russian defeat of 1904–5. It had been precisely this defeat which had created the basis for the Russian Revolution of 1905! Lenin, Trotsky, Martov had all welcomed the Japanese victory as a blow against those whom Russian Revolutionaries also regarded as their enemy. Examples like these could be multiplied a thousand times over.

The potency of history in current debates is registered by the slow pace of change immediately after Gorbachev came to power. When he spoke on the fortieth anniversary of victory in the Second World War, the new General Secretary paid tribute to his predecessor: 'The gigantic work at the front and the rear was led by the party, its Central Committee, and the State Committee for Defence headed by the General Secretary of the CC CPSU(b) Iosif Vissarionivich Stalin.' Did he not know about Stalin's crimes on the eve and during the war? Was this the new language of glasnost or was it a display of tactical virtuosity in the face of a recalcitrant Politburo? Several weeks later, the new Soviet leader marked the fiftieth anniversary of Stakhonovism and claimed that the same zeal was being exhibited today in designing new cars! There were no early signs of the speed with which events would move in 1987 and 1988. On 17 April 1987, Yakovlev spoke at length on the state of the social sciences to the Academy of Sciences. His report was interesting on a number of counts. He made a very sharp attack on the idealisation of *narodnost* (national spirit/nationalism) and condemned the constant 'efforts to whitewash the activity of pre-revolutionary Russia' by 'poetising what is reactionary in the culture of the past'. He was savage in his condemnation of religion and warned against utilising the 1,000 anniversary of Christianity as 'the mother of Russian culture.' On the history of the Revolution he called for a break with Stalinist historiography and attempted to establish a new agenda which meant 'a new approach to many important and complex periods of party history, learning the necessary lessons from each of them.' He concluded by condemning the violation of history and insisted that there should be no more 'blank pages and spaces' in Soviet history. Yakovlev's broadside provided the green light to historians, students and the Soviet press. Over the last two years not a day has passed without new revelations of one sort or another, including Stalin's destruction of the Red Army high command before the war and the killing of key officers during the war against fascism.*

Virtually the entire old guard of Bolshevism has now been rehabilitated. It started with Bukharin and the juridicial commissions investigating the show trials of the Thirties have concluded—fifty years later—that there was no basis whatsoever for any of the charges brought against Lenin's comrades on the Central Committee. Pen-portraits of Bukharin, Zinoviev, Kamenev, Radek and others have appeared in the Soviet press. Christian Ravovsky, too, has been given his proper place in history. Ravosky was an old friend and comrade of Trotsky. After the latter's exile, Ravovsky was the leader of the Left Opposition inside the USSR and served many years in prison. After Hitler's rise to power he made his peace with Stalin, understanding, as did Trotsky in exile, that it was only a matter of time before Hitler invaded the USSR. For this act of generosity Stalin had him tried, imprisoned and shot at the outset of war. Ravovsky it was who wrote some of the most important texts of the Twenties charting the rise of bureaucracy and the dangers of Great-Russian chauvinism. And what about Trotsky himself? The demon of the world Stalinist movement for many decades, the creator and first leader of the Red Army, has already appeared on Soviet television. He was shown talking animatedly to Lenin in documentary footage marking the latter's birth anniversary. On the same occasion, the *Literaturnaya Gazetta*, published for the first time since the Twenties the undoctored photograph of Lenin speaking from the podium with Trotsky waiting his turn at the foot of the platform. The journal explained to readers how the photograph had been falsified for years by removing the image of Trotsky. Another documentary commemorating the foundation of the Red Army showed Trotsky taking the salute, froze-frame on his face with the words, 'and that was Trotsky', before moving on. In June 1988, on the eve of the Nineteenth Party Conference, Yuri Afanasiev told a Moscow press conference:

*A documentary was broadcast on Soviet television in August 1988 about the advent of nuclear weapons to the Soviet Union. The programme asserted that Stalin had in fact known about the Allies' nuclear capacity far earlier than those in the West had suspected. But the documentary most particularly criticised Stalin's role at the beginning of the War—when he wouldn't actually appear in public or issue a statement about what had happened to the Soviet Union's pact with Hitler. It actually stated that Stalin had let his people down, and that after the War they became his main enemy. The narrator concluded by saying that Stalin would be remembered in history books as the second Genghis Khan!

We must not stop the process of rehabilitation and judicial review at any level. We have to rehabilitate all who were oppressed or wrongly accused and, as a matter of justice, Leon Trotsky stands equally with all the victims of Stalin... On the question of Trotsky's political rehabilitation, I think there will be a breakthrough in this direction. But it will depend on the deepening of perestroika in our historical sciences, and on the internal political struggle that is now under way in our party... I believe the works of Trotsky, and indeed of Stalin and of Khrushchev, should be published and made accessible to all, to teachers and students and citizens. It is very strange that professors and teachers try to criticise Trotsky when they have never read a word that he wrote. The same is still true of Bukharin, Zinoviev and Kamenev. We have to envisage a situation in the future when their works will sit in the bookshops and libraries alongside contemporary archive material, available for all to read.

This is the most forthright statement on the subject from a senior Soviet historian to date. There is, however, a great deal of resistance to this project. Why? In one sense, of course, Trotsky is almost entirely irrelevant: Trotskyism does not represent a significant force in world politics and there are no signs of it becoming so in the near future. There is, therefore, a very powerful argument in Afanasiev's statement. A debate has already begun in the USSR on the Twenties and Thirties and a great deal of nonsense is being written for the obvious reason that the historical record has been suppressed along with Trotsky's writings. If Afanasiev has his way this record will be put straight, but this should remain a matter for serious historical debate and research which should follow its own scholarly rhythms.

The question of Trotsky's importance, however, is not simply a subject for historians, but Soviet politicians and publicists too. Now some in the West and particularly Trotskyists may imagine that this reflects the power of Trotsky's ideas. After all there is something gratifying in the notion that the spectre of the old man killed on Stalin's orders in Mexico still haunts the hard-bitten infighters within the *obkoms* and *ispolkoms** of the Soviet apparatus. This is, alas, not the case. The problem is not Trotsky as such but one of legitimacy: how does the apparatus justify its right to govern before the Party millions and the hundreds of millions of non-party members in the Soviet Union?

Till recently they have argued that they—the apparatus—are the heirs of the October Revolution, which opened a new epoch in world

*Local and district committees.

history: the transition from capitalism to communism. This transition has its own laws of development. These laws are understood only by the CPSU, which is the leading scientific force in world communism. In short, for decades, the Soviet leadership has justified its rule by insisting on the continuity from Lenin's Bolsheviks to the present-day CPSU.

This is undoubtedly an extremely peculiar way to jutisfy one's right to rule. It is also a very weak basis. Bourgeois democratic states also utilise a mixture of appeals (monarchy, nationalism, war victories, danger of totalitarian threats from the USSR, etc) but their legitimacy essentially rests on the claim which may be largely bogus, but is undoubtedly effective, that the existing electoral system provides rule by consent: the state and its citizens share an identity of interests because the citizens have the right to choose their own leaders. The Soviet leadership can not use this argument, so they appeal to a higher court: history. For it is history that embodies the scientific-Communist role of the Party and this requires the establishment of an unbroken link between the Party of today and the party of Lenin.

Of course one of the functions of this strange form of legitimacy is to outlaw any questioning of the *key* role of the Party and its policies. This means that no public politics is permissible. If party policy is scientific, then it follows that those who question or challenge it are, in fact, wanting to oppose Truth and consequently they must be in error. Hence they must be removed. Also if party policy equals science, then there is no need whatsoever to consult the people on policy. How could the masses possibly express scientific truth? The people, after all, are by definition not the vanguard. The Party is the vanguard, the people only the followers of the vanguard. And if they refuse then they must end up in the guards' vans of the vanguard.

It is this tradition which makes party history such a central political question and which has made it necessary for the Soviet leadership to tell its citizens a pack of lies about the history of the CPSU. The Soviet élite would have loved nothing better than to tell the whole 'truth' about party history; to give all the facts and then say: you see? We have been right all along. No errors, leave alone crimes. We have always grasped the scientific truth and given the correct answer to each concrete situation. This may have been possible if the mistakes had been of a tactical character. What has made such an approach impossible is that *the* Leader of *the* Party in the Thirties and Forties did not simply make disastrously criminal errors of policy. That might have been possible to excuse. What Stalin actually did was to destroy the CPSU as a living force of Soviet revolutionaries. He simply wiped out the party of Lenin and the beneficiaries of the mass murders were the very people who became the Soviet élite in the Fifties, Sixties and Seventies. The entire Brezhnev generation of leaders had rocketted up the hierarchy during the *Yezhovchina** of 1937. And therein lies the rub.

The first serious attempt to shift the justification of CPSU rule away from the Party as embodiment of Science, Truth and the Future was during the Brezhnev period. This was attempted by the use of the concept of Actually Existing Socialism. The argument quite simply was that the Soviet people must obviously accept the existing political system because of the tremendous benefits gained from the existing social, economic and cultural order. This 'advanced socialism' was represented as the proof of the historical pudding. Whatever the past sufferings and agonies of the Soviet people the time had come for a new start. The past was over and the successes were visible in everyday life. Problems, naturally, remained, but these were easily surmountable through quantitative improvements, minor reforms, practical work and so forth.

This line of reasoning did permit a marginally more relaxed attitude to party history and a more pragmatic approach to current issues. It was also based on a certain reality: in the early Seventies Soviet people had really never had it so good. As the Seventies ended all this had already turned to ashes. The entire Brezhnevite framework had begun to crumble and the Soviet Union was on the verge of a multiple crisis. With the decision to embark on perestroika, the Soviet leadership set itself the task of persuading the people, especially the strategically placed and securely protected social group of industrial workers in the big plants, that things were now so bad that a drastic change was required. The media has been explaining every day that Actually Existing Socialism is really a dreadful mess which can only be cleared through radical changes, although we have still not been informed of the mechanism whereby a terminally ill individual (Chernenko), not at all popular in the Party, was put forward—and chosen—as the leader.

One easy way of legitimising the shift would have been to return to the old scientism which the neo-Stalinist authoritarians have never really abandoned. If they had decided on this course the scientist

*The beginning of the mass terror against old Bolsheviks. Yezhov was then Stalin's Minister for the Interior.

doctrine would have enabled them to denounce Brezhnevism as a terrible deviation from the scientific-communist line and maintain that the Party was now returning to the correct scientific path of Marxism-Leninism. Such arguments, however, cannot be easily fitted in to the types of reforms being proposed by the Gorbachev group. The reformers have, accordingly, been attacking the ideologies of Actually Existing Socialism as well as the scientist-Stalinist method of justifying CPSU rule. Gorbachev has repeatedly told the Soviet people that the greatest problem they need to overcome is the fear of making mistakes. He insists that perestroika is bound to result in mistakes: the Party will undoubtedly get some things wrong. Policy, argues the Soviet leader, is a matter of learning from experience and through debates and discussions. Gorbachev has also identified the source of the present problems and locates them in the structures established by Stalin in the Thirties. Far from being the touchstone of socialist orthodoxy these structures, Soviet citizens and party comrades are now informed, are gigantic obstacles to socialist progress and human emancipation. This line represents a radical break with the traditions of Stalinism. When Gorbachev decided to back the demands for 'no more blank pages' the crimes and horrors of the Stalin period flowed across the pages of the Soviet press like a stinking sewer.*

In these circumstances it is hardly surprising that many people are bewildered and wondering what the present crisis means in historical terms. How could it be that the supposed Brezhnevite culmination of soviet history turns out to have been a nadir? And if things have been going wrong since the Stalinist period, where does this leave the wise guidance of the CPSU? And it is in this context that the name of Trotsky crops up. It is not raised by the liberal intelligentsia, since most of them tend to be extremely hostile to Trotsky for the simple reason that they regard the crimes of the Thirties as stemming from revolutionary fanatacism and not from a counter-revolutionary consolidation of bureaucratic rule. Trotsky, for many, is the epitome of a fiery fanatic—even more so than Stalin precisely because he was so intelligent—and therefore a figure to be loathed. The same argument, however, could be applied to Lenin, but it is not. No one wants to go that far just yet! Trotsky's name is raised as a spectre by the Stalinist authoritarians. They argue that if Gorbachev destroys

---

*Although it should be noted that one of Stalin's major crimes—and the one which perhaps provided the pretext for the resulting Terror—has still not been admitted: namely, the assassination of Kirov in 1934.

Stalin's credibility totally, there is only one alternative *political* tradition available in the history of the CPSU for the party membership to turn to: Trotskyism.

Historically they are correct. Lenin died prematurely and therefore could not answer many of the problems faced by Communists in the late Twenties and Thirties. It is slightly absurd to pretend that Bukharin's political record contains an alternative political tradition to Stalinism. Although this is becoming a new orthodoxy for influential sections of the pro-party intelligentsia as we shall discuss later, it is a futile attempt as the historical record reveals. And notwithstanding the impressive credentials of Bukharin's biographer, Stephen Cohen (whose books will soon be officially published in the USSR), we doubt whether these claims will be repeated by Bukharin's widow, Anna Larina, in her forthcoming memoirs. During the Twenties, Bukharin was Stalin's ideologue and was used by him to destroy the Left Opposition. 'Bravo,' Stalin shouted during one such display, 'the others just attack them [the Opposition]. Bukharchik slays them!' Bukharin's writings in the Thirties amount to nothing of any political substance whatsoever. At one critical moment Bukharin did raise the banner of revolt against Stalin, over the forced collectivisation of 1928–29. But to attempt and transform that momentary and half-hearted resistance into a political tradition is a road to nowhere. Furthermore in the opposition to forced collectivisation Bukharin found himself on the same side as Trotsky and Rakovsky. Therefore to elevate the resistance to forced collectivisation does not dispose of the very real challenge represented by the stand of thousands of Bolsheviks, old and young, who fought and were killed for supporting the political programme of Trotsky.

However to imagine that the crisis of the Party could only be resolved by saying that Trotsky was right and Stalin wrong is ridiculously utopian. What is critically important for party members today is not to accept the agenda of the neo-Stalinists, to first of all resolve the dispute on party history. This is indeed an important issue, but the only real solution on this front lies in the vital first step which has already been called for by the Rector of the Institute of Historical Archives: publish the works of all the old Bolsheviks and the entire historical record of the period. The dominant question today is, as always, how to move forward in the present situation. Within this framework it is perfectly legitimate to inquire whether the theoretical writings of Lenin, Trotsky, Bukharin and others have anything relevant to say about the problems which the Soviet Union is confronting *today*. Lenin's writings have been used by the Gorbachev leadership selectively, but in a fresh and invigorating manner. The dead leader is not simply an icon, and many of his texts are vital reading for rebuilding the party. Bukharin's works are about to be published in the USSR and those who are using him simply as a tool to avoid the question of Trotsky might be surprised to find a great deal of ultra Leftism in the early texts. Trotsky's ideas are still unknown to all but a handful of people in the USSR. It is therefore worth considering some of his main ideas dispassionately and seeing to what extent they converge and diverge from the new reformism in the Soviet Union.

1. *The USSR is a proletarian state in transition to socialism.*

Like the present leadership and all the tendencies in the CPSU, Trotsky argued till his dying day that the fundamental character of the Soviet state was that it remained a product of the October Revolution, insofar that it had freed the Soviet people from domination by capitalists and landlords. He always rejected the notion that the real gains of the Revolution had been erased by Stalin. He consequently argued that socialists throughout the world needed to defend the USSR as a state against international capitalism and imperialism *despite* the victory of Stalinism. Simultaneously Trotsky insisted that the USSR was a primitive and backward proletarian state and very, very far from achieving what the Brezhnevites were to refer to as 'advanced socialism'. It was only at the beginning of the road towards a fully-fledged socialist society.

This view is not far removed from the essence of contemporary Soviet reformism. Gorbachev has been arguing and demonstrating this fact throughout the country. When one-third of Soviet schools have no indoor toilets, when the bulk of Soviet hospitals lack basic amenities, when there is evidently a fierce struggle for scarce goods among Soviet people, when primitive, reactionary ideologies like anti-semitism and great-Russian chauvinism are widespread, when tensions remain between major nationalities, it is somewhat grotesque to paint this reality under the title of 'advanced socialism.'

Trotsky would not have been in the least surprised or shocked at the idea that in the 1980s, nearly half a century after he was assassinated, the Soviet leadership was finding it necessary to introduce a new form of NEP, re-introducing market exchanges, reviving genuine co-operatives, returning agriculture to *de facto* family farming and other measures designed to revive the economy. All this is incomprehensible in terms of an 'advanced socialist' social formation, but is eminently sensible if the USSR is, as Trotsky believed, a primal socialist society. In the late Twenties Trotsky urged the maintenance of market relations while beginning a properly planned state sector. Above all he insisted, like Bukharin, in the necessity of maintaining the *smychka** through non-coercive economic exchanges between the peasantry and the urban, statised economy†. Despite all the changes over the last sixty years—and all the bombast from Stalin, Khrushchev and Brezhnev—this is the policy that now has to be revived in the Soviet Union today.

2. *The Soviet Union is locked in an irreconcilable struggle with the capitalist world.*

Trotsky's views here are fairly standard among Soviet communists. They are not, however, mirrored in the official rhetoric of the Gorbachev group. Gorbachev speaks of the USSR and the USA belonging to one single civilisation. For Trotsky this would only have been true in a superstructural sense: namely that, as Lenin always argued, the task of the Soviet people is to incorporate and make itself the master of bourgeois culture in order to raise itself to the point where it can transcend bourgeois culture and civilisation. The entire justification for the socialist project lies in the fact that it is *not* part of the civilisation of capitalism, but a higher civilisation. If Gorbachev really means that he wants to create a common capitalist-socialist civilisation then he is indulging in a utopian fantasy. The end result, if this view were taken to its logic in practical terms, would certainly be a single civilisation, but it would be a capitalist one and it would incorporate the USSR or rather the USCR.

If on the other hand Gorbachev is recognising a *fact* rather than a dream, and is basicly stating that whether people like it or not the USSR is part of a single world dominated by capitalism, then he is making a profoundly 'Trotskyist' point as opposed to a Stalinist one. Trotsky was not opposed to political and economic co-operation between the USSR and the capitalist world. What underlined his approach, however, was a fundamental irre-concilability of the two socio-economic systems. This was and

*The alliance between peasants and the urban population.
†Appendix II.

remains the view of all the leaders and ideologues of the capitalist world today.

3. *The road to genuinely advanced socialism in the USSR passes through the victorious political struggles against capitalism in the West.*

In Trotsky's view there was a basic contradiction which governed the conditions in which the Soviet state would have to survive and develop. On the one hand there was only one world economic system in which the USSR (and we could call COMECON today) had to insert itself. There was no escaping this reality through isolationism and autarchy. On the other hand this world economic system was dominated by capitalism and was deeply hostile to Soviet economic, social and political development.

The Stalin faction and especially Bukharin (who Lenin had criticised in his last testament for not understanding dialectics) drew from this dilemma the following conclusion: either the USSR must perish or nothing could be done internally except wait for the world revolution. Bukharin and Stalin asserted that the Soviet Union could confront the problem by sealing itself off from the world market, develop its own economy and properly exploit the inexhaustible material and labour resources of the USSR. All that was necessary to pursue this uninterrupted, smooth, contradiction-free internal development of socialism within the USSR was to build up sufficient military reserves to deter any capitalist aggressor.

This political trajectory led inexorably, despite Bukharin's refusal to accept the logic, to the forced collectivisations. The explosive contradictions of that process gave the lie to the absurd notion of autarchic socialism and led directly to the civil war inside the CPSU, when violence was used to destroy the cadres during the Yezhovchina. This violence gravely weakened the Soviet Union and damaged severely the ability of the Red Army to beat back the genocidal assault of the Third Reich. The entire postwar history of the Soviet Union is the story of the gradual awareness within the Soviet leadership that it was impossible to seal the country off from the massively superior forces of the capitalist world.

The autarchic mentality led to idiocies such as jamming Western radio stations at huge cost and ineffective results; making heroes of insignificant groups of human rights activists; harassment of quaint religious sects because they had international links; banning

Western rock music and numerous similar absurdities which symbolised the bunker years of Brezhnevism. The rise to power of the new reformers involves the final recognition that this policy—whose theoretical roots lie in Stalin and Bukharin's dreams of achieving advanced socialism via isolationism—must be abandoned and the Soviet Union engage openly and directly with the forces of the capitalist world.

The Stalinist authoritarian wing of the party today is deeply suspicious of this trend. They fear that the result of this open engagement will lead to a deeper penetration of the USSR by capitalist ideology, culture and finally politics as well as the economy where a serious Western intervention could unleash powerful centrifugal forces.

Trotsky was for open engagement (the Gorbachev line) but without any political illusions. He was always of the view that capitalism would never be reconciled to the USSR and would always constitute a threat to its survival (the Stalinist-authoritarian line). Thus in this debate he would have seen that both sides had a point. His solution? The development of the USSR and its engagement with the capitalist world could be achieved because, and insofar as, the USSR had indestructible bases of *political solidarity* within the capitalist countries, whereas capitalist countries had no significant bases of political support inside the USSR. Trotsky's solution to the contradiction lay in the field of world politics.

The survival of the USSR, as far as Trotsky was concerned, did not at all depend on the overthrow of capitalism in the advanced capitalist countries. Of course Trotsky, together with Lenin, believed that this was desirable and would accelerate socialist developments in the USSR. However in the absence of such a cataclysmic upheaval the only stable lever for effective engagement with the capitalist world was the existence of powerful working class parties in the advanced capitalist countries which had the capacity to prevent economic, technological or political warfare against the USSR. That was indeed the case in Western Europe at the end of World War Two. The gains were squandered in an extremely cynical fashion by the Soviet leaders. Of course that is only part of the picture. Some of the setbacks were the result of forces outside Soviet control: the enormous economic strength of American capitalism and the post-war economic boom, which enabled the United States to buy off the social democratic parties of Western Europe. But the responsibility on the part of the Soviet Union played a decisive part, namely the lack of moral insensibility with which the Stalinists trampled over working class interests and principles for the purposes of short-term diplomatic gains or in order to avoid any form of accountability to working people in the USSR and Eastern Europe.

The substitution of real-politik in place of even the most cursory internationalism, leave alone an emancipatory vision of socialism, undoubtedly affected the USSR's standing in the world. For example, in 1983 the USSR was faced with a serious military threat in the form of Pershing missiles being stationed in West Germany. In order for these and Cruise missiles to be comfortably introduced on to West German territory it became necessary to remove the Social Democrats from office. The FDP aided the Pentagon by switching alliances in September 1982. It became important for the French rulers to urge the West Germans to accept the missiles. François Mitterand made a very direct appeal to the working class base of the SDP to accept the missiles replete with cold war symbols and the 'evil empire' ideology. The Soviet Union was politically powerless. The CPSU leaders, led by Gromyko, did make a desperate, last-minute appeal to the West German electorate in the spring 1983 elections to vote against those parties which backed the new missiles. They were badly rebuffed. Gromyko's message proved to be largely counter-productive. If that situation recurred today it is very likely that the results would be different. Why? Because Gorbachev's prestige in West Germany is higher than that of any post war Soviet leader. A direct appeal from the present leaders would have been effective precisely because of their moral standing at home and abroad. Let us take another example. After thirty-five years of the Polish People's Republic, an ultra-reactionary Pope, elected after a vigorous intervention by the extreme right-wing Opus Dei current, has an infinitely greater authority amongst the mass of Polish workers than the leaders of the USSR. This poses a considerable ideological challenge to Polish-Soviet relations. This is not an academic question: the most important military-security zone for the USSR anywhere in the world is the North European plain from the Oder to the Bug. Of course one can blame all this on the reactionary Polish workers, but Catholicism did not have this appeal in the Forties, Fifties and Sixties. Brezhnevism drove the Polish working class into the arms of the Church. It remains to be seen whether Gorbachev can disentangle the embrace.

We will return to these themes later, but enough has been written to demonstrate the utterly irresponsible character of Brezhnevite policy, which totally ignored the political importance of oppositional parties and movements in the West and thus sacrificed the only real source of genuine, stable relations with both the West and Eastern Europe.

4. *The Bureaucratic Dictatorship lies at the root of all threats to Soviet Security.*

Trotsky was a relentless opponent of Stalinism on every level. Together with Christian Rakovsky he developed a theory of the bureaucracy as a new ruling caste. Rakovsy realised well before Trotsky that a struggle against Stalin and his supporters was vital. In 1923 at the Twelfth Party Congress it was Rakovsky who took up the cudgels while Trotsky remained silent. From 1924 onwards both men were in harness and collaborated politically. Trotsky then developed the theses on bureaucracy further, and did not deviate from these views.

The authoritarian political regime of Stalin was termed as the rule of a bureaucratic caste, terminology which led to a great deal of confusion. Trotsky did not mean by this that power was in the hands of a social group of desk workers, managers and the like—all those in white collar jobs outside the direct process of production. What he meant was the *political expropriation* of the mass of working people, white collar as well as blue collar, by a narrow, political élite of party and state officials claiming an absolute monopoly over political decisions. He referred to this distinct social layer as a caste, in order to draw a parallel with the officer caste in, for example, the nineteenth century Prussian Army, which was a self-selecting political élite.

Trotsky argued that there were powerful *objective* factors which aided this development and led to a reflux of the Soviet working class in the Twenties. These developments militated towards a concentration of power at the upper levels of the party and state apparatus. But Stalin, instead of combatting these tendencies, encouraged them, gave them a lead and turned them into a *system*. The only element of control over this bureaucratic élite which he permitted was his own authority. Once established during the Stalin period and based politically on police coercion, this political system became extremely difficult to remove. Trotsky believed that it could only be removed by the revival of a mass working class movement within the Soviet Union which was capable of asserting genuine popular sovereignty, genuine self-determination of the working class, making the goverment directly accountable to the people. He called this process a *political* revolution because he maintained that the basic character of the socio-economic system—basic, that is, in the sense of the social class located in a strategically dominant position within society—did not have to be changed. What was required was a qualitative break with the authoritarian political system, its destruction and replacement with socialist democracy. Trotsky did not believe that this qualitative transformation of the political system could only be brought about by civil war, barricades and a new storming of the Winter Palace/Kremlin. He thought that bloodshed could be avoided, but what was necessary was a thorough-going shift of the centre of gravity of power from the élite to the majority of working people. He did not believe that this change could come about without the emergence of new organs of power arising from below. He certainly did not believe that forces from within the bureaucracy could ever become the bearers of qualitative changes in the political system. What he was calling for was a popular sovereignty anchored in the soviets and he believed that this was only possible through Soviet pluralism.

Now it is not necessary to agree with every strategic nuance in Trotsky's thought in order to observe that his overall thrust is, in general, faultless. It is also worth remembering that he was developing and codifying these ideas from the mid-Twenties onwards, ie. over half a century ago. The fact that many of Trotsky's concepts are not so far removed from the concerns of the present leaders tends to make the latter far more hostile to the founder of the Red Army than they would have been if he had died a natural death in 1925 or had been killed by Stalin during the early Thirties. The fact is that Trotsky and the Left Oppositionists analysed Stalinism on a daily basis. The record is there in the *Bulletin of the Left Opposition*. They are stocked in the restricted section of the Lenin Library in Moscow. When they are published any student of history will be able to study them and form their own judgement. Some might indeed ask how it was that what the reformers of today have discovered only in 1956 or 1962 or, in the case of some, 1985 was not only known but savagely denounced in the Twenties and Thirties. It is to preempt such questions that Trotsky, of all Stalin's victims, is still under fire and from both sides in the present divide.

Mikhail Gorbachev is a political leader who prides himself, and with a great deal of justification, in pioneering a new political language based on straightforwardness, and unmarked by the fear of admitting mistakes. In 'October and Perestroika: The Revolution Continues', delivered on 2 November 1987, to mark the Seventieth Anniversary of the Revolution, Gorbachev delivered a rather dull and even conservative speech, which we've mentioned previously. Instead of using the occasion to rehabilitate Bukharin and asking his widow to join the leaders on the podium, he recalled Lenin's criticisms of Bukharin. These are of interest, but totally irrelevant in the overall context of Stalinism. Lenin criticised almost every leader of the party. Many of them criticised him openly and sometimes savagely. So what? All that this proves is that Lenin, despite his brilliance, was not treated as a deity while he was alive. Gorbachev's fire, however, was reserved for Trotsky. The speech was clearly designed to reassure the authoritarian wing of the party (it is worth remembering that most of the people who were in the process of rehabilitating Stalin in the late Seventies are still alive, well and in leading positions) that they had no reason to worry. It may be that this was actually a Politburo speech delivered by its General Secretary, but that does not excuse anything:

> The leaders in question continued to provoke a split even after the vast majority in the Party saw that their views were contrary to Lenin's ideas and plans, and that their proposals were erroneous and could push the country off the correct course.
>
> This applies first of all to Leon Trotsky, who had, after Lenin's death, displayed excessive pretensions to top leadership in the Party, thus fully confirming Lenin's opinion of him as an excessively self-assured politician who always vacillated and cheated.
>
> Trotsky and the Trotskyites negated the possibility of building socialism in conditions of capitalist encirclement.
>
> In foreign policy they gave priority to export of revolution, and in home policy to tightening the screws on the peasants, to the city exploiting the countryside, and to administrative and military fiat in running society.
>
> Trotskyism was a political current whose ideologists took cover behind leftist pseudo-revolutionary rhetoric, and who in effect assumed a defeatist posture. This was essentially an attack on Leninism all down the line. The matter practically concerned the future of socialism in our country, the fate of the Revolution.
>
> In the circumstances, it was essential to disprove Trotskyism before the whole people, and denude its anti-socialist essence.
>
> The situation was complicated by the fact that the Trotskyites were acting in common with the New Opposition headed by Grigori Zinoviev and Lev Kamenev. Being aware that they constituted a minority, the opposition leaders had again and again saddled the

ty with discussions, counting on a split in its ranks. But in the final
analysis, the Party spoke out for the line of the Central Committee and
against the opposition, which was soon ideologically and organisationally crushed.

    In short, the Party's leading nucleus headed by Joseph Stalin had
safeguarded Leninism in an ideological struggle. It defined the
strategy and tactics in the initial stage of socialist construction, with its
political course being approved by most members of the Party and
most working people. An important part in defeating Trotskyism
ideologically was played by Nikolai Bukharin, Felix Dzerzhinsky,
Sergei Kirov, Grigori Ordzhonikidze, Jan Rudzutak, and others.*

These slanders are straight out of the notorious *Short Course
History of the CPSU*. They are expressed in more moderate
language, but every single sentence is historically inaccurate. This is
not a question of agreeing or disagreeing with Trotsky's positions.
Any Soviet historian who knows the subject is perfectly well aware
of the facts. Trotsky did commit mistakes, but these were not them.
And many of Trotsky's errors, as we will discuss later, were also the
errors of a triumphant Bolshevism. Lenin is not immune. Critical
mistakes were made by the Bolsheviks after the seizure of power,
some of whose consequences still haunt the Soviet Union.
Gorbachev's remarks, including the gem that Stalin was safe-
guarding Leninism in the Twenties and Thirties, are an outrage by
any criteria. What is more, this will become obvious when Trotsky's
works are finally published in the Soviet Union. So what is the point
of telling lies? The only serious explanation is that Gorbachev wants
to maintain above all else the unity of the party and the stability of its
top cadres. This is understandable, but dangerous and seems to
underline Boris Yeltsin's fears that Gorbachev is too dependent on
the party authoritarians.

    Mikhail Shatrov, is also rather hostile to Trotsky, but from a very
different point of view. Basically a Bukharinite, his plays reveal this
streak. His critique of Trotsky is that at a critical moment in the
history of the USSR, Trotsky vacillated and manoeuvred but did not
behave as Lenin wanted him to or as Lenin himself would have
done. This is the critical period 1922–23 when Lenin lay paralysed by
a stroke and began to make new observations from afar. This whole
period has been brilliantly portrayed by Moshe Lewin in his classic
book-essay, *Lenin's Last Struggle*† and by Robert Daniels in *The

* Moscow News, No 45, 1987.
† Pluto Press, London, 1972.

Conscience of the Revolution*. The facts were, in brief, as follows. Lenin is extremely worried at the growing bureaucratic trends in the party and state. He is appalled by Stalin's personal behaviour and its extension into the political realm, and is shocked at how Stalin and Dzerzhinsky are treating the Georgian Communists by offending their political and national sensibilities. He therefore proposes that Dzerzhinsky and Ordzhonikidze (a camp-follower of Stalin and involved in the violence against the Georgian commuists) be expelled from the party and that Stalin be removed from the position of General Secretary. He wanted to shift the gravity of power from the Secretariat to the Central Committee, which he would then enlarge and make more representative. He proposed that Trotsky, who Lenin regarded as the member of the Politburo closest to his own views, should take up the fight on behalf of both of them in the Politburo and *in the party as a whole* at the Twelfth Party Conference. Compare this with the pathetic passages in Gorbachev's speech where he praises Stalin, Dzerzhinski and Orzhonikidze for the fight against Trotskyism.

Shatrov says that Trotsky failed Lenin at this juncture. I tend to agree with him on this particular point, which was also raised in the suicide letter of Adolphe Joffe (a veteran Marxist and Soviet diplomat who was a close comrade of Trotsky) in 1927. Trotsky is here under fire for not fighting Stalin sooner than he did, which is hardly what Gorbachev is saying. But Shatrov then moves beyond to a view very common in the Soviet intelligentsia which, is to treat Stalin and Trotsky as different sides of the same coin. Moreover Shatrov does not get too angry with Bukharin for serving Stalin loyally for almost a decade. It appears that the targeting of Trotsky requires differential criteria, and this of course is totally unjustified. Otto Latsis, a veteran party ideologue and Deputy Editor-in-Chief of the theoretical journal *Kommunist* told me in April 1988 that while he was certain that 'Trotsky should not have been tried or assassinated, but he should have been, to my mind, expelled from the ranks of the Party. At least this is a debatable question.' Latsis, however, did agree that Trotsky's works should be published, regardless of whether or not he was posthumously readmitted into the party and his historical role in the Revolution be made known. He was not in favour of revising the stance taken on any of the oppositions in the party in the Twenties. Vladimir Nikolaev of

*Simon & Schuster, New York, 1969.

Ogonyok magazine had equally strong views on the subject: 'If Trotsky had become General Secretary instead of Stalin he would have been a fit replacement. You say this is wrong? Well if you go through Trotsky carefully you will see many things which can be qualified as forerunners of the personality cult. Trotsky was for barracks communism like Stalin. Whether you're aware of the paradox I don't know, but you know that Stalin used Trotsky heavily in his own writings!'

TA: I think what you're saying is tragic. And you are saying this because you have actually read very little, if anything, by Trotsky himself. You've taken one tiny aspect of Trotsky's writings—the debate on trades unions—on which he was wrong, though it is worth pointing out that he came to that view only after his suggestion of a NEP was rejected by the Party in 1920. It's a totally incorrect way of looking at a person's history. You could apply similar methods to Lenin. After all Stalin used him a lot as well in his writings...

VN: Anyway that's not an issue for us today. The issue is perestroika and it's not really Trotsky we would like to be clear about, but Stalin and his legacy.

TA: Agreed. But you can't be clear about Stalin's legacy without understanding the fight that took place. It was not Trotsky alone, you know. It was most of the defendants of the Third Moscow Trial, who've now been rehabilitated. Rakovsky, now rehabilitated, wrote the first major text on the growth of a bureaucracy. It's difficult to grapple with the legacy of Stalin unless you grapple also with the writings of many old Bolsheviks who were liquidated and destroyed for grappling with Stalin himself.

VN: You are quite right. We agree on this.

TA: And that also means publishing the works of all these comrades. They should be made available. Because surely you can see that it is not a question of finding new idols or new heroes. It's just to make the truth available and this is usually best expressed in what people have themselves written rather than commentaries on the same.

VN: I agree on this too.

 Later on during this conversation, Nikolaev was shocked by the fact that when Hitler was in the process of seizing power, Stalin did everything possible to prevent a unity of social democrats and communists to resist fascism. It appeared to Nikoleav that 'Stalin did everything humanly possible to destroy socialism in Germany.' When I told him that Trotsky's writings on the rise and consolidation of fascism were peerless; that Trotsky had proposed a united front of communists, social-democrats and liberals against Hitler and had been denounced by the Comintern as a 'fascist agent' for his pains, he was clearly surprised. This Trotsky did not tally with his own image.

History remains a controversial science in the USSR. The past is only too present in all aspects of everyday life. There is still a great deal of caution, especially where a discussion of history might clash with the new orthodoxies. This point was stressed by the distinguished historian, V.P. Danilov at a roundtable discussion in London in 1988:

> A highly characteristic—and dangerous—fantasy is found in the novel by Boris Mozhaev, *Peasant Men and Women* where the responsibility for the violence the peasantry underwent in the course of collectivisation in the winter of 1929–1930 is transferred from those actually guilty (Stalin and his closest circle, above all Molotov and Kaganovich) to Trotsky, Zinoviev, Kamenev, Yakovlev and Kaminsky, of which the first three from 1927 had no sort of contact with any political decisions taken and Trotsky had already been deported from the USSR in 1929. All these fantasies are not the result of perestroika. Perestroika and glasnost only brought them to light.

In Moscow in June 1988, Danilov repeated this theme at a discussion on the rehabilitations at the Institute of Marxism-Leninism. He read out a speech by Trotsky at the Ninth Party Conference where he called for a new economic policy—the first Soviet leader to do so! Danilov's importance lies in the fact that he is a historian of the Russian peasantry and a supporter of Bukharin. Yet his objectivity as a historian will not allow him to listen passively to the slander which would paint a victim in the colours of his executioner.

Yuri Afanasiev, too, is determined that objectivity should prevail. He told me in Moscow in July 1988 that he was unhappy about the very idea that a single textbook jointly written by several authors was the way in which history should be taught. He was for letting the students read a wide range of material and assess it critically. He explained that history textbooks had contained not just a few distortions, but had 'contained a total falsification of history' (for full text of interview see Appendix IV). On the question of Trotsky, he gave a very clearcut answer:

The question of Trotsky is a very special one in many respects. At least this is my opinion. First, none of the Bolshevik Old Guard around Lenin played such a major role in both the Revolution and the civil war that followed as Trotsky. Secondly, Trotsky is the only one of Lenin's old guard who for many years has openly criticised Stalinism and Stalin. Thirdly, Trotsky is part and parcel of the history of the International as nobody else from the old guard, especially as concerns a study and appraisal of Stalin's regime. Getting rid of the stereotypes of Trotsky in the Soviet Union is a measure of getting rid of the vestiges of Stalinism in our society. That's why it's a special question. I am not a Trotskyist sympathiser, but I am in favour of an objective assessment of his role in our history. We should comprehensively report on his activities and have an open mind on the question. Getting rid of the Stalinist stereotypes of Trotsky is crucial for getting rid of Stalinist legacies. That is why I insist on objectivity on the question of Trotsky and attach special importance to this issue.

Afansiev confirmed that he had indeed read Trotsky's *History of the Russian Revolution* and strongly favoured its publication. In fact he stated that all the histories of the Revolution should be made available: both those like Trotsky's which defended 1917 and those by Milukov and Kerensky which were hostile. And, of course, he added: 'I am strongly in favour of publishing Sukhanov's history as well.*

Sadly, his hopes are still some way from being realised. In the prize-winning film *Repentance*, Abuladze ends with the following scene: a middle-aged narrator meets an old woman who asks her, 'Is this the Road to the Temple?' (The narrator's parents were burnt to death when the temple was set on fire at the end of that street), so she replies: 'No. This is Varlam's Street.' (Varlam is the Beria-Stalin figure who killed her parents.) The old woman replies with another question which remains rhetorical, 'But what is the point of a road which does not lead to the Temple?' In 1987, Igor Klyamkin, wrote an extremely powerful essay in *Novy Mir* (No 11) entitled, 'Which Road Leads To The Temple?' It was a wide-ranging text in which the author moved with considerable facility from literature to history to economics and philosophy. It was possible to disagree with many aspects of Klyamkin's article (and I found the attempt to justify 'national Bolshevism' somewhat unpalatable), but the general approach of the text was excellent, in that the author pleaded for objectivity and the ending of self-censorship. In particular he sought

*Sukhanov was an extremely talented Menshevik historian whose works were strongly recommended by both Lenin and Trotsky.

to rehabilitate Trotsky's reputation and rescue him from the opprobrium still heaped on his head. The response to this article from the official and semi-official writers and scientists was slightly unbalanced. What was especially noticeable in a number of replies, including one from the economist Seliunin, was a total failure to evaluate Trotsky objectively.*

This prompted a scholar, Leonid Volkov, at the Institute for Scientific Information in the Social Sciences (INION) to write an article defending Klyamkin on certain issue against his detractors. The central issue was, of course, Trotsky. Volkov's comments on Klyamkin were entitled 'Reflections on the Road that does not lead to the Temple' and took Klyamkin's fearless remarks on Trotsky's positions during the Twenties much further. Volkov defended Trotsky's strictures on 'socialism in one country' and his insistence on the necessity of a genuine internationalism. The debate on Soviet history is likely to continue for a long time. It involves, after all, not just politicians and historians, but the entire country. We have, for instance, yet to read reminiscences of workers whose families were wiped out. How far this debate will extend will depend very much on the emergence of a socialist democracy in the USSR.

Volkov, alas, was unable to have this text published in any magazine, though he had not given up all hope when I met him at the Writers' Club in Moscow in July 1988. He noted wryly that some people enjoyed the fruits of glasnost more than others.

*The most useful comments on Klyamkin's article were contained in Theodor Shanin's 'Roads Which Lead to Temples' in *Detente,* No 11, 1988.

Alexei Sundukov, *Station*, 1986.

5. ALL POWER TO THE SOVIETS
Is Democracy Possible in the USSR?

The main direction of the democratisation of our society and state is the restoration in full of the role and authority of Soviets of People's Deputies as sovereign bodies of popular representation. V.I. Lenin discovered in the Soviets, born of the experience of revolutions in Russia, a political form in accordance with the nature of socialism. At once representative bodies of power and mass organisations of the population, the Soviets organically combine the principles of statehood and self-government...

At the same time, we see serious shortcomings in the activity of the Soviets and dissatisfaction with their work among the working people. As a result of well-known deformations, the rights and powers of the representative bodies have been curtailed, and Party committees continue to exercise unwarranted tutelage over them. In many instances, ministries and departments resolve questions of economic and social development behind their backs. Executive committees and their administrative apparatus frequently unsurp the Soviets' functions, leaving to the Deputies only the sanctioning of what are in effect preresolved questions. It is necessary to change this situation fundamentally and to return real governing powers to the Soviets, turning over for consideration and decision by them all concrete questions of state, economic, social and cultural life, without exception.

Central Committee Theses passed by the Nineteenth Party Conference of
the CPSU, Moscow, June 1988

The debate on pluralism and democracy which began at the Nineteenth Party Conference in June 1988 and continues in numerous newspapers and magazines has suffered from one weakness. There has been a failure to evaluate the important period which followed the February Revolution and lasted till 1919-20. Thus any discussion on democracy in the Soviet Union entails a look back at history. Was there ever a period of soviet democracy? And if so, why and how did it come to an end? Was it just the civil war and foreign intervention or were there other, equally fundamental, factors at work? As 'unofficial' groups continue to grow and many Communist Party members become active within their ranks while maintaining their membership of the CPSU, how and where can political disputes and contradictions be resolved? The old Soviets (councils) were the result of a mass upsurge in a society without any parliamentary traditions. Are soviet-type institutions really democratic and can they fulfil the role demanded on them? These are the questions that need to be considered.

After the February Revolution in 1917 which overthrew the Tsar
and placed a provisional government in power, the principal
theoretician and leader of the Bolshevik Party returned from exile to
find his party totally unprepared for the tasks that lay ahead. Lenin
had to wage a fierce struggle to convince his comrades *on the
leadership* of the party that the dual power which existed offered
enormous opportunites for Russian revolutionaries to prepare the
basis for a new, *socialist*, revolution. This view clashed with the
theoretical orthodoxy of the party, which had been elaborated
largely by Lenin. 'Lenin has gone mad' was a common view
expressed in semi-public by Bolshevik leaders. The only other
political figure who had stressed that the character of the coming
revolution would be socialist was, of course, our old friend Trotsky,
whose book *1905** had contained the clearest exposition of his ideas
and had been denounced by the Bolsheviks.

The crisis of strategy which confronted the Party after February
1917 has been analysed and described in vivid detail by Alexander
Rabinowitch in *The Bolsheviks Come To Power.*† The failure of
Lenin's party to rise to the occasion for the second time (in 1905 the
Bolshevik faction had initially expressed a total hostility to the birth
of soviets) must have given its principal leader a great deal of food
for thought. Lenin had often defended his faction in sharp, even
sectarian language. When he had been reproved by friends for
splitting the Social-Democratic Party on the grounds that it was
totally incomprehensible to socialists working inside Tsarist Russia,
Lenin used to come out with his favourite answer, which was taken
from one of Tolstoy's short stories. From a distance a man is visible.
He appears to be making the most crazy gestures with his arms
moving up and down and sideways as if he were not in full
possession of all his faculties. But as one got closer it became obvious
that he was engaged in an important activity: he was, in fact,
sharpening a knife. The implication was obvious. The Bolshevik
faction was a sharpened, political instrument. This was not a totally
foolish analogy. Yet the Bolshevik theoretician must have wondered
how sharp the instrument really was if it needed him to explain
something which was happening before their very eyes. Lenin had
always liked Goethe's gentle assertion: 'All theory, dear friend, is
grey but evergreen is the golden tree of actual life.'

1905 by Leon Trotsky (trans by Anya Bostock), Allen Lane & Random House, 1971.
†*The Bolsheviks Come to Power* by Alexander Rabinowitch, New Left Books, 1979.

It was in this period — between February and July 1917—that Lenin started work on a new pamphlet, which was published two months before the October Revolution as *State and Revolution*. This text has often been described as 'utopian', 'Libertarian', 'justifying violence', but although all these descriptions have a grain of truth in them they miss the central point. *State and Revolution* is, fundamentally, an essay on the different forms of democracy. The 'destruction' which Lenin is obsessed with is not violence *per se*, but the necessity to destroy the bourgeois state. Why? Because it is bourgeois? Yes, but not that alone. It is because bourgeois democracy is based on the permanent separation of the masses from power. That is the reason a new state is needed and it can only be provided by the Revolution. But this state must not only be based on universal suffrage. There has to be universal participation in the running of the state. This meant a different kind of political institution to a bourgeois parliament. The soviets could provide this new basis provided that the right by the people to recall their representatives was enshrined in a soviet constitution. That, for Marx, had been one of the gains of the Paris Commune and Lenin was determined that the *soviet* State would soar to greater heights than the Communards could ever have done.

Despite the Bolshevik success in 1917 and his absorption in other projects, Lenin did not forget these ideas. At the Seventh Conference of the Party in 1918 he returned to this theme. He told delegates that he was aware of all the shortcoming of the soviets, which were 'crude and unfinished', but that was a reflection of the state of the country itself. What was important was that the soviet form had spread to the whole country which was populated by several nations. It was a new type of power and Lenin insisted 'that a definition of the new type of state should occupy an outstanding place in our Programme.'

Soviet power is a new type of state without a bureaucracy, without police, without a regular army, a state in which bourgeois democracy has been replaced by a new democracy, a democracy that brings to the fore the vanguard of working people, gives them legislative and executive authority, makes them responsible for military defence ... In Russia this has hardly begun and has begun badly. If we are conscious of what is bad in what we have begun we shall overcome it, provided history gives anything like a decent time to work on that Soviet power.

What Lenin was rejecting totally was the bureaucratic formalism of bourgeois democracy. He was to stress on another occasion that 'all restrictions on elections are abolished; the people themselves determine the time and order of elections, and are completely free to recall any elected person.' He continually stressed two interrelated themes. Soviet democracy already was 'an immeasurably higher and more progressive form of democracy than bourgeois parliamentarism', but all this would be frittered away unless the masses were involved in administrative work: 'Our aim is to draw *the whole of the poor* into the practical work of administration . . .' He knew that this was the most difficult of all tasks, but 'this transition alone can guarantee the consolidation of socialism.' In other words military might or coercion could prevail for a short period, but *socialism* could only function on the basis of active mass participation.

Theb role of the Party is virtually absent in Lenin's writings on the state and democracy. He assumes a pluralism, since the time when he was writing these texts was a period when the Menshviks and Left SRs (Socialist Revolutionaries) were represented in the soviets, the Bolsheviks in a coalition with the Left SRs in a number of soviets, while the Mensheviks actually had a majority in Georgia. Thus the critique of the bourgeois state centres on the limits which it imposes on democracy and this makes bourgeois democracy by definition a 'narrow and restricted' political system. The reasons for this, as far as Lenin was concerned, had already been spelt out in some detail by Marx in his writings on the Paris Commune of 1871. He stressed the continuity of his own writings with that of classical Marxism against the 'revisions of Kautsky'. A parliamentary majority by a workers' party in the confines of a bourgeois state could, on its own, never lead to socialism. Neither Kautsky, regarded by Lenin till 1914 as the Pope of Marxism, nor his latter-day mimics ever consider the links between the class structures of capitalism and a parliament existing within the framework of those structures. A parliamentary regime has no class character as such. It floats, presumably, above class. It is simply a question of a parliamentary majority, ie. of control in parliament to begin a solution of the problems confronted by the class divisions under capitalism. Lenin's writings in the period 1917-20 constituted a serious and mature rebuttal to these views, but—and this is critical—the only basis for rejecting the model of bourgeois parliaments was a soviet system that was superior in every way. This was certainly a very different Lenin from the one against whom Trotsky had polemicised so viciously though perceptively, in *Our Political Tasks* (1904):

Lenin's methods lead to this: the party organisation at first substitutes itself for the party as a whole; then the Central Committee substitutes itself for the organisation; and finally a single 'dictator' substitutes himself for the Central Committee.*

History, alas, failed to give the Revolution time to develop toward a Soviet system. The civil war and the intervention of the Entente powers made the entire country into a battleground. The White Armies, backed by the capitalist states, made a point of destroying the soviets everywhere they went. It was not simply a destruction of the buildings, but of the elected representatives who were the first to be lined up and executed.

The White Terror always followed up its victories by massacring communists, killing other members of the soviets and declaring them illegal. The brutalities of the counter-revolution were combatted by the Cheka (an abbreviation for the 'Extraordinary Commission for Combating Counter-Revolution and Sabotage') which had been established in December 1917. The spread of the civil war resulted in the Cheka being given extraordinary powers to arrest and execute. The late Belgian historian Marcel Liebman in his classic *Leninism Under Lenin,*† has charted the course of the decline of *soviet* power in some detail. After listing the crimes of the counter-revolution, Liebman wrote 'more paradoxically, however, the soviets also fell victim to the organisation that was specially charged with the struggle against the "Whites" — the Cheka'. The roots of the subsequent degeneration of the Soviet state can not be ascribed to any single factor, but to a combination of subjective and objective conditions: the defeat of the German and Hungarian Revolutions; the death of Lenin; the absence of soviet democracy; the exhaustion of the working class as well as the absorption of its leading cadres into the administrative apparatus of the state; the defeat of the Left and Right Oppositions. The virtual transformation of the Leninist Politburo into a Stalinist Committee of Public Safety, however, was facilitated by the growth of the secret police and its utilisation in first harassing, later imprisoning and ultimately executing, communists who opposed what was taking place inside the country and the party after the victory of the Stalinist faction. Liebman does not pass

---

*Trotsky was later to disown this book, but not completely. He admitted that he was unfair to Lenin, but he insisted that the book contained several insights into the narrow mentality of a number of Bolshevik committee-men of the period. In the event this was a slight understatement.

†*Leninism Under Lenin* by Marcel Liebman, Jonathan Cape, 1975.

immediate judgement. With an exemplary objectivity he notes the facts.

On 28 August 1918, the headquarters of the Cheka actually instructed its local agencies to refuse to submit to any interference by the soviets: on the contrary, it was these local agencies that were to impose their will upon the soviet bodies. They succeeded in doing this in the many areas that were affected by the military operations. The institutions that competed in authority with the Cheka were no longer the local or regional soviets but the new administrative institutions born of the civil war...

The 'de-Sovietisation' of political life developed quickly, and made itself felt at the centre as well as the local level. The All-Russia Congress of Soviets, which was supposed to meet every three months, and whose frequent gatherings—October 1917, January, March and July 1918—reflected the intense activity of the soviets during the first few months of the new regime, began to space out these occasions over longer intervals. From the end of 1918 they became annual, and also acquired an increasingly academic character. The Central Executive Committee of the Congress had been conceived as a permanent, or quasi-permanent body. However, it did not hold a single meeting between 14 July 1918 and 1 February 1920—though decrees continued to be issued in its name. In general, the militarisation of the whole of public life had suppressed the soviets as really functioning bodies.

Lenin was forced to acknowledge at the Eighth Party Conference in 1919 that 'the Soviets, which by virtue of their programme are organs of government *by the working people*, are in fact organs of government *for the working people* by the advanced section of the proletariat, but not by the working people as a whole.' This was a very serious admission for the author of *State and Revolution* to make, but his great quality as a leader was always to look truth in the face. Demands were constantly made by Communists and Mensheviks for the only really democratic institutions produced by the Revolution to be revived. There was some hope that this might happen. Elections to the soviets were held in 1920 and the Mensheviks participated in great numbers, winning a number of seats. Their leader Julius Martov, a friend and comrade of Lenin during the old pre-split days, commended the fact that soviet democracy was functioning well, 'except in Petrograd, where Zinovievite elections were held in the old manner.' The reference here was to Grigori Zinoviev, a veteran Bolshevik who was the Communist party chief in Petrograd and who had soon after October 1917, begun to acquire the reputation of an effective manipulator: 'his' section of the Party always voted 'unanimously' and he had clearly extended this principle to the soviets. This revival, alas, was only the last flicker before the flame was finally extinguished. In 1920-21 the Whites mounted a new offensive and the Poles attacked Soviet Russia. The economy deteriorated resulting in growing unrest in both town and countryside. Soviet democracy was among the first casualties.

There is a general impression that the Bolsheviks had a master-plan for banning every other party and ruling the country by themselves. This was not the case during the critical years of 1917-21. A number of historians of the Russian Revolution, despite very strong criticisms of the Bolsheviks, acknowledge that the other political parties virtually excluded themselves from the revolution. The Kadets (Constitutional-Democrats) were hostile to the soviets and opposed to the revolution. They soon made this clear by taking up arms against the new regime and calling for a restoration of the monarchy. The other main parties were the SRs whose support was based in the countryside. The SR historian, Radkey, described them as the voice of a rural intelligentsia and stated that the core of the party was composed of 'village scribes, the children of priests, the employees of the *zemstvos** and co-operatives, and, above all, the village schoolteachers.' The SRs were divided internally. The right-wing of the party had collaborated with Kerensky after February 1917; the left-wing had collaborated with the Bolsheviks and had participated in a coalition government. The Left SRs, disgusted with the refusal of their own party to support the Revolution had seceded from the parent organisation after the October Revolution. Lenin was in constant negotiation with them to join the government and this happened in December 1917: the Left SRs were given seven places (as opposed to the eleven held by the Bolsheviks) in the Soviet cabinet: the Council of People's Commissars. They left three months later because of their refusal to accept the Treaty of Brest-Litovsk which brought the war with Wilhelmine Germany to a conclusion, but at heavy costs in terms of territorial concessions. In July 1918 the Left SRs resorted to open terrorism, thus ending the period of co-operation. However they were not excluded from the soviets at that stage.

The Mensheviks were, like the Bolsheviks, concentrated in the towns. They had a strong base in the working class in the years

*Municipal Councils.

between 1905 and 1917. After the February 1917 revolution, however, they began to lose ground very rapidly to the Bolsheviks. For a working class party to have lost most of its support in the ranks of the proletariat was a disaster. It is often forgotten that the Bolshevik decision to make the revolution was *determined* by the fact that their party had won a majority in the key soviets of Petrograd and Moscow, and this process was showing signs of being repeated elsewhere in the country. It was these soviet elections which provided the Bolsheviks with a legitimacy as far as the Russian working class was concerned. The right-wing SRs had refused to accept this verdict and had decided on 26 October 1917 to undertake armed struggle to overthrow the new regime. Abraham Gotz the SR leader had made a pact with Kadets and Monarchists to achieve this aim. The Right Mensheviks were veering in the same direction. For years many of the Menshevik High Command had been obsessed with 'legality' to the point of timidity, but the Bolshevik triumph made the moderate Mensheviks into militants. Right-wing Menshevik chiefs openly stated that the only way to deal with the Bolsheviks was with guns and Lieber, their leader, called on the party to participate in the 'fighting alliance of all anti-Bolshevik forces.' This view was defeated at the extraordinary congress of the Mensheviks in December 1917. Martov refused to join the 'anti-communist camp'. His comrade Dan agreed that since the '*force of arms*' had failed they should begin talking to the Bolsheviks again. At the very dawn of the revolution, Trotsky and Martov had clashed bitterly on the floor of the soviet assembly. Martov had denounced the seizure of power as a plot, a military coup. Trotsky had defended the revolution, explaining the art of insurrection and ending with a fateful sentence: 'You are pitiful isolated individuals; you are bankrupts; your role is played out. Go where you belong—into the dustbin of history.' 'Then we will go,' Martov had replied angrily and walked out. Trotsky was later to refer to him more affectionately as the Hamlet of democratic socialism. A year later the Mensheviks had reappeared in the soviets and participated vigorously. Martov was the Leader of the Opposition in the soviets and it was anything but a tame opposition. Menshevik newspapers continued to be published. Outside Russia itself the Mensheviks had strong pockets of support. In Georgia they had a majority in the soviets and formed the Government, which was later overthrown by force: an early mistake with bad consequences. How would soviet democracy have functioned if the Civil War had ended in December 1918? But history willed otherwise. The Kronstadt revolt was seen as a strategic threat to the revolution. 'This is our Thermidor,' Lenin said as he decided to preempt the possibility of further attack and heightened the Red Terror. Having banned all the other soviet parties, the Bolsheviks began to censor themselves. At the Tenth Party Conference in 1921 all factions inside the party were banned. This was to have been a 'temporary measure', but it is still in force today. Stalin was to utilise that temporary measure with great effect, to drown the old Bolshevik party in blood. The talented Menshevik historian, Sukhanov, had described Stalin in 1917 as 'a grey spot which could sometimes give out a dim and inconsequential light. There is really nothing more to be said about him.' The revenge of the 'grey spot' against history was truly phenomenal.

All this history, as the present Soviet leadership understand only too well, is anything but a digression. Development in the USSR has been very uneven. Moscow, Leningrad, Kiev, Riga, Tallin, Vilnius, Tblisi, Yerevan and a dozen other towns have many amenities, but in the glubina there is still misery and hardships. Its economy, as we discussed in Chapter 3, is lopsided. A space exploration of the red planet, Mars, can be organised with all the technology and resources that are necessary, but in a small town a hundred miles from Moscow, Zaraisk, there is a shortage of sugar. There is only one cinema and drunkards and pregnant women jostle each other outside, waiting for the next show to begin. Hospital facilities are inadequate and patients sleep in the corridors. Studies usually end in the secondary school. Why, it could be asked, is it necessary to explore the red planet when the red countryside needs urgent attention? The revival of the soviets could mean that all these matters are publicly discussed and debated. And this brings us back to Gorbachev and his plans for modernisation of the country's political structure. Now it may be that the Lenin of *State and Revolution* was a hopeless utopian. But by the late Twenties the counter-revolution already had been decisively defeated. It is at this time that Lenin's absence became a key element in the evolution of the Soviet Union. This is not to suggest that sheer will-power could have transformed objective conditions overnight. It is simply that other alternatives were possible and that Stalinism was not a pre-ordained necessity. In any event, regardless of whether or not soviet democracy was possible in the Twenties and the Thirties, there can be little doubt that all the objective conditions are present for its rebirth today. In the years that followed the revolution the soviet democracy that

existed operated under very serious restraints of foreign intervention, civil war, and economic blockade by international
capitalism. As a result it could only be a moth-eaten and truncated
version of the ideals of the Revolution. This is not the case today.
Now the problem exists only on the subjective level.

Mikhail Gorbachev's weakness may well be his refusal to debate
his opponents within the party *in public*, a problem which never
worried the old Bolsheviks. In Gorbachev's favour it has to be said
that he is engaged in an extremely delicate operation which did not
confront Lenin. He has to effectively dismantle a gigantic
bureaucratic apparatus, and he wants to do this with the agreement
of those whose privileges will be swept overboard. The Soviet élite
has been built up over the last fifty years through a long process of
formal and informal selection and conditioning. It starts with the
family, goes through primary and secondary education and
continues in the allocation of jobs and posts inside the apparatus.
These members of the élite are, generally speaking, alienated from
ordinary people and their living conditions. In their work styles a
complete subjugation to higher authority is instilled; in carrying out
a task delegated to them they reckon with nothing else.

Why do these bureaucrats feel threatened? Because like the old
feudal war-lords they live in a different, isolated world. They stay in
special regions, in apartment blocks of a better quality at medium
rank and have entire floors to themselves or, at higher ranks,
individual houses. They have special facilities for health care, for
vacations. They have higher salary scales. Their children are sent to
schools which cater to élitist families and later to special institutes,
such as the Moscow Institute for International Relations, which is
run by the Foreign Ministry to train Soviet diplomats who are
carefully selected from amongst the children of high officials. At
medium rank, they merely have to dial a number for free transport;
at a higher rank they have a limousine permanently at their disposal.
The shortage of labour could be alleviated if the chauffeurs assigned
to these bureaucrats were cut down drastically and put into
productive labour. They shop at the special shops at special prices.
Most of these activities and services are managed by a special
organisation termed *Upravleniye delami* (Affairs Administration),
which indicates the importance of 'such affairs'. This bureaucratic
estate lives totally segregated from the everyday life. They observe
problems, certainly, but in a dehumanised fashion. They can not
relate to these problems because the conditioning process for half a

century has been such that they simply execute the will of the higher authority, treating the people as they would a gift of nature. This is the élite which used to say in the pre-Gorbachev era that 'advanced socialism' had been achieved. Perhaps one is misinterpreting them. Perhaps what they really meant was that *they* had achieved a form of 'advanced socialism'. The reformers realise very well that in these conditions it is impossible to ask the workers to make sacrifices. Politics and economics are such that only a thoroughgoing democratisation could permit large-scale economic reforms, and technological innovations in the economy. In brief, to win over the workers means, and there is no way to avoid this, antagonising the *nomenklatura*. Gorbachev understands this well but proceeds with care. Yeltsin understands it just as well but wants to clear the obstacles immediately, if necessary by mobilising support from below.

Mikhail Gorbachev's speech to the Central Committee plenum in January 1987 was truly astonishing, especially to people like myself who had long given up hope of anything genuinely radical or progressive ever emerging from the lips of a General Secretary of the CPSU. He told the plenum (who must have been even more astonished and wondered what on earth he was babbling about) that the ultimate goal of socialism was not democracy, but *freedom*. Now it is true that this word has been devalued and debased by the Nixons, Reagans and Thatchers of this world, just as much as Stalin, Brezhnev, Chernenko muddied the image of socialism. Gorbachev, however, made it clear that he was using the word in its classical Marxist sense. He meant free human creativity in the community. The objects and subjects of such creativity are the people themselves. This was the authentic voice of the cantankerous old man in the British museum who was working on texts which were designed to set humanity on the road to self-emancipation. Who would have expected his voice to be echoing in the chambers of the Kremlin in the late Eighties?

By 'free' human labour Marx meant labour freed from the realm of necessity, from the struggle for existence in a world of scarcity. The world today is far removed from any of that. Capitalism dominates the globe with its starving millions in the 'third world' ('third' because it is starving!) through its enormous machinery of military terror. And the strength of this beast remains far stronger than that of the states where capitalism was overthrown. This means that what is on the agenda today in the USSR is *not* the radical freedom of communism as envisaged by Marx, but a *renewal of socialist dynamism* amongst the Soviet people. This means democratisation and the refounding of the socialist project amongst Soviet people. Gorbachev made no bones about this. 'We need democracy,' he declared, 'as much as the air we breathe' and he explained that more democracy means more socialism, not less.

As I have already argued here, this does not make sense to cold-war liberalism, leave alone conservatism, which has been mobilised and educated in the seventy-year war of 'democracy' against 'socialism' (ignoring for the moment the fact that when this war was first declared, half the population of Britain and the United States ie. women—did not have the vote, whereas their Russian counterparts were active participants in the February and October revolutions and voted eagerly in elections to regional and local soviets). The supposed gulf between democracy and socialism has played such a strong part in the ideology of the West that it has not only affected attitudes towards socialism, which is understandable, but it has created serious misunderstanding as to the nature of the socialist critique of actually existing democracies. It is, therefore, useful to take a brief look at the models on offer before discussing what a reborn soviet democracy could look like in the USSR.

The defence of existing democracies by bourgeois theorists rests on a piece of ideological juggling with three concepts: popular authorisation, representation and politically neutral spheres of life which must be permanently safeguarded from the intrusion of politics. The first entails the view that the public interest—which is identical to the national interest—is decided democratically through multi-party elections. As a result of these competitive elections state policy is a direct reflection of the desires of the people. Because of this legitimacy people obey the state. If they don't the state has every right to punish them. This notion is fundamental to liberal democracy. Government policy and, therefore, its laws emanate from the people or, at least, are voluntarily and actively approved by the people through electoral choice. And it is this that results in the 'political obligation' of citizens which is a moral justification to obey the state. Thus the fact that there is not a permanent mass mobilisation against the enormous military expenditure which is needed for the 'defence of the realm against world communism' is taken instead as indicating mass approval.

So far as representation is concerned the idea here is a simple one. Because people have voted for Ms X or Mr Y they are henceforth obliged to obey whatever their representatives decide in parliament or Congress. At the same time it is stressed that parliamentarians should not consider themselves mandated in any sense, or feel as if they are simply delegates. They should behave as they see fit and not be manipulated by particular constituencies. (It is well-established that there are powerful lobbies at work on these representatives, but that does not matter since the lobbyists represent the powerful monied interests in the land.)

Then there is the so-called non-political sphere. This is supposed to include the economy, culture, intellectual and domestic life, social activities on one side and the administrative, legal, police apparatus of the state on the other. If politicians start taking control of any of these fields the tocsin is sounded since we are on the road to a totalitarian communist state. This 'civil society' is apparently unmarked by politics and because politicians are excluded from these fields the people are under no constraints in choosing their representatives! In brief, because civil society is free from the political state, there is freedom of thought, speech, assembly and organisation. And because the police and the judiciary are not under the control of politicians the rule of law exists. Politically neutral guidelines apply to everybody. Nobody is oppressed. It all sounds good.

But what does all this really mean? If one takes the authorisation of governments by the electorate the mechanism is supposed to work as follows. The candidates make promises to voters (and, incidentally, I have *never* known of any candidate promising mass unemployment) and because of these promises or because the other candidate's promises are less convincing, the voters vote for them. In return for this privilege, the voters must obey the laws. Yet if we then look at the repesentation principle we see that this is exactly what the candidates must not be bound to do: *they* can do as they please once they are elected. So if they can break their promises why should voters keep their side of the bargain? The answer often given here is that voters authorise governments by the simple act of voting. In other words, mere participation in the electoral process indicates approval of the system. Some would say: provided that there is a choice. If we use the same criteria in the Soviet Union we would find that people do go and vote in the elections. True they have had, until recently, hardly any choice at all. But, say, the one-party structure is preserved, with a choice of different candidates then, according to the criteria established by the liberal theorists of capitalist

democracy it would be difficult to argue against the notion that the
Soviet Union had embraced democracy. Because of these problems
many political scientists in the West have dropped the matter of the
obligations of a state to its citizens as a contentious issue in political
theory. This question, which has bedevilled the discussion on
democracy for centuries, has simply been buried by mainstream
writing. Democracy is now equated with the existing electoral
systems in the West. In this universe no other system is possible.
That is the voice of liberal orthodoxy in the West today.

Two points are stressed as fundamental to 'democracy': it is
strengthened by political apathy on the part of the population and its
strength depends on shared values, rather than a sharp division,
between the parties. It is preferable, in other words, that political
parties in competition with each other fight for power underneath a
common ideological umbrella. Democracy, according to this view,
is best when people are passive outside elections—when they can go
and cast a vote—and when there is a consensus between the main
political competitors for high office. Where there is a substantial
choice, as there was between the Socialists and the Christian
Democrats in Allende's Chile, then 'democracy' is really under
threat until the choice is removed. That great political theorist,
Henry Kissinger, was not deviating too much from liberal theory
when he attacked the Chilean people for being 'irresponsible'. Their
punishment was General Pinochet. In Italy 'democracy' is under
threat until the Italian Communist Party is removed as a serious
contender. Heaven knows the poor Italian communists have tried
hard to prove their loyalty to the Italian State, the Vatican and
NATO, but that isn't good enough. Promises, as we know, can be
easily broken.

If we look at the United States today the crisis of democracy is
very profound. Let us leave aside the fact that a very large percentage
of the American population simply does not vote in elections, the
personalist character of a Presidential choice is become more and
more of a farce, dominated by everything except politics. The
manifest vacuity of Presidential electoral choices saw the emergence
of the so-called pluralist theory. This made a positive virtue of the
beauty contest character of US Presidential elections by arguing that
the candidates don't stand for anything at all except getting the
maximum number of votes. The real way in which citizens control
the system is through independent pressure groups which offer the
votes of their supporters in return for Presidential support for their

particular policies. A classic case of this is the support provided to Ronald Reagan by the born-again, fundamentalist Christian sects in the United States. The millionaire divine, Jerry Falwell, provided money and ideology. Reagan began to play the part. Gore Vidal takes up the story:

> On 20 September 1970, an evangelical Christian, George Otis, and several like-minded folk visited Reagan when he was governor of California. They spoke rapturously of Rapture. Then, according to Otis, they all joined hands in prayer and Otis prophesied Reagan's coming election to the presidency. According to Otis ('Visit with a King') Reagan's arms 'shook and pulsated' during this prophecy. The next summer (29 June 1971) Reagan asked Billy Graham to address the California legislature; afterwards at lunch, Reagan asked Graham, 'Well, do you believe that Jesus Christ is coming soon, and what are the signs of his coming if that is the case?' Graham did not beat about this burning bush. 'The indication,' he said, 'is that Jesus Christ is at the very door.'*

The politics of the pressure groups means abandoning any formal idea of the 'public interest' or what is best for the nation. Everything is determined by which private interests can deliver votes. Thus the argument that representatives should be independent of sectoral pressures and take their own position on the 'national interest' collapses without a trace. The Christian fundamentalists perhaps can be treated as a zany nightmare, but what about General Motors? In the event of a tussle between this giant multinational and the carworkers' trade union, the UAW, it is obvious who will win. General Motors will go into battle with a veritable army of full-time staff engaged in open political activity. They lobby; they advertise; they spend money; they cajole; they threaten to close plants (jeopardising, in this fashion, the careers of local politicians, not to mention the workers concerned). GM can withdraw funds from Senators who need millions in these days of modern technology to mount an effective electoral campaign. Add to this the fact that the entire weight of the system—its political agenda and its laws—is stacked in favour of General Motors: it can sack, close down, ruin the lives of tens of thousands of ordinary families, all without the fear of any political comeback. All this led Charles Lindblom, the doyen of liberal political theory in the United States, to ruefully conclude at the end of the Seventies that US politics is entirely dominated by big business.

Armagedolon by Gore Vidal, Andre Deutsch, 1987.

If we now look at civil society—which is supposedly the realm of freedom crowned by a set of neutral institutions—we see, as numerous authors have pointed out, a sphere where ordinary people are dominated by extremely authoritarian business organisations, with their unlimited mania for wealth. The people are totally dependent on the will of the owners of these organisations for their livelihood: that is, for the means of all the private ends they may wish to pursue in their lives. There are millions of people out of work in the United States and Britain alone, where urban decay goes hand in hand with violent gangs and Crack culture. One of Britain's least successful exports, for instance, is a sizeable section (though by no means a majority) of the soccer hoodlums who have taken the Falklands ethos to the rest of Europe. Surely all this is a matter of concern to the whole community, a case of public interest if anything is? But no, not a bit of it. Politics, we are informed, can not and should not solve these problems. Leave all that to the police, the judiciary, the prison system, the churches and social workers (preferably of the voluntary sort) and, in the last instance, the army.

It is, of course, well-established that the legal system is totally neutral. Now and then judges and magistrates might well turn out to be fascists, but all that is irrelevant. Law is based on the principle that all are equal before its majesty. It is true that the poor are not allowed to steal from the rich, but then it is equally true that the rich are not allowed to steal from the poor. Both rich and poor have the equal right to fund political parties or launch newspapers and cable television channels. Both rich and poor can buy TV time to put across their point of view or lobby Capitol Hill and Westminster. But we do all have the vote. Once every five years or if we're lucky once every four years. Through this we exercise power, indirectly of course. And yet electoral surveys regularly reveal in the United States, in particular, that people vote out of a sense of public duty, not because they feel it gives them power. They vote because they feel they should. They are persuaded to vote. In the United States just about half the population takes time off from its daily chores to do its duty and vote, since voting is as American as apple pie. Friedrich Hayek, the guru of the Thatcher-Reagan counter-revolution, was totally correct when he wrote in *The Road to Serfdom* that economic control is *not* just one part of society amongst others, but 'it is the control over means to all other ends.' And in conditions of capitalist democracy, capital has economic control, and therefore it controls the means to any political group's ends. It is not that capital is inflexible. If it is confronted by a wave of general strikes which it cannot defeat, leave alone semi-insurrections, it will permit a surprising amount of concessions—only to claw them back when the time is right. Small wonder then that neither German social-democracy nor the British Labour Party nor the people in power (Mitterand in France, Felipe Gonzales in Spain, Andreas Papandreau in Greece) neither pledge to nor can get rid of unemployment. They simply do not have the means to control that end. And yet an overwhelming majority in every capitalist country wants to end unemployment; but this majority view clashes with the requirements of a stable 'democracy'. Is this the democracy that one should hope for from the Soviet Union under Gorbachev? We think not.

However, before leaving our models and moving on to discuss the concrete application of the democratisation proposals in the Soviet Union today, it is worth mentioning how orthodox Stalinists viewed democracy. It is easy to dismiss their views with contempt, since that avoids the luxury of a debate, but the points made by various Stalinist writers are not without interest. Four basic points are made:

1. That democracy can not be considered in isolation from the social structure of the country. How can there be a truly democratic society in a country where capitalists exercise a social dictatorship over the population? Politics is defined by the character of the state. If the state has a socially oppressive function because it defends capitalism, then *ipso facto* it cannot be a democratic state. In the USSR on the other hand, capitalists and landlords do not exist. Workers, peasants and intellectuals dominate society and since the entire people rule, the state is democratic in character. The political monopoly of the Communist Party, far from contradicting democracy, confirms it. After all parties represent classes. The Soviet workers lead the rest of the country. The Party leads the workers. Thus CPSU hegemony guarantees the democracy of the state.

2. The democratic character of the state is also defined by its public policy. To ascertain whether or not a state is democratic one has to ask the old question. *Qui prodest*? Who benefits? Western states benefit *only* a rich minority. In the USSR the central thrust of governmental policy is geared to the welfare of ordinary working people just as the capitalist state guarantees the profits of the wealthy. It is this substance of government policy rather than the

formal mechanisms of decision-making which is the real test of the character of states and governments.

3. During the Khrushchev period a very heavy stress was laid on public political participation by all social classes and strata in government activity. Khrushchev's utopian view that a short transition to communism was possible led him to the conclusion that it was important to transfer public administrative functions from state bodies to social organisations. Brezhnev played down this aspect but the stress on popular participation in political and administratve work was continued. The numbers of people voting, engaged in public discussions during election campaigns, participating in the work of local soviets or writing letters to the newspapers—all this was treated as democratic involvement—was far greater than in the West.

4. Soviet orthodoxy has entailed a strict attitude to ethnic representation within representative bodies. Thus if there is a local soviet in an area with a mixed Russian and Ukrainian population then the soviet has to reflect a proportionality. [In this area the major void is the lack of representation of women. In fact women are totally under-represented in the Soviet pyramid on every level.]

These ideas are flawed, but no more so than liberal orthodoxies in the West and they deserve a response. Stalinist theory continued to stress two ideas which are indeed substantial preconditions for an authentic popular democracy. These are (a) that instead of economic and social power being treated outside the sphere of 'politics', but in reality in the West, controlling the options in the political arena, it stressed the equality of economic and social power and (b) it mocked the notion that popular apathy is the most stable form of democratic rule as opposed to popular participation.

The sleight of hand involved here, however, treated these two *preconditions* for political democracy as if they were political democracy itself. What this view left out of account was the not unimportant question of the mass of ordinary people being able to use their formal social equality as the basis for their own political sovereignty and being able to participate as the makers of decisions. These matters, in other words politics, were to be left in the secure hands of the 'cadres' whose stability, as we have pointed out before, was to be defended against all attacks.

For many decades now we have been offered two alternative models of popular democracy. In the West the formal procedures of democratic choice are, in practice, drained of all substance because of the lack of even the most minimum social power of the average citizen. In the East some of the substantial preconditions for political democracy exist, but without the crucially important democratic political forms. What underlies much of the excitement generated by perestroika throughout the world is the expectancy that events in the Soviet Union might lead to the emergence of a higher model of democracy which combines substantial equality and participatory rights with the procedures of democratic choice. Such an advance would simultaneously mark a return to the original impulse of the Revolution and transform the terms of the battle of ideas between East and West and between socialists and supporters of capitalism.

In recent months attention has been rivetted on the attacks within the CPSU itself, not least from the leaders of the party, on the 'democracy' of cadre departments. What is at stake inside the party is the bureaucratic monopoly. But one that is successfully challenged and destroyed the monopoly of information and ideas which has been jealously defended by party ideologues from the late Twenties onwards will itself begin to wither away. This has, amazingly enough, emerged from within the CPSU itself. Mikhail Gorbachev and Alexander Yakovlev have stessed repeatedly in virtually every forum that what currently exists is completely insufficient and their open encouragement to party members on every level to think aloud is beginning to spread. Thus Boris Kibirev, Secretary of the Party Committee in Krasnodar Territory, a giant agro-industrial complex, washed by the Black Sea and the Sea of Azov, stated in 1988 that a central problem was the selection of cadres:

> Leaders, including Party and government ones, were selected on the basis of fellowship, nepotism and personal devotion. Leaders were protected against criticisms, shielded against Party accountability and quite often criminal liability, moved from one leading post to another. In such an atmosphere there were regular distortions of results achieved, bribery and abuse of authority thrived. This adversely affected the development of the economy and the social sphere; the moral and psychological climate in the Territory worsened. People ceased trusting leading cadres. A sociological study made in Krasnodar in 1982 produced dismal results: about 60 percent of residents of the city had no faith in the possibility of putting things in order and restoring social justice.

Readers may be surprised that Kibirov is talking about using sociological studies to find out what people are thinking. Not only are these common in the Soviet Union, but the research methods are

designed to ascertain real needs and complaints. In that sense they
are the polar opposite of opinion poll surveys in the West! Another
point worth noting is that already in 1982 with Andropov in power,
serious moves were afoot to reform the party and society. Kibirov
explained how open nominations, discussions of the same and
competition for posts had resulted in 'younger workers and a large
number of women [coming] to hold leading posts.' Yet he was not in
the least complacent. He admitted that in a number of cases in the
factories the workers had rejected the party candidate and elected
their own representatives. Why? Because

> many party workers, for example, lack adequate public knowledge,
> and have no proper understanding of personnel policy amid growing
> democracy and openness. In the run-up to the election of people to
> leading positions, Party committees sometimes fail to give serious
> thought to the conditions in the workplace and have not enough
> contacts on the grassroots level.

The situation elsewhere in the Soviet Union varies, but, in general,
it is accepted that the problems for the Party are the same. The time
is obviously coming to dissolve this party and elect a new one. It is in
the application of democracy *inside* the Party that perestroika faces a
severe test. Will the party be able to renew itself from below?
Gorbachev is clearly banking on this taking place. This helps to
explain his reluctance to clear the Central Committee and make
room for the reformers. If, however, this happens on the *obkom* level
because of pressure from below then the new party secretaries of the
regions will automatically come on to the central committee and
replace the old guard. This process has already begun, but it is in the
key areas—such as the Ukraine, the Central Asian Republics, the
Baltic states—where it will have the greatest significance if the
political structures of the entire country are going to be transformed.

The Nineteenth Party Conference approved the principle of
encouraging more mass participation, via a real choice in elections to
the soviets. This marks a very important step forward, especially
when it is coupled with increasing the powers of the soviets and
enhancing their political status. I have no doubt that very real
political debates will take place there, but the separation of the Party
from the state requires far more than these tentative and somewhat
cautious first steps. It is obvious that from Khrushchev onwards the
ideologues of the Party have understood the problem. The situation
now is the total reverse of what it was in the 1917-20 period. Then the
leaders of the Party were centrally involved in the soviets, at both

assembly and executive level. Simultaneously they were immersed in running the country and waging a civil war. The consequence was that the Party was actually downgraded in importance. This had two immediate effects. Local parties became far more independent and often did not even bother to send reports of their activities to the centre. This was not such a bad thing, but the major effect was that party organisation in this critical period was (after the premature death of Sverdlov), left increasingly to Stalin. He did all the 'shit work' and everyone, including Lenin, failed to see what he was up to until it was almost too late. By the time the civil war ended the soviets were dead and as party leaders took a renewed interest in the Party they discovered that while Zinoviev controlled Petrograd/ Leningrad and Moscow veered between Stalin and Bukharin, the future dictator had built an effective network throughout the country. Lenin's testament stated that Stalin should be removed because, among other things, he was 'too rude' to party members. Did Lenin mean that Stalin's verbal violence foreshadowed something more sinister? I doubt it. Trotsky later wrote that if Stalin had been told in 1924 that his political methods would lead to exterminating the entire Bolshevik old guard he would have been disbelieving. Left on its own the charge of 'rudeness' was a mild, one might say, even a shallow, psychological criticism. True Lenin's solution seemed drastic: Stalin should be removed from his position as General Secretary. This indicates that Lenin knew or feared what might happen if Stalin stayed in place, but the real problem was the political structure both of the party and society as a whole which could be so easily manipulated by the merged and powerful apparatus of party and state.

The question which is posed is the following one. Is it possible to separate the party from the state in a one-party state? This returns us to the Stalinist conceptions of democracy that we discussed above. The argument for a one-party state used to be that it was this party alone which represented the interests of the working class: past, present and future. Since parties were representative of classes, the argument went and there was only one class in the USSR therefore there should be only one party. The obvious fallacy here is that social classes themselves are never homogenous. It is not even necessary to look at the situation in existing democracies where, in many cases, the social democratic parties vie for influence with Communist parties, far-Left grouplets and, especially in the case of Britain, the Conservative Party. The Russian workers were never possessed by a monolithic consciousness. During the Tsarist days the more politically backward section of the Russian working class were under the influence of monarchist and Black Hundred propaganda; the more advanced were attracted to revolutionary social-democracy. After the split between the Bolsheviks and the Mensheviks their working-class supporters, too, divided into differing currents of thought. There was, of course, a great deal of movement. Changing material and environmental circumstances brought about shifts in consciousness. The defeats of the Tsarist army during the First World War resulted in a growing disenchantment with the monarchy. The senseless slaughter of that conflict combined with the food shortages (which were the result of a massive economic and logistical disorganisation) laid the ground for the February Revolution. The inability of Kerensky to either end the war or take measures to create a new basis for the distribution of food created a further demoralisation. The Bolsheviks were in a minority in many soviets in the period between February and October 1917. It was only *after* they had gained a majority in the two key soviets of Petrograd and Moscow and while their strength was growing in soviets elsewhere in the country, that the decision was taken to mount an insurrection 'Lenin,' wrote Trotsky in his epic *History of the Russian Revolution,** 'very studiously followed all the elections and voting in the country, carefully assembling those figures which would actually throw a light on the actual correlation of forces. The semi-anarchistic indifference to electoral statistics got nothing but contempt from him.' There wouldn't have been much point in analysing election results if the polls had been confined to a single party.

The Stalinist belief that the 'leading nucleus' of the 'leading party' is the only force capable of scientific knowledge and hence infallibility is pure mumbo-jumbo. Its purpose is to preserve the bureaucracy's monopoly of politics and information. This view has an obvious corollary: the population at large is incapable of political thought. The workers themselves can not see what is in their own social interests and therefore the party or rather its leadership or, just to be extra careful, its 'Leader' are the only people/person capable of taking the correct decisions. What flows from this theological conclusion is that since 'the party' and it alone represents the immediate and future interests of a class which is permanently

History of the Russian Revolution (3 vols) by Leon Trotsky, Gollanze, 1933.

homogenous then that party, too, must be totally monolithic in character. And from this it is only a small step towards authoritarian control over all spheres of social existence. These pernicious ideas reflected the inability of those who developed them to engage in a battle of ideas with opponents outside or inside the party. Such views had nothing in common with any theories by Marx or Engels. In fact the victory of Stalinism in the USSR led to the debasement of Marx's thought, and what could have been a critical science became a state religion. The consequences of this was an ideological famine in the USSR. The poverty of creative thought deprived Soviet social scientists of their life-blood. It created a generation of talentless time-servers who rose to the top. Of course there were others who carried on the battle for critical thought through Aesopian means or retreated to a study of the Ancient World.

In normal conditions a country has one *real* centre of power: the state. If the country in question has only a single party then it is extremely difficult, if not impossible, to separate the party from the state and provide the latter with a meaningful autonomy which enables it to act as an arbiter of competing political and social interests. As we discussed earlier the decisions of the Nineteenth Party Conference reflected this problem in very graphic detail. The decision to put local party bosses in charge of the soviets had the effect of pruning the potential powers of the soviet from the very beginning of an attempt to revive their status in a country which bears their name. I am not suggesting that the reformers are unaware of this dilemma. The problem is that their own positions will remain under constant threat unless and until there are institutional safeguards. The revival of soviets entails the rebirth of mass politics. Pluralism can not be restricted to ideas alone. After all they do not drop from the sky. Ideas flow from differing perceptions of reality. In that sense they reflect material conditions. Suppose the proponents of a particular idea X decided that the only way to pursue their publicly-expressed thoughts to a logical conclusion was by the formation of a political tendency inside the CPSU. What then? Mass expulsions? If so then there is nothing to prevent the supporters of X from forming a new organisation Y and challenging the CPSU in the election to the soviets. Let us suppose that they win a majority in the Moscow soviet. This would give them the right to elect an executive. Obviously they could not possibly accept the head of the Moscow CPSU as the head of the Soviet. This could, speaking technically, happen even within the confines of a single party state.

Suppose non-party individuals won a majority and did not accept the person imposed on them by the decisions of the CPSU. What then? Police measures?

The question of a multi-party soviet system is being openly and privately discussed throughout the Soviet Union. Its staunchest opponents are the diehard defenders of the *nomenklatura*, symbolised by Yegor Ligachev. The preservation of party unity forced a compromise, but many supporters of the First Secretary are deeply divided on this issue. Otto Latsis told me in April 1988 that while he agreed that there was nothing in the theory of Marxian socialism that outlawed multi-party democracy he—and he stressed that this was his opinion—simply could not see how 'other parties could be formed, could function and exist on an everyday basis.' I asked him why.

> Because in the entire seventy-year history of our state it happens that we had pluralism only for several months after the revolution. Seven months or so out of seventy years! And it wasn't our party that abolished this system. The other parties walked out ... In any event nowadays it would seem to be an artifical matter, out of place. Don't misunderstand. We are not against pluralism as such in principle, but I just don't believe that this could be through a system of universal democracy. There is a natural quest as far as any human being is concerned for freedom and democracy and this quest must be satisfied, but this can be done by other means. Different countries decide in different ways. Our task today is to revive the activity of the one party that we do have because it doesn't function as it should. It very often substitutes for the state and unsurps its functions. This is partly a historical tradition which was necessary during the Civil War, but, in the main, it is the legacy of Stalin. So I think that the most logical thing is to ensure the proper functioning of our one party so that it does not substitute itself for state and economic instruments.

This view probably reflects majority thinking inside the CPSU and unites supporters of both the apparatus and the reformers. When I pressed Latsis on this question I suggested that the implementation of the economic reform was bound to lead to big differences, especially if there was working class resistance to the price reforms, which would undoubtedly be reflected inside the Party. How could such differences be contained or resolved?

> The very fact that our party was the mastermind behind perestroika testifies to its health. I mean if the Party pushed it through and is carrying it out it attests to the fact that a one-party system is sufficient and our party will survive the tests that lie ahead. As for the difference

of opinion on economic renewal: this certainly exists inside the Party, but a one-party system does not preclude a discussion between the different groups. Of course you are quite right in saying that perestroika can't go on smoothly and it isn't going smoothly, but this demands even more than before the leading role of the Party. If differences keep increasing I can't tell at this moment what to do. We shall see. If one tries to foretell now it's pure guesswork.

There is a sense in which Latsis in articulating an alternative conception of democracy. During the Khrushchev period a very heavy stress was laid on the Soviet definition of democracy. This was, in my opinion, a flawed argument, but nonetheless one which deserves to be discussed seriously. The argument was that a key criterion for assessing whether or not a society was democratic was not the formal mechanisms of the ballot, but the public political participation by all social layers in the activity of government. Khrushchev's 1961 programme had talked of a short-term transition to communism. It therefore became necessary to insist on the transfer of public administrative functions from state bodies to social organisations. This aspect was played down during the Brezhnev period, but continuing popular participation in political and administrative work was continued. The numbers of people voting and involved in public discussions during election campaigns, participating in the work of local soviets or writing to the newspapers—all this was taken as a sign of democratic involvement far greater than that in the West. These processes have multiplied a hundredfold under Gorbachev. In fact one can almost see quantity beginning to be transformed into quality.

Just to take one example: the range of people who write letters to the media is far greater in the USSR than either in Western Europe or North America. We have already referred to some of these letters in Chapter 2, but this is now a phenomenon on a very large-scale which supplements and sometimes supplies information in the myriad complex of the Soviet print media. The letters published in the *New York Times* or the *Washington Post*, for example, usually come from a tiny layer of the population. It would not occur to a worker made redundant or a black victim of random police brutality or a battered housewife to seek retribution in the letters column of the press. It is exactly the opposite in the USSR.

Nonetheless the view that a one-party state can co-exist with genuine soviet democracy is untenable. This is already becoming obvious in the USSR. Since the Twenty-seventh Party Congress there has been a mushrooming of 'unofficial groups' of almost every variety. The group which tends to receive the most publicity in the West is the one which produces *Glasnost* magazine, a glossy outfit funded by the Heritage Foundation and patronised by the US Embassy in Moscow. The second most-publicised group is the Democratic Union, which explicitly disavows socialism. The fact is, however, that the most lively and largest unofficial organisations have been the Federation of Socialist Clubs and the ecological groups. The Socialist Clubs sprang up in 1986. They were composed largely, though not exclusively, of people in their twenties and thirties. The pattern of activity in different towns was similar: packed meetings, intense discussions, a desperate urge to seek and find the truth about the society in which they lived, to openly debate taboo subjects and through this activity to strengthen the thrust towards perestroika. The socialist clubs consisted of people who were ardent supporters of Gorbachev's reform programme and had very consciously situated themselves within that particular framework. They viewed themselves as the left arm of the reformers, but they tended to stress different aspects in different parts of the country. When I attended a meeting of the Moscow Federation in April 1988 the discussions were very reminiscent of the Sixties in Western Europe. There was a long discussion on a programmatic document which was to be presented at a meeting the following weekend before delegates from clubs all over the country. The debate centred on the economic reforms. There was no disagreement on the need for a degree of marketisation, but it was emphasised that this needed to be carefully monitored and regulated. The fact that the workers would not be prepared to give up their *social rights* was underlined by a number of speakers who wanted amendments to the draft. This was followed by the usual complaints from the Clubs in Omsk and Leningrad: the paper (*Left Turn*, a cyclo-styled thing) was not arriving on time. Other regions demanded better quality paper, all of which was discussed in a jovial fashion. A brief debate continued on the absolute necessity of establishing links with the factories and the meeting ended just as my sense of *déjà vu* was complete!

One of the most important issues drawing young people into activity within the clubs is ecology. This is both a direct result of Chernobyl and the pollution of Lake Baikal, and the cavalier fashion in which many historic buildings have been destroyed by the mafiocracy. There is little feminist discussion in any of these clubs, although this is probably because Soviet women are still finding their feet and concentrating on women-only environments. Racism as a topic for discussion is also not common.

The Moscow clubs were in the forefront of the public campaign to defend Boris Yeltsin after his removal as party chief in Moscow. This brought members of the Clubs in touch with many young and old members of the CPSU and friendly relations were established on a horizontal level. In May 1988 the Clubs merged with various ecology groups and others to establish the Popular Front For Perestroika. This movement has spread to many parts of the country and has even received official blessing in Estonia. Many of the big public protests against the rigging of delegates to the Nineteenth Party Conference were the results of a joint effort by the Popular Front and rank-and-file party members. The new organisation is clear on its organisational structure: 'We are not a party, but a united front from below. If we call ourselves a party we just cut ourselves off from the masses. We want legality for ourselves throughout the country as we have obtained in Estonia.'

Mikhail Malyutin, a party member, is one of the major voices of the Popular Front in Moscow. He said that many of their ideas were having an undoubted impact on the upper reaches of the party intelligentsia. 'Even Alexander Yakovlev, I'm sure, is glad that we exist. There is a terrible poverty of creative thought in the secretariat of the Central Committee.' Malyutin has been engaged in a series of negotiations with the Moscow Procurater to have the group formally registered since this would considerably facilitate legal activities. The legal officer concerned is a Stalinist stereotype. Malyutin told me in July 1988, after the Conference that:

> I did not address Baranov as comrade, but called him Citizen Baranov. We told him that the Popular Front believes in democratic, self-managing socialism which unites workers, students and artistic groups. We said that we wanted to accelerate the process from below and that we would fight every violation of the law, small or big. Citizen Baranov listened carefully and then said: 'We don't allow perestroika from below.' I asked who the 'we' was. He replied, 'the Party!' I asked where is this party registered. How is it that it can exist without being registered? What became very obvious is that the party apparatus is scared of any mobilisation from below.

On the far-right of the political spectrum is an organisation known as *Pamyat* (Memory). While some of the reformers tend to dismiss it as an ephemeral collection of psychological misfits who are politically irrelevant, this view is not shared by the Popular Front activists. Boris Kagarlitsky analyses the phenomenon as potentially very powerful and with supporters in the apparatus of party and state as well as sections of the literary intelligentsia: Valentin Rasputin and Yuri Bondarev, for example, hold views which are similar to those of Pamyat. The group is a political organisation in the full meaning of the word. It has a rigorous internal structure, local branches in almost a dozen Russian cities as well as individual members. The actual membership consists of several hundred people, but the group acquired national prominence when Yegor Ligachev agreed to meet its leaders and instructed Boris Yeltsin (at that stage still Secretary of the Moscow Party) to do the same.

Pamyat's genealogy can be traced straight back to the pre-revolutionary Black Hundreds. Its Führer is a man called Emilyanov, who murdered his wife some years ago, was imprisoned for a period and after his release he founded Pamyat. It is a proponent of Great Russian chauvinism, and its activities and propaganda are quasi-fascist: anti-semitic and anti-asiatic, some of its vocabulary is reminiscent of the pre-revolutionary Orthodox Church. In Moscow one of its major campaigns is to the effect that it was the Jews who destroyed all the churches in the city during the Thirties. Stalin is not openly praised, but his anti-semitism and his strong sense of pan-slavism makes him a popular figure in private. The novelist, Anatoli Rybakov, whose *Children of the Arbat* will have sold two and a half million copies in the Soviet Union alone by the end of 1988 described in an interview with *Moscow News* in 1987 how some of the letters he received criticised him for using 'foreign sources'. He rejected such criticism with contempt and went on to say: 'Nor can I accept Valentin Rasputin's advice which appeared in the press that I write about, for example, Stalin's henchman Kaganovich, rather than Stalin. By the same token I could suggest that Rasputin go ahead and write, say, about the Tsarist politician Purishkevich!' The point here being that Kaganovich is of Jewish origin and faithfully carried out Stalin's orders during the late Twenties and Thirties: Purishkevich was an ardent monarchist who founded the union of the Russian People (URP) in 1905 as a rightwing response to liberal and revolutionary groups. It was violently anti-semitic and the Black Hundreds became its storm-troopers, fomenting pogroms and murdering political opponents. Purishkevich was the first Russian fascist and Rybakov's reference to him indicated his utter contempt for the crude nationalism and anti-semitism of Valentin Rasputin.

The changes within the party and the emergence of public political organisation of one sort or another is bound to have an effect on how pluralism is viewed by the ideologues of the reform movement. Yuri Afanasiev expressed a different view to Otto Latsis when I talked to him in July 1988. In the past the students who entered the portals of the Institute (of Historical Archives) did so out of a sense of duty: the place resembled a morgue. Since 1986 it has had applications from more students than it can accommodate and the foyer was crowded with young aspirants desperate to study here on the day I met the Rector. The following exchange on socialist democracy was part of a longer interview, but it is an accurate summary of Afanasiev's opinion:

TA: At the time of the Tenth Party Conference in 1921 *all* the leaders of the Bolshevik Party stressed *that* the banning of tendencies and factions inside the party—in other words the outlawing of dissent within the ranks of Bolshevism—was a temporary measure. Stalin was to utilise this ban to institutionalise authoritarianism in the country. As I see it it was the banning of other Soviet parties such as the Left Mensheviks and the Left SRs which paved the way for barring pluralism inside the party itself. Now we can see the film being reversed. Surely if pluralism within the Party leads to the emergence of other parties the heavens will not fall? Don't you think that it is perfectly possible to accommodate other parties within the soviet system? I would have thought that it was perfectly possible to move towards a form of soviet democracy which was much more real in terms of mass participation than any existing capitalist democracy?

YA: Well I must say in the first place that I agree with you. For me what you've just said is perfectly acceptable. I have the same assessment as you of the Tenth Party Conference. It was meant to be a temporary measure. This was indeed the spirit in which that resolution was passed. This 'temporary measure' has lasted from 1921 till 1988. It is impossible to regard this situation as normal. The Party must not represent a monolith, because a monolith is like a boulder. It is something total—inanimate. Of course differences of opinion are perfectly normal in a political party. I think that at the present stage there is very great scope for the development of a pluralism of ideas even within the framework of a one-party system. Of course only if the Party itself is radically transformed. What does this mean? It means the Party must abandon the commandist and administrative methods of rule and instead offer guidance through persuasion and participation. In other words a party should lead not by the authority of its physical force, but rather through the force of its moral authority. That is what we are moving towards and that is why this whole subject was much debated at the Nineteenth Party Conference.

Secondly I believe that tendencies and factions should exist inside the Party which should represent a community of independent ideas. We should have differing platforms articulating differing political positions and that's what will happen soon. I think the existence of tendencies and factions is a positive phenomenon. It's healthy provided that the factions do not behave organisationally in a way that is contrary to the constitution.

As for the presence of other organisations it is already a fact. In Estonia there is the Popular Front for Perestroika which is legally registered. There are over 1000 unofficial groups in our country. They are part of the new political realities. On the eve of the Nineteenth Party Conference I was present at a conference of the independent, unofficial groups in Moscow. They had studied and discussed the Theses of the Central Committee which were presented to the Conference and worked out their positions on them. I must say I was impressed by their seriousness. The Party has to see this as part of the growing process of democratisation which has to be taken into account. It must not be ignored and nor should the Party treat these groups in a condescending fashion. I think our life is beginning to manifest what you said, but perhaps not in as clearcut and succinct a fashion as you. There are still problems. There remains a hostile attitude to the mass movement and its leaders, but things are moving in the right direction ...

And yet, despite this note of optimism, Afanasiev struck a more prudent note when I asked whether Gorbachev and Yakovlev were secure in the Politburo. In other words if a serious crisis developed over the next couple of years could not the apparatus organise a palace coup to remove the reformers as had happened in the case of Khrushchev? 'There are no guarantees,' replied the historian and went on to stress that the only way to protect the gains that had accrued since the Twenty-Seventh Party Congress and to safeguard the reformers at the top was to create and revive institutions which could channel support from below. Without regular mass participation in the running of the state nothing was safe. This question is undoubtedly preoccupying the leaders of the reform movement. Their more euphoric supporters at the base of the party are confident that there can be no going back. Any attempt by the apparat to topple Gorbachev would, I was told, unleash a civil conflict. But what if Gorbachev became a prisoner of the bureaucracy and agreed to call a halt to the whole process? Very few people believe that this is possible and one hopes that they are right, but there is this danger in leaving it all to Gorbachev. Afanasiev's stress on the necessity of institutionalising the democratic gains is, clearly, absolutely decisive if the political revolution is to succeed.

Changes are already under way in the legal sphere. The Soviet functioning of the Soviet judicial system has, since 1930, been determined by the 'theories' of Yudin and, more notoriously, the dreaded Andrei Vyschinsky. After 1917 there was a rather creative discussion on what the legal basis of the new regime should be and a young vice-commisar of Justice, Evgeny B. Pashukanis, a Lithuanian who joined the Bolsheviks in 1912, produced *The General Theory of Law and Marxism*, which soon became a cult book and even today is regarded outside the Soviet Union as a classic Marxist study on law. Pashukanis strongly criticised all notions of 'proletarian law', arguing that in the period of transition from capitalism to socialism many of the advances of bourgeois law needed to be preserved. As society moved away from the old patterns then the old law would be totally demystified and ultimately abolish itself as the community began to live in a different way altogether. In the Thirties this talented legal theorist's books were banned and he was executed in 1937. The Procurator-General of the USSR, Vyshinsky, had denounced him as belonging to a crazed 'band of wreckers' in the pay of 'Trotsky-Bukharin fascist agents'. Vyshinsky developed the concept that a court could never establish ojective truth since no crime could be reproduced. Thus practice was not a criterion of truth. It followed that there was no real need to become too obsessed with notions such as truth. 'Maximum probability' of guilt was sufficient cause to conflict. In his book *Criminal Process*, Vyshinsky argued that the very aim of trying to establish courts as independent of outside influences was 'bourgeois through and through'. The function of law was not to establish any objective criteria, but to 'mercilessly suppress the remaining enemies of the people'. This 'theory' was enshrined in the Soviet law on 'terrorist activities' which was passed on 1 December 1934.* It

*Ironically, this was the very same day as Kirov was assassinated.

rejected every humane advance since the birth of Roman Law: there was no right to a defence council or to summon witnesses; the only possible sentence was death by firing squad and there was no right of appeal against the sentence. In this fashion did Vyshinsky, a one-time right-wing Menshevik, get his revenge against the Bolshevik Old Guard. As constitutional and legal rights are slowly restored to Soviet citizens it is surely time for a student of law to write Vyshinsky's biography as a lesson and warning to future generations. There is only one possible title for such a work: *The Criminal's Progress.*

A small, but significant sign of the shift in the legal system took place when I was in Moscow in July 1988. In the Sverdlov District Court a remarkable trial took place. The Plaintiff was our old friend Boris Kagarlitsky. In November 1987 he had been denounced by the *Komsomolskaya Pravada* (the newspaper of the Young Communists) as an 'imposter' and a former criminal. He had been imprisoned for several months during the Brezhnev period for writing a socialist critique of the system, *Dialectics of Hope.* The KGB had seized both the manuscript and the author. He had been released when Andropov had replaced Brezhnev The slanderous attack published in the paper of the Komsomol was hardly original, but Kagarlitsky refused to ignore the attack. He refused to subdue himself or stifle his own song, so decided to sue the newspaper for libel. In the preliminary examinations the newspaper claimed that it did not know who had written the article and that its signatories were not members of its staff. At the actual trial, the defence council admitted that the information had been provided by the KGB: Kagarlitsky won. The newspaper was instructed by the court to apologise or face a fine. This is the first time that this has happened in a Soviet court since the early Twenties. Kagarlitsky's 'little' success is an important watershed. A precedent has been established.*

---

*It is true that there was another case in 1918, but that had ended rather differently. Julius Martov, the Left Menshevik leader, had published an article in his paper *Forward*, which had alleged that Stalin had been expelled by the Russian Social Democratic and Labour Party because of his involvement with gangsters and criminals engaged in expropriations. Stalin had taken the case before a Tribunal. Martov had insisted on calling several Bolsheviks as witnesses, especially Bolsheviks from Georgia, Stalin's home province. This request had been denied, but the Tribunal dismissed Stalin's case. Some months later Stalin had successfully manouevred and manipulated the apparatus to get the Menshevik newspaper banned on some spurious charge. Lenin, probably for misguided reasons of party patriotism, had failed to defend Martov. Nor had Trotsky or Bukharin. It could be argued that this was Stalin's first small victory: the realisation that it was possible to use the apparatus to get rid of personal 'enemies'.

We have argued that sovialist democracy, far from being a utopia, is perfectly practicable in the USSR today and, for that matter, in Eastern Europe, China, Cuba and Indo-China. The monolithic model is utterly discredited. The question is what to put in its place. As far as the Soviet Union is concerned there are many political scientists who closely observe the functioning of politics and economics in the United States. The decision of the Nineteenth Party Conference that the Supreme Soviet should elect a President of the Soviet Union is an interesting proposal and it poses a number of questions whose solution, however, is dependent on the ultimate success of democratisation. For what is being considered very seriously in the Soviet Union is the separation of party and state and it is a matter of fundamental importance. What are the existing models which could be of use to the Soviet Union? There are, of course, some features of the American system which could be developed further and transplanted without difficulty in the Soviet Union; there are also many aspects of the Indian Federation which need to be examined in some detail. But neither the United States nor India offer an overall model of an exemplary democracy. The system in the United States is, as we have already noted, deeply flawed. As the New York weekly, *The Nation*, noted in an editorial on 25 June 1988:

> The Soviet Union is playing with pluralism, France is preparing for a new parliamentary coalition and Mexico suddenly has a real opposition party. Only in America does one-party rule have a lively future. Returns from the primary precincts were hardly complete when Governor Dukakis and Vice President Bush let it be known that nothing of substance separates them. Oh, Bush loves liberal-baiting and Dukakis gets a big response from his Noriega lines, but as *Time* aptly put it last week, 'The contest... will be less about ideas and ideologies than about clashing temperaments and styles.'

So both *The Nation* and *Time* are, in this instance, agreed that the Presidential beauty contest hardly offers a serious choice. In Western Europe there is, of course, a much greater choice because of the existence of large working class parties. The Italian Communist Party, the German Social Democratic Party, the Austrian and Swedish socialists and the British Labour Party are *not* the direct instruments of capital. Nonetheless they agree to operate within a certain consensus. With the exception of the Italian Communists, who have never exercised power, the social-democratic parties have proved themselves to be loyal upholders of the economic and social system. This does not mean that they have not pushed through certain important reforms. The Scandinavian social-democrats, for instance, have provided the workers with public housing of a very high quality indeed when compared to similar projects in either Britain and the United States or, indeed, the Soviet Union itself. In fact Soviet planners could learn a great deal on this front from the Danish, Norwegian and Swedish socialists. It could be argued that public housing in Scandinavia used the Soviet model of the Twenties: the Constructivist architects had undoubtedly produced workers' apartments and clubs which displayed a rare creativity. Architecture here was not alienated from the needs of those for whom it was intended. Despite important reforms, however, no social-democratic party has ever challenged the economic monopoly of capitalism or its basic priorities. This is not an empty digression. If social-democracy has failed to challenge the capitalist system, but has rather tried to prettify and humanise it (with limited successes), how would social-democratic currents operate in Eastern Europe and the Soviet Union if they were allowed to operate legally? Would the Eastern equivalents of Willy Brandt, Bruno Kreisky, Olaf Palme and their successors take up arms against these states in order to re-introduce capitalism? Would they be Trojan horses for the World Bank and the International Monetary Fund? It is of course difficult to be categorical about a hypothesis, but I think they would behave in the East as they do in the West with one difference: they would be able to operate in a far more positive fashion without the constraints of capital. Ironically enough social-democracy in Eastern Europe and the Soviet Union coupled with the reforms already under way could help to ignite unforeseen sparks in the West European labour movement.

The Indian Federation provides a prototype on another level. Despite the fact that the Congress Party has ruled from the Centre almost continuously since Independence in 1947, this has not been the case in the provinces. In Bengal and Kerala there have been elected communist governments. In Tamil Nadu and Andhra Pradesh regionalist formations have exercised power and in the rich Punjab the Congress has had to alternate with the Akali Dal. Far from weakening the Indian Federation this process has actually strengthened it (excluding the Punjab today where there is a great deal of outside interference) because it has shown that India is a voluntary Federation. Even in the Punjab today a large majority are *not* for independence. I have been asked by Soviet sociologists on a number of occasions as to why the army has never tried to seize power in India. There are a number of reasons which explain the resilience of Indian democracy, despite its many weaknesses, but the point I have always stressed is that given the size of India a military dictatorship could lead to Balkanisation. In other words democracy is the main preserver of the Indian Federation despite attempts to destabilise it in the past by both the United States and China. Soviet colleagues have always smiled at this explanation. In the Soviet Union, you see, it is believed that democracy could encourage secessionist forces. It is not an argument to be dismissed out of hand, for it is obvious that the West would use every non-military means possible to gain a foothold in the USSR, but this fact of global political life should not be allowed to hamper the democratisation process. If Soviet political parties are permitted to develop a moral authority and revive political life in the community and the factories then the attractions on offer from Washington or its favoured satellites in Western Europe would begin to lose their drawing power.

So, speaking objectively—there are no roadblocks to impede the smooth passage of soviet democracy. There is the bureaucracy, which numbers over 15 million men and women. The top layers of this strata number between two and three million people. If they were wholly united against the reforms then clearly things would not have reached the stage that they have today. Whether or not Mikhail Gorbachev would command a majority vote in the event of a no-holds-barred struggle for power is an open question. The Soviet élite may be a parasitic excrescence, but it is certainly not stupid, and is constantly on the lookout for new and intelligent recruits.*

An example of this was provided by a friend in Moscow, an architect immersed in the exploration of new possibilities in his field because of perestroika. He recounted an amazing tale. I had mentioned that Lazar Kaganovich a member of Stalin's Politburo was still alive at ninety-five. 'Ah yes!' Eydar's eye's lit up. 'I remember Lazar Moisevich well.' He then described how in 1957 he was one of five students selected by the powers that be to be interviewed for a special assignment. They were taken to an office

---

*This facet of the bureaucracy was sensitively but sharply portrayed in a remarkable Hungarian film of the Seventies, *Angi Vera*: the story of how a young woman cleaner in a hospital is sucked into the apparatus after she assumes the role of a spokesperson for the workforce and confronts the hospital director.

and questioned. Three out of the five were chosen for the task that lay ahead. It was stressed to them that they were very privileged to be selected. The three, which included Eydar, were told to report early next morning outside a house on the Leninsky Prospect. It was a large mansion with guards at the gates. They were let in and informed of their task: they were to clear and clean the garden thoroughly for this was the house of party leader Lazar Kaganovich who was still on Khrushchev's Politburo and his removal together with Molotov as an 'anti-party group' lay a few months ahead. The young students had no idea of this as they cleaned the garden. They were treated as slaves. Eydar recalled that when, exhausted and thirsty, he found his way to the kitchen it took a great deal of explaining to even obtain a glass of water. Later he realised that this was all part of a process. He had been talent-spotted as a potential recruit to the *nomenklatura* and the Kaganovich garden had been a first test.

The crucial question is whether the existing political institutions in the USSR can be democratised and transformed without an open conflict within the party hierarchy. Clearly Gorbachev's entire strategy has been premissed on avoiding a showdown. It is not that he is 'soft'. When events have played into his hands he has acted with despatch. The removal of Grigory Romanov in Leningrad was one example of his ability to seize the time. The utilisation of the Mathias Rust escapade in 1987 to change the military high command was another. However what is at stake now is to maintain mass support while engaging in delicate manouevres at the top to neutralise the opposition. The reforms in the political institutions of the USSR are going to be pushed through slowly and yet one has a strong sensation that if his conservative opponents step out of line, Gorbachev will give no quarter and then speed the process so that a point of no-return is reached before any crisis that erupts reaches unmanageable proportions.

As for the structures themselves they are already in place. All that is needed is a number of examples which demonstrate that the old-style candidates can be defeated. Once this begins to happen and the 'opposition' deputies begin to use the local, regional and Supreme Soviet as a political arena where discussions can take place and where decisions can be made. The Soviets of Working People's Deputies comprise 55,000 Soviets. These include the Supreme Soviet of the USSR, 15 Supreme Soviets of the Union Republics, 20 Supreme Soviets of the autonomous republics and almost 50,000 local soviets on a district, city and village level. Formally speaking these are the political institutions of the Soviet state. Their social composition is not without interest. Nearly fifty percent of deputies are workers and thirty percent are collective farmers. The gender ratio is interesting: 51 percent men and 49 percent women. It would be wrong to see these organisations as nothing more than a rubber-stamp for Politburo decisions. Many non-political issues are regularly discussed and sometimes hotly debated. As a result of the Nineteenth Party Conference these bodies will be given more powers and budgetary responsibilities, but the decision to make Party secretaries in the regions and localities head of the soviets indicates the compromises that were pushed through at the Conference. The fact that the conservatives insisted on this shows how worried they are at the thought of a real devolution of power. Nonetheless the next elections to these bodies might well produce some extremely interesting results.

What is required is democracy from the base upwards. This means that party secretaries must not be appointed by the Central Committee secretariat, but be elected by the membership as must local and regional executives. This not only produces better results, but prepares the basis for real politics in the soviets if the candidates to the soviets are elected by the party or the workers in a factory or a collective of housewives or the university. It also means the beginning of institutionalising a democratic culture. Even within the Institutes a new spirit is discernible. I was told of a small incident where the Director proposed a person to become Head of a section. The man suggested was a talentless timeserver regarded with contempt by most people in his section. One of the latter, let us call him Y, proposed that there be an election. He was very straightforward and explained that he wanted to put himself forward. This was agreed. An election took place and Y won by a large margin. Panic at the top. The Director refused to recognise the result and insisted that only the Academic Board of the Institute could confirm such a rash decision. The Board met and confirmed the election though by a tiny majority. Y was told that since it was such a small majority there should be another vote. This was organised when some of those who had voted for Y on the first occasion were on holiday. In the second vote Y's election was declared null and void also by a small majority, but this time the Director accepted the decision. Why the over-reaction? Because the Director felt threatened. He is a former diplomat with a limited

intelligence. If elections become a regular procedure there is no way
in which the Director would be elected and he needs the Directorship
of this particular institute to improve his chances of becoming an
Academician. Then he can retire in comfort and tend to his dacha.
One tiny incident, but multiply it by a million and the scale of the
problem becomes obvious.

We could take another more generalised example. As we've seen,
the number of women elected to the soviets is truly impressive. So is
the number of women in the professions or in leading positions in
certain industries. Yet the law is broken every day by women being
compelled to work on night-shifts; conditions in factories are
abysmal: sexual harassment is universal and sexual 'favours' are
regarded as an important male bureaucratic perk. The worst
offender is the textile industry, where women work in appalling
conditions and the health and safety regulations are disregarded
with impunity.

The overwhelming majority of Soviet women, while identifying
real grievances we could call feminist, ironically tend to see their
problems as the result of *not* being treated like women *enough*, much
to the exasperation of Western feminists. Nearly everyone is
expected to work, and women who work in unskilled jobs often tend
to believe that they would be happier not working (the 20 percent
according to opinion polls who would leave work if family income
were large enough). They still shoulder the whole burden of
motherhood and domestic responsibilities. Women do most of the
incredibly wearing amount of shoping in Soviet conditions, where
minor purchases can be a triumph and everything is catch as catch
can. [If they are 'giving out' children's shoes of a decent style today,
you had better be there at once, or even for items like baking soda or
paper napkins.] Career-orientated women have not seen their
problems as coming from discrimination, possibly because there is
much active, open discrimination. Rather, there is an *ideology* of
equality, coupled with the incredible difficulty of combining a high-
level job with motherhood.

All these problems, coupled to the official ideology on women and
sexuality—a combination of Victorian morality (absence of decent
contraception, rags in place of sanitary towels) and Stalinist
hypocrisy—can the number of women in the soviets therefore be
seen as no more than a case of window-dressing? There is not a single
woman on the Politburo and this is not because there are no female
equivalents of either Ligachev or Yakovlev. It is simply that they

have been consciously stopped at a certain level. In December 1979 a samizdat journal, *Almanac: Women and Russia*, began to circulate in Leningrad. It was one of the first explicitly feminist bulletins to reach the West and it was free. It reflected differing opinions on the social level, but it expressed an anger at the conditions of women in the USSR. The Manifesto harked back to the hopes of the Twenties when it had appeared possible that new relations between men and women would be possible. It argued that Lenin always referred to women when discussing the problems that lay ahead and argued that 'The Russian Revolution had a resonance throughout the world and the world changed under its impact. The liberalisation of society as a whole also gradually liberalised attitudes to women. But in Russia this process came to a halt at the time of Stalin...' The description of women's lives retains its power and is extremely apposite even today:

In Russia, life's major problems have reached such a dead-end that scepticism is becoming the normal mode of behaviour. And this is particularly visible in the case of women, who are the most sensitive element in society. The real ideal of a good old patriarchy—subject women, resigned mothers, household angels—no longer exists. But the weight of tradition and ossified mentalities continues to make women the caryatid of the home—or, to be more precise, of the communal apartment... Women do not have the possibility of escaping these inhuman constraints: if they free their hands, then the house collapses. However, the myth of woman's 'frailty' is still very much alive, so that she has to pay if she leaves the home. Since the obligation and responsibility of reproduction rests upon women, together with participation in social labour and that domestic labour which is still unashamedly called 'female', it is quite normal that such an excessive burden should arouse frustration in woman; just as it relegates her to the background, according to a conception cultivated by patriarchy which sticks like glue to her skin. Formally, equal rights were proclaimed long ago; but in reality, women's legitimate demands are branded as too pretentious. Fear of competition (above all for the top jobs, which are given to women only drop by drop) and fear of losing prestige: these are what drive the very same men who flatter the exclusive roles of mother and wife. These pharisees pretend not to see that it is women who drag the cart—which men spur on from the driver's seat. Feverishly yet insidiously, the ever-moving steamroller of everyday life crushes women's personality. Her slave mentality is still with us, and it is taking a more concealed and monstrous form. The humiliating conditions in the maternity and abortion clinics and in the communal apartments are an affront to human dignity. The values are still male: women's social evaluations and self-evaluation depend on their similarity with men. This warped relationship demands ever new sacrifices from women—yet it is from society as a whole that one might expect these to be made. For the so-called 'woman problem' is a key point in the general struggle for a new world. Although it should not be denied that women's cultural level has increased, their conditions of existence are still antediluvian. Genuine, not just superficial, liberation is becoming apparent as the most important social requirement of our time. It is absolutely necessary to determine what is specific to woman's position in the family and production: so that, instead of accumulating both domestic and social labour at the cost of innumerable sacrifices, she may at last feel herself to be a human being with equal rights.*

The journal was swiftly suppressed by the KGB, and its editors warned not to produce a second issue. A number of women connected with it were arrested, including the founder and Editor-in-Chief, Tatyana Mamonova. She was exiled in 1980, but it is difficult to believe that Soviet feminism has simply disappeared. All the conditions are ripe for its re-emergence in much more favourable conditions. The democratisation process should benefit all sections of the community, including women.

If Soviet democracy is permitted to take root, the incredible confidence which is starting to emanate from the literary world (see Chapter 1) could easily become part of the political sphere, although for that to happen the Soviet leadership will have to accept Rosa Luxemburg's critique of the Bolsheviks in 1918. More than that, they will have to inscribe it into the programme of the CPSU. It could be argued that conditions in 1918 were not propitious for soviet democracy. Today, all the conditions are present to facilitate what Luxemburg wrote about one year after the victory of October 1918:

Freedom only for the supporters of the government, only for members of one party—however numerous they may be—is no freedom at all. Freedom is always and exclusively freedom for the one who thinks differently. Not because of any fanatical concept of 'justice' but because all that is instructive, wholesome and purifying in political freedom depends on this essential characteristic, and its effectiveness vanishes when 'freedom' becomes a special privilege.

We are still some distance from a world of popular sovereignty, of democratic soviet power in the Soviet Union. There is still plenty of evidence that powerful currents within the bureaucracy reject

*The manifesto was first published in English by *Labour Focus on Eastern Europe*, February/March 1980.

socialist pluralism. They refuse to accept the fact that although 20 million people in the USSR may be communists it is impossible to imagine that *all* 285 million are communists. Surely among the Soviet peasants, for example, there must be some anti-communists. There must be millions who are neither communists nor anti-communists. Why should these millions be denied a voice in the reshaping of Soviet society? Why shouldn't they have their say without fear of the future? And if they are to speak out confidently within a soviet framework, then they must be allowed to unfurl their own flags, wear their own badges and symbols and use all the paraphernalia of everyday political life to convince others of their point of view.

Soviet law is already being altered to guarantee individual authors whose works are rejected by state publishing houses to publish an edition of their book which will be distributed in several thousand copies by the state distribution network. If the book sells then the state publishing house will be obliged to print a larger edition. The same principle could and should be applied to political rights. If a grouping gets over a particular percentage of the popular vote it should be provided with state subsidies to function and produce its publications. If social-democratic Sweden can provide such guarantees then so can the Soviet Union. All this could happen. These are still early days.

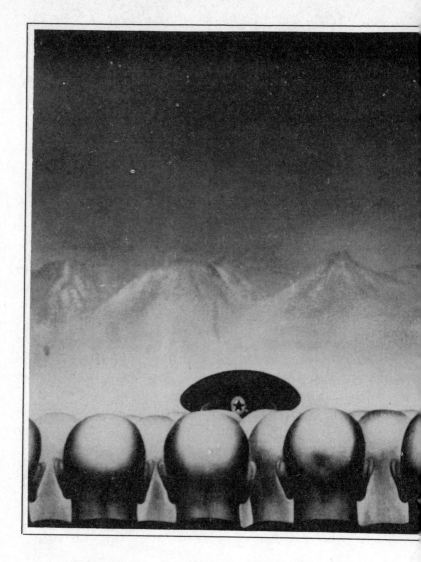

6. THE SOVIET UNION IS FAR TOO IMPORTANT TO BE LEFT TO THE SOVIETOLOGISTS

Whenever I see the movement of a locomotive I hear the whistle and see the valves opening and wheels turning; but I have no right to conclude that the whistling and the turning of wheels are the cause of the movement of the engine.

The peasants say that the cold wind blows in late spring because the oaks are budding, and really every spring cold winds do blow when the oak is budding. But though I do not know what causes the cold winds to blow when the oak-buds

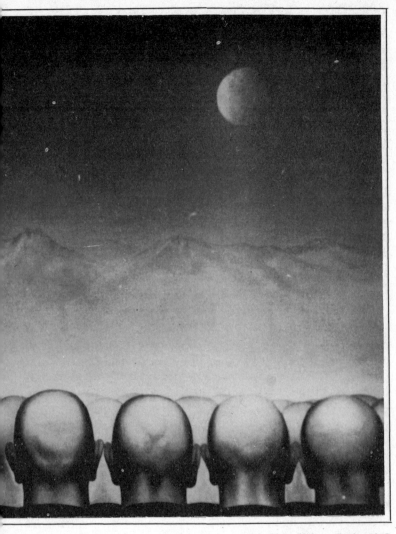

Alexei Sundukov, *Peaks*, 1987.

unfold, I cannot agree with the peasants that the unfolding of the oak-buds is the
cause of the cold wind, for the force of the wind is beyond the influence of the buds.
I see only a coincidence of occurences such as happens with all the phenomena of
life, and I see that however much and however carefully I observe the hands of the
watch, and the valves and wheels of the engine, and the oak, I shall not discover the
cause of the bells ringing, the engine moving, or of the winds of spring. To do that I
must entirely change my point of view and study the laws of the movement of
steam, of the bells and of the wind. History must do the same.

Leo Tolstoy, *War and Peace*

Before we go on to discuss the question of how the USSR perceives the world, it is useful to review some of the analytical writings which have dominated discussion and policy-making in the United States for several decades. It is true that revisionism is slowly capturing the American academy, but there are still many hangovers from the past and the needs of the State Department and the Pentagon remain paramount. If Gorbachev were to fail, we should be in no doubt that the ugly old thing—totalitarian theory—would rear its head again.

The writings of Deutscher stood out in the Fifties ad Sixties as a clarion call to anyone prepared to listen, not to be taken in by the seductive voice of yesterday's fellow-travellers. One can learn a great deal more from Deutscher's mistakes than from the outpourings of cold war warriors. In a powerful essay written in 1965, he described the Soviet bureaucracy thus:

> It is true that the Soviet bureaucracy dominates society—economically, politically and culturally—more obviously and to a greater extent than does any modern possessing class. Yet it is also more vulnerable.... It has been something like a huge amoeba covering post-revolutionary society with itself. It is an amoeba because it lacks a social backbone of its own, it is not a formed entity, not a historic force that comes on the scene in the way in which, for example, the old bourgeoisie came forth after the French Revolution.

The disparity between this view and the dominant approach of Kremlinologists in the West could not have been greater. One image of the Soviet system overshadowed all else: of a State that crushed every single aspiration of the Soviet population. This is a view held not only on the Right, but also on the Centre and the Left of the political spectrum in the Western world. Some groups on the far-Left, despite their total hostility to their own States, nonetheless share this attitude to the Soviet State. The term they would use to sum it up is totalitarianism, and the Soviet State is a totalitarian state par excellence. For the Right it can be toppled by keeping it under constant seige militarily and economically in order to ensure that a large chunk of the Soviet budget is swallowed up by military spending. The hope here is that the failure to satisfy consumer needs will detach the population from the hierarchy and lead to massive revolts which favour a restoration. From the extreme on the Left the hope is often expressed that a revolution from below will sweep everything away. Events in the Soviet Union seem to be contradicting these analyses.

The severest blow, however, has fallen on the shoulders of the

totalitarian theorists in the United States who first developed this
theory during the late Forties and early Fifties, a period when the
United States had embarked on its own drive towards global
hegemony. During the Sixties when the Vietnam war was at its
height these theories came under severe attack from more critical
members of the academy who denounced the cynical manipulation
of political theory to serve US policy interests. The new criticisms,
which were extremely sharp in tone, focused particularly on the
abuse of scholarly standards in order to equate the USSR with the
Nazi regime in order to justify war preparations and military threats
against the Soviet Union.

The use of 'totalitarian theory' to shape US public opinion had
impressive intellectual credentials. The creators of Cold War
Liberalism were ex-Marxists of one variety or the other. Max
Eastman, Bertram Wolfe, Sidney Hook and Dwight MacDonald
were talented writers and propagandists. Their journal, *Partisan
Review*, became the voice of the Pentagon intelligentsia. In 1955, on
the very eve of the Twentieth Party Congress where Khrushchev
exploded his bombshell, Eastman wrote:

> Stalin's police state is not an approximation to, or something like, or
> in some respects comparable with Hitler's. It is the same thing, only
> *more* ruthless, *more* cold-blooded, *more* astute, *more* extreme in its
> economic policies, *more* explicitly committed to world conquest, and
> *more* dangerous to democracy and civilised morals.

In the weeks preceding the Congress, Wolfe was even more
explicit. Totally blinded by the cold war he refused to accept that
Khrushchev had released hundreds of thousands of prisoners and
that the camps were gradually emptying. On the eve of the Twenty-
second Party Congress in 1962 which took de-Stalinisation much
further than before, Wolfe wrote:

> The Soviet State has existed longer, is more total, the power of Stalin
> and his successors more absolute, the purges bloodier and more
> sweeping and continuous, the concentration camps larger... than
> anything Mussolini dreamed of or Hitler introduced. Only in the
> crematoria did Hitler's imagination exceed the deeds of Stalin.

The instrumentalist character of these ravings became very clear
when Hook spelt out the significance of all this for US foreign policy:

> Whoever believed that Nazi expansionism constituted a threat to the
> survival of democratic institutions must conclude by the same logic
> and the same type of evidence that Soviet Communism represents

today an even greater threat to our survival, because the potential opposition to totalitarianism is now much weaker in consequence of World War Two.

The logic is clear. What is needed is a heavily-armed state on a permanent war-alert and ready to strike at the first sign of aggression. Now all these statements would make sense on one condition: that Nazi Germany and the USSR are in fact two faces of the same beast, a totalitarian Janus. The entire thrust of the totalitarian theorists has been to prove the existence of such a monster.

The team from *Partisan Review* were given strong backing by a much more influential trinity of scholars, namely, Hannah Arendt, Carl Friedrich and Zbigniew Brezinski. Here again the link between theory and the needs of US foreign policy was far from invisible. Arendt's pioneering work, *The Origins of Totalitarianism*, was published in 1951 when the Korean War was at its peak. Arendt, a German-Jewish intellectual had grown up in the ultra-conservative intellectual world of the German Philosophy faculties of the Twenties. She was a student of Heidegger and became his lover, their passionate love affair coming to an end when Arendt, who was Jewish, had to flee Germany. Heidegger sought consolation in the ranks of the Nazi Party, becoming its most eminent philosopher and most vigorous recruiter of academics to its ranks. Arendt and Heidegger re-established contact in 1949 soon after she had completed *The Origins of Totalitarianism*.

The book itself had an interesting genealogy. Its first two outlines written in 1945 and 1946 concentrated exclusively on fascism as a form of 'Race Imperialism'. In both these drafts Arendt argued that the essence of Nazism was anti-semitism. Memories of the epic Soviet resistance to fascism were still fresh as was the size of Soviet casualties during the conflict. In 1949 the post-war phase of the Cold War was a year old and it was now that Arendt incorporated the Soviet Union into her book, using the concept of totalitarianism as the unifying theme. She went further and responded to the mood of the time in Washington by arguing that the United States should organise a combined military attack on the USSR to get rid of Stalin's concentration camps. This thoughtful proposal necessitated regarding Hitler's Germany and Stalin's Russia as totally identical. A few problems arose. Arendt had insisted that the essence of Nazism was anti-semitism, but the 1951 edition of her work contained no reference whatsoever to Stalinist anti-semitism. This was corrected in the 1966 edition as by now (thanks largely to Khrushchev) Arendt had discovered the strains of anti-semitism in the so-called Doctors' Plot in the Soviet Union.*

These were relatively trivial problems. Arendt had maintained that Nazism was a grotesque aberration which had no antecedents in Western culture and its intellectual traditions. In her opinon, Nietzsche and, needless to add, Heidegger, had nothing whatever to do with Nazi totalitarianism. Even if one accepted this to avoid an argument the Soviet Union posed other problems. Was not Marxism a part of the Western intellectual tradition? Were not leading members of the Bolshevik party which led the revolution, exemplars of the most radical wing of European thought (in addition to the fact that many of them were of Jewish origins)? In the 1949 edition of her work Arendt solved this problem by erasing it from her agenda. Marx/Marxism, Lenin/Leninism, Trotsky/Trotskyism had nothing to do with the Soviet state. Not unnaturally this led to some criticism of her book and she spent the year preceding Stalin's death studying Marxism to try and prove that it had a theory of *man* as 'worker-animal.' This was an impossible task as the editors of *Partisan Review* should have told her before she began, but she persisted only to acknowledge failure. As she wrote to the Guggenheim Foundation, which had funded the project: 'Marx's dignification of labor as an essentially creative activity constitutes a decisive break with the entire Western tradition for which Labour had represented the animal, not the human part of man.'†

The theory of totalitarianism then rested on the similarities of Nazism and Stalinism: concentration camps and terror. The distinction between the crematoria and Soviet labour camps was unimportant. What was key was simply their existence, although Arendt was, however, careful to insist that these camps were quite different from concentration camps used by other states.

*On 13 January, 1953, Tass announced the arrest of a group of doctors. It stated baldly that a terrorist group of physicians had decided to kill off selected Soviet leaders and that Andre Zhdanov (a Stalinist cultural commisar) had fallen victim 'to this band of monsters in human form'. Most of the doctors arrested were of Jewish origin and, at least one of them, Professor Boris Kogan, was an old Bolshevik. The interrogation was conducted by the well-known torturer and sadist, Ryumin. Fortunately Stalin died two months later and the doctors were released. Without his protector, Ryumin was trapped. He was executed a few months later as a criminal and forger. It is obvious that the 'Doctors' Plot' would have been the forerunner of a new and vicious anti-semitic campaign.
†*Hannah Arendt–For Love of the World*, by E. Young-Bruehl, Yale University Press, New Haven and London, 1982.

The problem with this definition was that it could not survive Khrushchev's decision to open the camps and let the prisoners return home during the Fifties. Thus 'Terror' became the crucial word. Friedrich and Brezinski stressed in *Totalitarian Dictatorship and Autocracy* in 1954 that terror was absolutely central to the existence of the totalitarian regime. A year later, Brezinsky produced another colourfully entitled volume, *The Permanent Purge*, in which he was sure that terror was the *essence* of totalitarianism. The banner he nailed so firmly to the mast bore the inscription: Without Terror There Can Be No Totalitarianism! Within a year this particular thesis had been bypassed by history. The Twentieth Party Congress of the Soviet Communist Party denounced Stalinist terror, rehabilated many of its victims and opened the doors of the camps. It soon became obvious that the Khrushchev reforms were not simply cosmetic. A full-blooded democratisation was not the goal of the regime at the time, but it had clearly renounced the use of mass terror. Brezinski's unpleasant encounter with the quickening pace of history seems to have soured his entire relationship with the concept of totalitarianism. His next major work, *Political Power USA/USSR* (1964) does not contain a single entry for totalitarianism in the index. By now the changes in the Soviet Union were making many Western academics nervous and they were resigned to discarding the entire hypothesis. Totalitarianism was periodised, consigned to the years of Stalin's dictatorship. This was, at least, debatable, but it seemed that the idea as such had now become inoperable as a weapon of the cold war.

Carl Friedrich was not prepared to give up so easily. As late as 1969 he insisted that not only was Soviet totalitarianism alive, but it had never been stronger. Why? Because its essential characterisitc was neither the camps nor the terror nor anti-semitism, but the concentration of all power in the hands of a single party.* He pointed out, accurately, that under Stalin the party had been much smaller and its penetration of Soviet society far less extensive than under Brezhnev. It followed, didn't it, that under Stalin we could only observe the contours of the beast. Its skeleton was visible, but it had only become a normal, mature, fully-fledged totalitarianism under Brezhnev! As Friedrich saw it the Stalin/Hitler regimes 'far from providing the typical model of a totalitarian dictatorship, were

*It is worth noting that this is the definition of totalitarianism used in most Western dictionaries.

rather extreme aberrations.' This raised more than a few laughs at the time and Friedrich's reputation undoubtedly suffered.

For good measure, Friedrich had added another idea in 1969: totalitarianism is at its peak when the monopolistic party is striving for 'totalist intentions under modern technical and political conditions.' The logic is unmistakeable. Any force trying to thoroughly change the world has 'totalist intentions' and is *ipso facto* totalitarian. But let us suppose that the entire world barring North America became Communist. Friedrich's theory would actually prevent his masters from embarking on a global counter-offensive to overthrow the red scourge since such a project would clearly entail 'totalist intentions.'*

Could the concept be salvaged? Leonard Schapiro entered the fray to see if this was possible. He put forward the view that the central feature of totalitarian regimes was the destruction of the power of the party. Hitler had destroyed the autonomy of the Nazi Party. Stalin had systematically broken the old Bolshevik Party and smashed its spinal chord. This enabled Schapiro to preserve the concept for Hitler/Stalin, but ditch it as an adequate response to the Soviet present. New problems arose. If totalitarianism equalled strong leader plus terror, then the bulk of regimes backed by the United States in Latin America, Asia, Africa and occasionally in Europe (Greece under the colonels, Turkey under the Generals) would have to be categorised as such. This was not good. For the great virtue of earlier theories had lain in this: by stressing concentration camps or the single mass party they had established a clear difference with all pro-American dictatorships. Schapiro was conscious of this anomaly, and decided to square the circle by taking up a sub-theme which underlay much of the earlier writings on totalitarianism. This was the marked hostility to democracy! So, Schapiro's basic explanation for totalitarianism is that such regimes are plebiscitary-democratic; that they arise when the old, traditional institutions keeping the masses in check break down, allowing counter-éites to seize power; and that unlike the pro-American dictators these 'totalitarian counter-élites' are *democratic* in their appeal.

Thus the word 'democracy' is deployed regularly, but never in a positive way. His reasons are revealing. Democracy, in the sense of mass, popular power is proto-totalitarian. It is a 'mass society':

Totalitarianism in Perspective by Barber, Curtis and Friedrich, 1969.

What then is the value of totalitarianism as a concept? The evidence that has been adduced suggests that it stands for a distinct and new form of government, which first became possible in the age of mass democracy, of modern technology and of twentieth-century national-ism.*

So, totalitarianism seems to be a conceptual harlot of uncertain parentage, belonging to no one, but in the service of all',† yet it would not really solve the problem. There is a widely held view on Left and Right which sees the actually existing system in the USSR as qualitatively worse than the system in the West. It is true that there are certain ideologues like Jean Kirkpatrick who prefer Pinochet's Chile or Botha's South Africa to the USSR, but since this second-generation parody of the *Partisan Review* collective has now virtually collapsed we can save both space and time.

The two crucial ideas justifying the superiority of the West to the USSR are usually expressed as follows: (a) In the Soviet Union the bureacracy is master of everything. All dimensions of people's lives are controlled by the élite and (b) the interests of the majority are trampled underfoot by the bureaucracy because the people have no means of influencing, leave alone controlling the state/party bureaucracy.

What this is really about is the scope of political decision-making and the locus of power in Soviet society. Who takes the real decisions? The mass of people or a tiny élite? Now the standard view which embraces the entire political spectrum in the West is that on both these issues the USSR is a totally and thoroughly negative example in comparison with liberal capitalist democracy. This is what unites 'public opinion' with what is at the core of most of the writings of the postwar totalitarian theorists.

Yet if one views both political systems dispassionately these assumptions can be easily challenged. The point here is not to permit the numerous atrocities of the bureaucratic regime to destroy any objectivity whatsoever. *If we look at how decisions are made the picture is quite revealing.* A fashionable view is that individuals should have a separate sphere, a space which permits them to shape their lives freely and without restraint or interference from other people or the state. It has been argued that this sphere exists in the West, but not in the Soviet Union. Let us look briefly at the lived

---

Totalitarianism by Leonid Schapiro, Macmillan, 1972.
†Barber, op cit.

experience in the West and the USSR. On one level there are many things in common: sports, TV, cinemas, personal freindships, children, sex, pursuit of hobbies. The differences, of course, are far greater in the two key areas of economics and cultural/political expression. In the economic realm, despite the permanent shortage of consumer goods, Soviet people have guarantees of job security. This provides an assured economic framework for all individual activities. In the West no such secuirty exists. Mass unemployment jeopardises all other choices related to individual activities.

On the other hand there is much greater political and cultural freedom for the individual in the West. Groupings and journals of the far-Right and far-Left are not prohibited, bohemian lifestyles are tolerated, religous cults are allowed to peddle their wares and, occasionally, voices opposed to the very basis of the capitalist social order are heard on radio and television. These rights have been traditionally banned in the USSR since the Twenties.

It could be argued therefore that the balance-sheet is mixed. Yet theorists of liberal capitalism would not accept this for a single moment. They have a peculiar way of dividing the public from the private sphere. For liberalism the economy (and therefore jobs) are in the private sphere. If they are not, then oppression exists and germinates totalitarian tendencies. Unemployment may devastate individuals, but it is unavoidable and even therapeutic, the price which has to be paid for avoiding political control by the state over economic life. This grotesque insistence by the ideologues of liberalism and their latter-day apologists that control over the economic levers of social existence should be treated as a private matter outside the public sphere is, of course, a naked defence of capitalism and its priorities. This view has been most clearly expressed by the guru of the Thatcher-Reagan counter-revolution, Friedrick Hayek in *Road to Serfdom* where he writes that 'economic control is not merely control of a sector of human life which can be separated from the rest; it is the control of the means for all our ends.' This is true. Hayek draws the conclusion that any form of state control of the economy is or leads to totalitarianism. But surely the argument works both ways? If those who control the levers of economic power control society and the individuals who make it up then it is bizarre to demand that economic control under capitalism should be a *private* matter. It is a supremely public matter which concerns the entire character of social life of the entire community. It therefore needs to be brought under public control in such a way that those whose skills are vital to any economy have the ability to determine how decisions are made.

Charles Lindblom, the doyen of American liberal pluralist theorists, in his disillusioned old age has recognised that public power in the USA embraces *both* state and private enterprise managers. He has come to the conclusion that the top managers of private businesses dominate public life in the capitalist world and therefore also Hayek's version of private life. They control the means to every individual's personal ends.*

The totalitarian theorists could respond by arguing that even if one accepted that economic control should be in the public sphere, the particular type of public control in the USSR is simply the exercise of absolute power over the masses by a state élite. This poses the question of political power, where it lies and how it is structured. Most of the Kremlinologists who have been in the forefront of policy-making and policy-guidance in the United States have tended to an extremely crude and fantastical picture of their enemy. As they see it all political power is concentrated in the hands of a single party. Within the Party power lies exclusively at the top and the *nomenklatura*, through the agency of the General Secretary and the Politburo, can make any decision they please in any area of economic, social or cultural life. They don't need to consult anyone; they can ignore ordinary people's interests at will since they don't have to face re-election and if problems arise the KGB or the army are ever ready to move into action. By contrast, in the West, political power is fragmented. There are different branches of government and the executive and legislative branches can not ignore the popular will because they face competitive elections.

It is a seductive argument and we all (both in the West and the USSR) now know how Stalin utilised this concentration of power to organise massive extermination campaigns, which removed all potential opposition within the party and state apparatus. The true extent of Stalin's crimes *against* socialism are being revealed daily in the Soviet media.† Yet the fundamental economic and political basis of the system itself has not seen any qualitative changes, though these are certainly under way. What is obvious is that the dominant Western view (as formulated in the academies) doesn't work very well for either the East or the West.

*Charles Lindblom, *Politics and Markets*, Basic Books, 1978.
†See Chapters 2 and 4.

As far as the West is concerned, let's take the question of unemployment which stands at over twenty million in the seven major capitalist countries. Opinion polls in Britain, to take one example, have indicated for years that the majority of the population regards this as the most serious problem to be tackled. The majority of people want an end to unemployment. Yet there is not a single major party—Right or Left—in the West which promises a statutory right to work. Why? Not because the leaders of the socialist parties want to maintain unemployment. Simply that a statutory right to work would be *unrealistic*, not to say utopian, in the conditions of late capitalism. If legislation was passed in Parliament guaranteeing everyone paid employment and compelling employers to take on workers, there would be an enormous economic crisis. The capitalist economy would take another plunge making the present bad situation even worse. In this case we see that political power can not be simply understood in terms of what one individual can order another individual to do; power is also embedded in the socio-economic structure of the society. And this social power *determines* the limits of what politicians can achieve within the present system.

This also appears to be the case in the USSR. The public ownership of the great bulk of the economy does not, strange though it may seem, give the political leadership the ability to do what it pleases. The Gorbachev leadership today undoubtedly wants to speed up economic growth, improve economic efficiency and modernise the country on every level. The simplest way of doing this would be to create unemployment, end the vast subsidies on food prices, stop subsidising housing, gas, electricity and transport, etc. If the élite has total power why don't they just go ahead and do it? There are enormous social-structural constraints preventing them from doing so.

In a publicly-owned economy where there is no capitalist market, economic reproduction and exchange is effected through the conscious *activities* of millions of people mobilised through the Communist Party and state institutions within the economy. In other words if a real attempt is made to push through certain changes, many of which are badly needed today, by the threat of unemployment and consequent impoverishment and without the support of the millions of workers then there will be mass explosions which will make Hungary 1956, Czechoslovakia 1968 and Poland 1981, look like harmless picnics. The social weight of the proletariat inside the USSR is such that very few leaders of the USSR would be inclined to antagonise this crucial layer, which constitutes a majority of the party rank-and-file.

The two systems share a social-structural reality in common. In the West any attempt to undermine, leave alone destroy, the basis of the economic security of private capitalists involves the entire system in a crisis. In the Soviet Union any attempt to destroy the basis of the economic security of the workers does exactly the same as we have seen elsewhere in Eastern Europe. The way events unfold is very predictable. The workers in the big factories resist and are joined by Communist Party members in the same factory. This throws the political system into catastrophic convulsions. When such crises occur in the West, formal political representation is cast to the winds. Democratically elected leaders might imagine that they are in control, but in reality it is the administrative bureaucracy and the police and military apparatuses which are in *de facto* control of the situation. In the East the formal powers of the party chiefs evaporate overnight. Party leaders find themselves prisoners of the forces and event they supposedly control in the *total* sense of the word.

What all this reveals is the fallacious character of arguments premised on the autonomy of the political system from its socio-economic basis of power. On the contrary, the formal mechanism of political decision-making is only one subordinate element within the overall system of social power. This applies to the United States just as much as the Soviet Union. There are, therefore, some major problems with the dominant image of the Soviet state as a totalitarian dictatorship. Such a characterisation automatically assumes that the determining feature of a state is its formal political system. In reality what governs the *substance* of the issues, agenda, choices and policies that the political system processes is the economic and political structure. In order to understand the dynamics of Soviet politics we have to understand the rules of its socio-economic system, albeit a changing one (See Chapter 3).

It is axiomatic in the USSR that anything and everything to do with the economy is a matter for public, political choice. Any person who attempts to exploit state resources for private gain is considered a criminal. People who misuse public property face the death penalty. Thus when prices change or priorities are revised to favour hotels and computers rather than cars or higher pensions or whatever then these choices are seen by people as political choices by the leadership and not as 'natural' processes determined by the market. Unemployment is for Soviet citizens not a natural, inevitable phenomenon, but a deliberate choice by those who exercise power. The entire public, political sphere extends over the deployment of economic resources, what Hayek calls 'means governing all ends.' This is the rational core of the totalitarian theorists. They correctly point to the fact that the sphere of public politics, of what governments can and should tackle, is far wider in the USSR than in the West. As for their insistence that extending this sphere to include the economy means the death of civilization, one can only say that it is somewhat narrow-minded of them to equate civilization with capitalism...

The capacity to impose political choices in the USSR and the West depends on the character of the decisions. The formal centralisation of power in the USSR and the formal fragmentation of power in the USA does not alter the fact that in the USA and other capitalist countries governments have the power to hit ordinary people's lives in a way that no Soviet government could dream about. No Soviet leader could pursue a policy on interest rates and currency—as in Britain today—which threw millions of family into a crisis and destroyed the means governing all their ends. Western governments can do this because such policies reflect the requirements of their respective capitalisms.

In the USSR on the other hand, governments have the ability to arrest and imprison people, sack them from their jobs, use enormous powers of patronage across the whole field of public life. They do so on the pretext of fighting against 'enemies of the people' or similar rubbish. In the West under functioning norms of liberal democracy this is far more difficult without suspending the constitution. The fragmentation of power and the requirement of protecting private property and individual rights makes this difficult. The coercive power against rebellion, subversion, heterodoxy, rests largely in the supposedly 'non-political sphere' in the West. Sackings, blacklists, victimisation, denial of promotions in private or state corporations and the control of the lower orders by magistrates, social workers, DHSS officials, police, judges are all outside the sphere of politics, or so we are asked to believe. In this fashion credibility is placed on the torture rack.

The official Kremlinologists have, in recent years, come under heavy attack within the American academy. The revisionists have mounted a formidable counter-attack. In this connection the work of Robert Daniels and Stephen Cohen has been extremely influential in restoring objective standards of scholarship. Jerry F. Hough in

The Soviet Union and Social Science Theory* has effectively torpedoed the claims of the totalitarian theorists by challenging the notion of the USSR as a passive, inert society dominated by an all-powerful élite. He writes that

> even the form of participation that is thought to be the most exclusive—membership of the Communist Party—engages approximately 22 percent of all men between the ages of thirty and sixty, a broader group than the 'attentive public' as usually defined in the United States on the basis of survey research. Participation in various commissions and committees at the place of work (groups that deal with housing distribution, passes to resorts, dismissal of personnel, planning of social–cultural affairs, and so forth) is even wider.

Hough's description of the pluralistic features that existed even before Gorbachev is very useful because it helps to understand how Soviet society actually functions. It also demystifies Gorbachev's rise to power.

Hough and Daniels have argued in their books and articles that the Soviet Union in the post-Stalin period began to stop functioning exclusively from the top down. They have demonstrated that during the Khrushchev and even more in the post-Khrushchev phase ideas and power have flown in both directions. Daniels has written of the USSR as a society in evolution attempting to discover a new form of politics, a

> participatory bureaucracy... In any complex modern bureaucratic organisation, it is impossible to function properly from the top down: all manners of influences—information, advice, recommendations, problems, complaints—must flow upwards... The problems of managing a complex economy and technology have made it abundantly clear to the Soviet leadership that they must allow this reverse stream of influence to flow freely, and their main concern is that the flow be kept within the organisational structure of the Communist Party.†

Both Daniels and Hough insist on a corrective. The diversity is limited to the party and state apparatuses. Hough, however, goes beyond Daniels and essentially puts forward a strong case for the view that pluralism in the Soviet Union and the United States shares a number of features in common. For him the main difference

---

**The Soviet Union and Social Science Theory* by Jerry F. Hough, Harvard, 1977.
†'Soviet Politics since Khrushchev' appears in *The Soviet Union since Brezhnev and Kosygin* edited by John W. Strong, New York, 1971.

'centres on the framework in which the political process takes place and on the types of political behaviours that are tolerated.' Despite this he sees Soviet politicians as 'men who are driven to represent many interests of their clientele and low-level subordinates...[and] who take the danger of popular unrest into account as they mediate conflicts among the political participants.'

Daniels and Hough are describing a regime which we could characterise as *bureaucratic pluralism*. The contours of such an administration first became visible during the World War Two. With the onset of the cold war the Zhdanovschina reversed the wheel and returned to the frozen political landscape of the late Thirties. After the death of the dictator and the summary execution of Beria the situation gradually changed till Khrushchev's victory against Malenkov. From the release of the prisoners to the Twentieth Party Congress and Khrushchev's speech, there was a new mood in the country. The first victory of bureaucratic pluralism lay in the very fact that a Soviet leader had been removed by a vote of a leading committee. More importantly Khrushchev was neither executed nor imprisoned.

None of this should be taken to imply that the system does not need fundamental and structural reforms or, in other words, a *political* revolution.

The political battles currently taking place in the Soviet Union could be seen as a re-staging of the long wars fought by the liberal bourgeoisie against the absolutist state. Or it could be regarded as a mere tinkering with the system. But such views are, in my opinion, myopic. As I have already strongly indicated there is another way of seeing things: as the first serious attempt by the Party reformers to renew the system by returning to *some* of the ideals proclaimed by the Revolution of 1917. Most of the revisionists in the US academy as well as Marxist writers usually critical of the Soviet Union failed to foresee the developments that have already taken place. As late as autumn 1985, Jerry Hough could write: 'As in the mid-Fifties, political change will be contradictory and gradual, if it comes at all.'* Writers on the Marxist left have, by and large, not paid any serious attention to *political* developments within the Soviet apparatus for many decades.

Gorbachev's success will depend on both domestic and

*'Gorbachev's Strategy', *Foreign Affairs*, Fall 1985.

international factors. The main representative of authoritarian orthodoxy on the Politburo, Yegor Ligachev, has issued a public warning to the reformers. In a speech at Gorky on 5 August 1988 he spelt out in some detail that he was opposed to letting the market determine priorities; he was opposed to 'nihilism with regard to the past' (ie the ferocity of the de-Stalinisation campaign which does indeed challenge the ideology of the present-day CPSU!); he was opposed to strikes since 'socialism is the system of working people, and going on strike against themselves is quite simply an absurdity' and that 'participation in strikes and illegal assemblies is, I would say, quite simply incompatible with party membership.' Simultaneously he insisted that 'Active involvement in the solution of general human problems, and primarily in the struggle against the nuclear threat, by no means signifies any artificial braking of the social and national struggle—the national liberation struggle. It does not mean that class contradictions and antagonisms are being ignored.' On paper one can agree with the latter sentiment, in particular, but essentially the apparatus, and Ligachev defends its interests vigorously, wants to scuttle the reforms and just make a few necessary adjustments. The reformers are by no means united on everything, but it is in the field of world politics that they are the most vulnerable and unless they develop a serious strategy on a world scale they will be outmanouevred by enemies at home and abroad.

(p 173) Konstantin Zvezdochetov, *Perdo,* 1987.

7. WAR AND PEACE
The Soviet Union and the World

Let the last inscription then run
(That broken slab without readers):

The planet is going to burst.
Those it bred will destroy it.

As a way of living together we merely thought up capitalism.
Thinking of physics, we thought up rather more:
A way of dying together.

Bertolt Brecht, Swansong

The success of the Russian Revolution in 1917 transformed the
nature of world politics. The Bolsheviks survived the wars of
intervention but at a price. The White Terror was followed by the
Red Terror. The brutalisation of society as a whole could not but
leave its mark on the victors of the revolution. Lenin and indeed the
entire Bolshevik leadership believed that the fate of Russia depended
on the world revolution. This was not simply a statement of hope,
but a firmly fixed Bolshevik belief. It was for this that the
Communist International was organised to replace the Second

International which had proved incapable of preventing the First World War. Most Russian communists were of the opinion that the very act of seizing power in backward Russia was an irrelevance if seen outside the context of a global revolutionary process. Lenin, above all, stressed this fact time and time again. He repeatedly stated that 'the basis of the whole of our policy' was dependent on 'the swift and direct support of the working people of the world.' All the 'efforts and sacrifices' only made sense as 'an essential step towards world revolution.'

*That the Socialist revolution in Europe must come, and will come, is beyond doubt. All our hopes for the final victory of socialism are founded on this certainty. [January 1918]
*The final victory of socialism in a single country is, of course, impossible. [January 1918]
*Regarded from the world-historical point of view, there would doubtless be no hope of the ultimate victory of our revolution if it were to remain alone. [March 1918]
*At all events, under all conceivable circumstances, if the German revolution does not come, we are doomed. [March 1919]
*The victory of the socialist revolution ... can only be regarded as final when it becomes the victory of the proletariat in at least several advanced countries. [December 1919]
*Until the revolution takes place in all lands, including the richest and highly civilized ones, our victory will only be a half-victory, perhaps still less. [November 1920]

In *Better Fewer, But Better,* the very last article that he wrote in March 1923 the Soviet leader was haunted by the same question—

Thus, at the present time we are confronted with the question— shall we be able to hold on with our small and very small peasant production, and in our present state of ruin, until the West-European capitalist countries consummate their development towards socialism?

He did not believe that this would happen in the way the Bolsheviks wanted it to happen. He saw how democratic reforms coupled with colonial plunder were keeping the working class at bay, but he always believed that the socialist project would sooner or later be realised in the heartlands of capitalism. He regarded Soviet Russia's survival as being partially the result of inter-imperialist antagonisms and he expressed the hope that if these were repeated the Soviet Union would get a 'second respite'. The key was not a belief in the inevitability of the total victory of socialism, but a correct working out of a strategy to 'prevent the West-European counter-revolutionary states from crushing us'. And then, in a remarkably perceptive sentence, Lenin dropped another hint: 'In the last analysis, the outcome of the struggle will be determined by the fact that Russia, India, China account for the overwhelming majority of the population of the globe.'

Soviet foreign policy from the late Twenties onwards was marked by a series of disasters. Stalin's policy on China led to a bloodbath in Shanghai in 1927 and a crazed coup attempt in Canton a few years later. This defeat of China's fledgling working class negatively affected the course of the Chinese Revolution. In the entire period preceding the victory of Hitler, the Comintern policy was a grotesque display of ultra Leftism. The German social-democrats were denounced as 'social-fascists' and placed on a par with the fascists. The only Soviet politician who predicted the disaster and for three whole years appealed for a united front between German social-democracy and German communism against Hitler was Trotsky from his Prinkipo exile. In 1936–37 the Stalinist decision in Spain to engage in a civil war against the anarchists and the POUM laid the basis for Franco's victory, a sordid chapter in European history which has been movingly described by George Orwell in *Homage to Catalonia,** amongst others.

The defeat in Spain prepared the stage for the Second World War. One should not underestimate the effect that a defeat for Spanish fascism would have had in reviving working class opposition to Mussolini and Hitler, and possibly even Stalin. The cynical display of real-politik in the face of Hitler—which finally resulted in the Hitler–Stalin pact—was another nail in the coffin of Lenin's foreign policy. This is not to say that Stalin could or should have remained passive in the face of Anglo–French appeasement of the German dictator. The reason for Chamberlain's policy had very little to do with Stalin's beheading of the Red Army General Staff as was recently argued by a Soviet historian, V. Dashichev, in *Izvestia* (18 May 1988). Instead, it had everything to do with the desire of the British and French ruling classes to convince Hitler that his real enemy was in Moscow. It is not that the fascist leader was unaware of this, but simply that as a student of the Monroe Doctrine in the Americas he wanted to establish German hegemony in Western Europe before embarking on a costly war in the East. Stalin had no

Homage to Catalonia by George Orwell, Penguin, 1968.

option, but to conclude a pact with the Germans and foil the Anglo–French plans, but the price he paid was a heavy one. Dashichev's assertion that 'it was hard for them [Chamberlain and Daladier] to do business with a supreme ruler who trampled on all human morality and who committed unprecedented repressions, using brutal, criminal methods...' is touching, but reflects an incredible naïvety. It was hard for them to do a deal with Stalin, but perfectly possible to abase themselves before Hitler and hand him Czechoslovakia on a plate? An odd display of human morality.

Since the late Thirties, Soviet foreign policy abandoned all pretence of internationalism. With the formal dissolution of the Comintern* in 1941/3 the stage was set for an unashamed national–Stalinism. The priority from now on was to put the interests of the Soviet state as defined by Stalin before everything else. The conclusion of the war saw a demonstration of this at Yalta. The 'gentleman's agreement' between Stalin and Churchill was blessed by Roosevelt. Europe was divided into 'spheres of influence'. The deal certainly safeguarded Soviet frontiers, but the Stalinisation of Eastern Europe turned out to be a gangrenous sore and the legacies of the Forties still haunt the new men in the Kremlin. Would it not, a socialist could ask, have been far better to aid the victory of socialism in Italy and Greece rather than impose a model on Poland or Rumania? Bulgaria and Czechoslovakia had strong traditions of socialism and communism. In both these countries it would have been perfectly possible to establish a pluralist socialist democracy. Yugoslavia was already in the throes of a revolution and Stalin's attempt to preserve the monarchy was a failure. In Greece, Stalin actively prevented the victory of the partisans. A Balkan Federation of Greece, Bulgaria and Yugoslavia would have been a much better defence of socialist interests than what ultimately took place.

Stalin was taken by surprise at the turn of events in China. The wartime Allies had give the right-wing Kuomintang leader, Chiang Kai Shek, an enormous boost, but the Chinese Revolution dispelled all such illusions. After much hesitation the Soviet Union provided aid and technicians and, of course, their particular brand of the single party, single leader model. Objective conditions in China, unfortunately, aided such a model, but if a different one had existed

---

*The Communist International (Comintern) was established in 1919 to promote the world revolution. It was dissolved by Stalin in 1943. Interestingly enough this is one thing for which he has not yet been criticised.

in the USSR itself then China, too, might have been spared most of the Thoughts of the Great Helmsman.

The reason for summarising recent history, albeit in a few paragraphs, is to show that, despite its twists and turns, there has been a continuity in Soviet foreign policy since the victory of Stalin. On this front the break with Lenin's conception—regardless of whether one considers them to have been realistic options—was total. Soviet historians are now admitting that Stalinism was not inevitable. This is true, but how much more true is the fact that *Hitler's* victory was not inevitable either, nor was the defeat of the Spanish Republic. The entire pattern of European development might have been different if Germany and Spain had not come under the iron heel. And would that not have had an impact inside the USSR itself? At the very least Soviet historians have a responsibility to seriously consider the alternatives and not transplant present-day priorities on to the world situation of the Thirties.

The Soviet Union today, as we have seen, is full of a desire to 'return to Lenin': the speeches of Gorbachev and Yakovlev; the plays of Mikhail Shatrov, the novels of Anatoli Rybakov; the films of Abuladze and Klimov; the new atmosphere in Yuri Afanasiev's institute; the mushrooming of new organisations, all testify to this. But in the field of foreign policy a return to Lenin would entail a drastic reorientation which appears inconceivable. There are, of course, new problems which were not foreseen by either Lenin or Trotsky. The nuclear age undoubtedly imposes new responsibilities and only a fool or a lunatic could argue that a simply nuclear war is a continuation of politics by other means. Not that exporting revolution on the point of bayonets was ever a useful principle. Lenin's decision to invade Poland in 1920 (opposed, incidentally, by Trotsky) was an unusual lapse and the price is still being paid.

A hallmark of Soviet foreign policy is that it has essentially been a reaction to the West and, in the post-war years, to the United States in particular. Virtually every major Soviet move has been a response to a real or perceived Western threat to its security interests. There are basically two interrelated interests at stake here. These are not new, and obsessed the founders of the Soviet State just as much as they preoccupy the present leadership: the necessity to trade with the capitalist world at the same time as helping to develop socialist forces in the West which neutralise the war machines and, perhaps, even prepare the basis for a different type of state. In the nuclear age this becomes even more important. Political co-operation between the USSR and the capitalist world is both possible and even desirable. There are real global issues that need to be discussed in a positive framework: nuclear weapons and ecology are only top of the list. Human rights in South Africa, Chile, Pakistan, Malaysia, Guatemala as well as Rumania, North Korea and China certainly need to be put on the agenda together with elementary violations either in the United States or the USSR and their respective allies in Western and Eastern Europe. Economic co-operation is also possible because of the rivalries of various capitalist states, each trying to steal an advantage of the other. Such an attitude stretches back to Lenin and Trotsky. The Rapallo Treaty between Germany and the USSR in 1922 undoubtedly helped the Soviet Union at a time when it was isolated by a virtual trade blockade designed to bring the revolution to its knees. The most famous alliance, of course, was the wartime concordat between the USSR, the USA and Britain. But since the victory of 1945 US dominance of the world became an established fact. It is worth reminding ourselves that the United States emerged from the war full of vigour and strength. They had revived their industries, there was greater wealth than before and this was coupled to the fact that their losses compared to those of their allies were minimal. Hardly a scratch compared to the prostrate colussus, Russia, which had lost over twenty million people and whose adult population was full of war wounded and war-traumatised people. It was this Soviet Union which was seen as a threat and against whom NATO was set-up. Prior to the announcement of the Truman Doctrine, the USSR had demobilised its armies from eleven-and-a-half million to less than three million. The remobilisation was begun *after* the formation of NATO. Many years later, in 1965, George F. Kennan, an architect of containment, a defender of the Truman Doctrine and a one time US Ambassador to Moscow coolly informed *The Times* that

> after the Second World War, American policy makers could see Communism only in terms of a military threat. In creating NATO... they had drawn a line arbitrarily across Europe against an attack no one was planning.... After the war the Soviet Union did not want or need to overrun other countries.

He could have added that until the end of 1947 the Russians were prepared to accept a unified Germany on the Austrian model. It was the West which rejected this plan. Kennan's turnabout was the result of observing that the mistakes of the West had enabled the USSR to extend farther West than might have been the case. 'The Atlantic Pact,' wrote Kennan, 'was unfortunate because it was quite unnecessary'. This is certainly true as far as the USSR is concerned, but it ignores the fact that NATO had a dual function. Its structures were considered necessary by Washington to keep Western Europe, and particularly Britain and Germany, under firm US control.

The cold war alternated with periods of detente from 1947 onwards, but the detente never represented, even remotely, a historic reconciliation between Western capitalism and the USSR. Yet time and again, Soviet leaders have acted in a fashion which indicate their belief in the possibility of such a reconciliation. They were quite happy to trample on the unity of the communist movement in search of a deal with the West. The Sino-Soviet dispute was not just about bilateral disagreements between Moscow and Beijing. It was just as much about the cavalier fashion in which Khrushchev was ready to ditch the Chinese efforts to preserve their independence in order to reach a deal with Washington on global military detente. The net result of this was that the Chinese outflanked Moscow at its own game. The Soviet Union has, as a consequence, paid the enormous price of Chinese hostility and Sino-American co-operation over the last quarter of a century. And the result? The threat of Star Wars, permanently dangled over the head of the Soviet leadership by a recalcitrant imperialism.

Another case is the invasion of Czechoslovakia by the Brezhnev leadership in August 1968. There were three pressures at work in this instance. There was the Adeunauerist Ostpolitik thrust by the West Germans, who were taking advantage of the fact that the United States was bogged down in Indo-China to extend their wings. The West Germans were proposing a number of extremely favourable trade deals to Eastern Europe. Then there was the veteran Stalinist Führer of East Germany, Walter Ulbricht. He felt threatened by the sheer exhilaration which was growing in Eastern Europe as a result of the Czech events. He did not want the Dubcek model in East Germany. He threatened Moscow: either you go in and sort out the Czechs or I'm flying to Bonn to do a deal with Adenauer. The third actor in this drama was Washington which was observing the West Germans from afar with growing anger. They did not want Adenauer to play any independent role in Europe. Washington fully approved the Soviet invasion of Czechoslovakia. Brezhnev overthrew the reformers in Prague and proclaimed the Brezhnev Doctrine. A grotesque mimicking of the US model of a 'great power' had now begun. But what were the consequences? In the short-term, of course, the invasion of Prague led to a flowering of detente (compare this to the invasion of Afghanistan) with Nixon and the development of a new Ostpolitik from the Grand Coalition in Bonn which was more favourable to the security interests of the USSR.

However by 1979 these short-term gains were shown to have amounted to very little: the American political steamroller had crushed the forces of detente and had harnessed the entire capitalist world for a new global coalition against the Soviet Union. And how did it achieve this? A critical factor was the perception of the USSR as an imperialist oppressor (by this time Kabul had been added to Prague) and this perception totally undermined the authority of the USSR across the Left in the USA and Western Europe, saw a massive weakening of the Communist Parties and marked the end of any organised communist movement on a world scale. It also destroyed the credibility of reform communism throughout the USSR and Eastern Europe. If Gorbachev's team are worried by the rise of a cynical, semi-Thatcherite monetarist current inside the Hungarian Socialist Workers' Party they do not need to look too far for an explanation. The invasion of Czechoslovakia destroyed reform communism inside the Hungarian party. Whenever detente has happened it has been brought about by the sharpening of differences within the capitalist world. The speed with which Reagan abandoned the 'evil empire' scenario has something to do with the emergence of Gorbachev and his undouted successes. But this should not blind us to the fact that the United States is also extremely nervous of the economic strength of Japan and West Germany. The stock market crash of October 1987 brought home to US strategists the importance of the Soviet Union as a factor in the world situation. There are two trump cards which the USSR holds: German re-unification and return of the Kuriles* to Japan. Can anyone doubt that in return for concessions on these two issues the West Germans and the Japanese would be prepared to offer very favourable economic agreements despite US displeasure? The Japanese could computerise the USSR within a year. The West Germans could follow Italy and quadruple their trade. It is these factors which explain the turn of the Reaganites which took their own supporters by surprise, and is an indication that regardless of the incumbent in

*The Kurile islands were granted to the USSR by the Allies after the Second World War.

the White House there are hard-headed realists in the United States who defend the overall interests of their state. To jettison the 'evil empire' ideology is an important move, but it does not represent any qualitative breakthrough.

Is there today any prospect of a new reconciliation between capitalism and Gorbachev's Soviet Union? The very reverse is the case. The reasons for this are simple and were cogently spelt out by Politburo member Alexander Yakovlev in his important *On The Edge Of An Abyss*, in 1984. Yakovlev understands how the West functions better than probably any postwar leader of the USSR. In his book he explained the hollowness of the two-party system in the United States which he compared unfavourably to Western European democracies. For him in the United States there was no attempt to disguise the close connections between the giant corporations, the military and the government of the day:

The postwar period has also been highlighted by the following phenomenon. The monopolies have become far more active in their efforts to seize control over government affairs. The process through which the merger of the two mechanisms—that of the monopolies and that of the state—takes place has accelerated. Political mediators are pushed aside or ousted altogether whenever that suits the monopolies.

After naming names in various US administrations from F.D. Roosevelt onwards who were direct or indirect representatives of big business interests, Yakovlev has this to say about the Reagan regime:

The present Washington cabinet is made up of representatives of major corporations, above all, those connected with the military business. Its composition is indicative of the balance of forces in the economic élite.... Significantly, Reagan is backed up by a new generation of the rich who have made fortunes by underhand dealings, graft, bribery, Mafia connections and the like.... The Reagan Administration is often dubbed the 'Bechtel Power Corporation government' because many of its members come from the California construction company specialising in large-scale power and industrial construction projects, some of which are developed in foreign countries.

If this is the case then what possible basis could there be for a 'historic reconciliation' with the giant corporations who regard even Keynesian social-democrats as a threat and who see the preservation of a socialised economy within COMECON as a permanent reminder that the Socialist option could be revived in the West at some time in the future? How much greater would this threat be if it were combined with a genuinely democratic political system? The Moscow Summit of Spring 1988, leaving aside the showbiz, showed only too clearly what the United States is up to: the Reaganite propaganda machine is busy reviving Christian obscurantism and a Solzhenitsyn-inspired theocracy as well as promoting the break-up of the USSR through a combination of nationalist antagonisms and demands for free-trade zones in Estonia. The only basis for a genuine reconciliation between the Soviet and American leadership would be if the reformers were really heading towards a restoration of capitalism inside the USSR. There are undoubtedly elements within the Soviet élite and intelligentsia who would like to travel down this particular road. Their voices can be heard from within the Soviet media as well as amongst the Heritage Foundation dissidents. But a restoration of capitalism is not on the agenda of Gorbachev or Yakovlev, leave alone Yeltsin. Apart from all other objections it would provide the basis for a new civil war or at the very least a military take-over.

None of this, of course, should be taken to mean that there cannot be temporary and partial agreements between the USSR and the USA or Western European states. The current negotiations are examples of this and would have been welcomed by the old Bolsheviks. But it is important to note the backdrop to these limited deals. The United States is under pressure within the capitalist world: the budgetary crisis, the chronic weakness of American domestic capital in the field of inter-capitalist competition, and so on. The United States wants a more stable relationship with the Soviet Union as part of an attempt to shift the burden of the world economic crisis onto the shoulders of West Germany and Japan. As in the early Seventies, the deals with the USSR can provide a valuable framework within which fierce assaults can be mounted on the *economic* interests of rival capitalisms. But at the most these new deals are nothing more than a phase in American policy and there is no reason to assume that it will not be followed within the next decade by a renewed attempt to isolate the USSR.

Before discussing some concrete proposals which could, if properly debated and implemented, totally alter the course of world politics, it is necessary to summarise what Gorbachev's foreign policy priorities reveal. There is no doubt that there is a strong revulsion inside the Soviet Union against the high military expenditure, the indiscriminate provision of military supplies to third world states and Soviet military presence abroad. If there was a referendum on these questions I have no doubt that a majority of the population would vote for what would amount to an isolationist stance. This poses problems for those who believe in democracy and are therefore loth to disregard popular opinion, but would be deeply unhappy if the Soviet population voted to cut off aid to Nicaragua or the freedom-fighters in Southern Africa. I belong to this category, but the point is to change this perception within the Soviet Union and that necessitates the revival of a popular internationalism. However few could disagree with Gorbachev's offensive against nuclear weapons which has given the Soviet Union the moral superiority throughout the world and put the cold war warriors on the defensive. The withdrawal of Soviet troops from Afghanistan in 1988 was a belated recognition of a dreadful error. To those on the Left who shout 'betrayal' one can only say that the only thing that has been betrayed are their illusions. Gorbachev's *de facto* repudiation of the Brezhnev Doctrine marks another step forward. It is now difficult to conceive of a Soviet military intervention to defend bureaucratic interests in Eastern Europe. Add to this a growing discussion on whether supplying arms to Ethiopia, Iraq, Uganda and numerous other states of this sort is justified or not, and one begins to appreciate the changes. Of course there are other cases. What should the USSR do in the event of a popular revolution which the United States attempts to crush by organising a counter-revolutionary army, arming it to the teeth and funding it despite legal restraints? Should the Soviet Union ignore the pleas for help from the victim of a sustained military attempt aggression? To do so would be an act of immorality and while there is a great deal of talk there is no clear evidence to suggest that the Soviet Union is going to leave black South Africa, Nicaragua or Cuba to the mercy of the wolves. Though it should be added that the billions of rubles of Soviet economic and military aid to Cuba helped to save the Revolution on that island but at a price. The Cuban regime was Brezhnevised: Castro was compelled to defend the criminal invasion of Czechoslovakia and as President of the Non-Aligned Movement, Castro was left to watch and justify the Soviet intervention in Afghanistan. In other words the aid had a crippling ideological effect on Havana.

One of the great liberal illusions of the late twentieth century is that foreign policy is unrelated to domestic priorities. There are some groups on the West European Left who sincerely believe that Gorbachev is just waiting to bring down the living standards of the

Soviet working class. Such a view is beneath contempt. Nothing would please the Soviet leadership more than to implement perestroika in such a way that it would involve the least possible short-term costs to Soviet workers. But everything depends upon the economic and financial-budgetary reserves at its disposal. And no single *domestic* political factor has more influence on that question than the core executives of Western capitalism. *If* there is a START deal, *if* there is a deal on short-range nukes in Europe, *if* there is agreement on a reduction of conventional forces in Europe, *if* there is a relaxation or flouting of the COCOM system for economic warfare against the USSR, and above all, *if* the US administration scraps SDI: if any one or a combination of these steps were to be taken by the West it would transform the domestic equations of Soviet economic policy.

Washington's foreign policy towards the USSR has everything to do with directly intervening in internal Soviet politics. This is done by utilising the economic and military strength of the United States itself, as well as by pressuring the allies to remain firm. Nothing would please Washington more than the spectacle of a Soviet leadership launching a draconian austerity policy against its working class and gravely weakening the links between the base of the CPSU and the leadership. Why? Because this would make the leadership more dependent than ever before on deals with the West.

The emergence in such a striking fashion of a reform communism in the Soviet Union has divided the politicians of the Right and Left all over the world. The question, which is of some interest to Western socialists in particular, is how the Soviet Union fits in with *their* socialist project and how they can help to influence the course of events in the Soviet Union. Ronald Reagan and Margaret Thatcher intervene in the Soviet Union on a regular basis. The parties of the Left: social-democracy, communism, greens and far-left grouplets have not yet come up with any serious discussion of an international response to the possibilities opening up in the USSR.

As far as a number of Marxist/Trotskyist currents are concerned one has to say that their attitude borders on parasitism. Instead of developing their own positive stance on international affairs they rely on the Socialist or Communist parties to come up with their policies. These are then criticised as inadequate. This leads to utterly sterile comparisons of, for example, existing Labour Party policies in Britain or CPSU policies, with an abstract ideal of socialist internationalism. This technique always produces happy results: the policy on offer can be denounced as a betrayal.

Gorbachev's foreign policy is subjected to a similar treatment. There is an ideal. The Soviet leadership is believed by some to embody that ideal. But in fact it is moving away from that ideal, moving to the Right, collaborating with capitalism, taking a line that is undermining the Communist Parties in the West by aiding the social-democratic parties. And so the litany continues. The implication that Brezhnev and Stalin were to the Left of Gorbachev is, of course, a joke in bad taste, but let us assume, for the sake of argument, that all this were true. All it tells us is that Gorbachev and Yakovlev in 1988 are not Lenin and Trotsky in 1917. True enough. But what then constitutes an effective socialist policy in Europe?*

What is to be done?

It becomes much easier to understand the Soviet Union if we view its developments from the perspective of some shift in Europe as a whole. What are the realities which stare one in the face? For over a decade now tens of millions of people in Western Europe have either been out of work or have faced the threat of unemployment. Social rights and welfare have been seriously eroded. The Right argues that the reason for this is because people have priced themselves out of jobs and because the welfare state has drained the wealth away from 'wealth creators' (ie big business). But the fact remains that the capitalist organisation of economic life in Western Europe and the United States, not to speak of the developing world, is not able to deliver a minimum level of economic security and welfare to the people of these states. Capitalism did succeed in guaranteeing most of these things—and to a far greater extent than the Left had thought possible—during the long post-war boom of the Fififties and Sixties. Since the mid-Seventies, however, the system has been failing.

There has been a great deal of talk as to how the electronic revolution coupled with the policies of the New Right would generate sufficient new economic impetus to enable capitalism once again to provide the minimum requirements for a civilised social and economic order. Yet, if we are to take the policies of the Thatcher

---

*Unfortunately the positive policy content of most Marxist currents in Western Europe today amounts to a romantic subjectivism. Limitless possibilities are projected onto every mass movement or strike. When these supposedly unlimited possibilities are not realised the leaders of the strike or mass movement are denounced for failing to live up to the subjective hopes of the particular groups. Once the group in question has recovered from one disappointment it gives full reign once again to its imagination in readiness for the next set of limitless possibilities.

government as a guide, it is obvious that the British state does not believe that we are on the verge of a new harmony-producing wave of economic growth. If it did it would not be accelerating measures to erode democratic rights and centralise power: essential requirements to deal with potential disorder. This suggests that the powers that be are not at all convinced that tomorrow's capitalism will be compatible with all but the most minimal rights of citizenship.

These issues are not unrelated to the political threat posed by the growth of the new Right throughout Western Europe. The manipulation of electoral laws in France may have temporarily reversed the rise of Le Pen's fascists, but their earlier successes evoked a great deal of enthusiasm amongst some of Mrs Thatcher's more innovative supporters in Britian: unmistakeable emblems of what could lie ahead. The growing racist murders and attacks, the resurgence of anti-semitism, the barbaric inroads of the Armageddon Christian Movement on the Reaganite base in America, the growing hysteria against homosexuals helped on its way by Clause 28; these are all issues which need to be discussed in preparation for a new Helsinki-style Charter.

Add to this three other key problems which confront the world today. First, the strangulation of hundreds of millions of people in the three continents of Asia, Africa and Latin America by an economic mechanism controlled by the metropoles in the West. And even as the transnational corporations maintain a tight grip on the digestive tracts of the peoples of the third world, resistance movements against differential tyrannies are slaughtered with immunity in South Africa, Chile and Israel—the world watches on its television screens. Secondly, there is the threat posed to the ecology on a regional and a planetary scale. And third is the threat of nuclear annhilation. Despite the pseudo-detente atmosphere which has followed the ratification of the INF treaty the threat to the planet is as real today as it was in the early Eighties. Indeed the economic and political clout of the war industries in the United States has never been greater in American politics and the novelist Gore Vidal has argued on a number of occasions that this military-industrial complex has eroded democracy in the United States beyond recognition.

If these are the main issues confronting humanity then it is obvious that they can not be solved by any single country or on a country by country basis. There are three alternative frameworks available to try and deal with these problems. The Atlanticist solution, the European Economic Community model or a new Pan-European framework:

1. *The Atlanticists*
This was the orthodoxy of Western European social-democracy in the postwar years and appeared to offer tremendous scope for the working people of North Western Europe throughout the Fifties and Sixties. The quid pro quo was based on accepting US hegemony (military bases and economic dominance) in return for massive reforms for the labour movements, symbolised by the welfare state of the post-war period. This worked during the boom years, albeit under strict conditions. The Communist Parties could not be legitimised within the Atlantic Order, but if you were a social-democrat, then apart from some massaging with CIA funds and agents, you could be treated as an acceptable participant. Social-democracry was acceptable because Washington still faced difficulties with the Nationalist Right and because some of the aims of social democrats fitted in with US interests. Moreover they could be used to undermine the communists in the trades unions and factories. The empire loyalists of the European Right were regarded as a terrible irritant by the United States throughout the Fifties and Sixties. Whether it was the Suez Conservatives trying to defend the Empire against the Yankees or the French Gaullists or the Adenauerist Right in Germany dreaming of dragging NATO into a Drang nach Osten, it was all regarded as an awful pain in the posterior. The European Right liked America's anti-Communist policies, but loathed Americans; the European Left loathed many of the policies, but liked Americans. The key point of congruence between the social-democrats and the American corporations lay in the following fact: the social-democrats wanted full employment and the US corporations were industrially geared up for a mass working class market which could provide better working conditions and mass access to Ford cars and refrigerators. Add to this the social-democratic dislike of high defence spending, support for the welfare state and a nervousness of nuclear weapons and you have something coinciding with American attempts to block the European Right's efforts to develop its own nuclear weapon programmes (in order to escape US hegemony). A third factor was that the economic boom was fuelled largely by the enormously powerful domestic US economy. The pragmatic socialists were

attracted to this more than anything else: America could deliver both goods and dollars for badly-needed reforms.

Now this may all have been very nice in the Fifties and Sixties, though it was not without its problems, but the situation is totally different today. Not only has the threat from the powerful nationalist, Empire-centred conservatives evaporated, but the United States is desperately keen to get its European allies to shoulder much heavier military expenditure in order to ease the budgetary strain in America itself. This is the main pressure for slashing welfare programmes throughout Western Europe. The US foreign policy élite regard the growing desire on the European Left for a serious detente with the USSR as the major problem today. They hate Gorbachev's popularity in West Germany in particular, seeing this as the threat of the Finlandisation of Western Europe. In other words they do not want Western Europe to cease to be a militarist vanguard in the cold war; cease to provide a domestic political base for joint ventures in the third world, especially the Middle East; become committed to using domestic wealth for civilian and welfare development; and treating the USSR like a normal state. As for the US economy, far from being the locomotive of European prosperity it is, in fact, the prime source for threatening the destabilisation of economic growth in Europe.

As a result of all these changes most of the leaders of the Socialist parties know fully well that it would be madness to expect any significant support from Washington in their efforts to form or manage a government. Even a cursory glance at the foreign policy journals of the American think-tanks will disabuse any notion that Atlanticism offers a positive framework for even the most mildly reformist strategy. This does not mean that Washington's *power* can simply be ignored. It means that it has to be a recognised as a hostile and destabilising power for any party that wishes even to implement some major social reforms. The emergence of Jesse Jackson as a major, though minority current within the Democratic Party is a fact of great significance, since it provides an important layer which will back many projects which unite all sections of the Left in Europe. The Jackson Democrats are the natural allies of social-democracy, but they are still a long way from achieving victory within the democratic camp.

2. *The Common Market Wallahs*
This seems to have become a fashionable option for the Left in

Western Europe. Much to Mrs Thatcher's irritation, the year 1992 is being packaged by the EEC bureaucrats in pink wrapping paper as a step towards a 'social' Common Market in which trade union rights and welfare spending will be enhanced. The realities of the drive towards 1992, however, belie this public relations image just as the great EEC declarations of 1973—about regulating and taming the multinationals—turned out to herald a diametrically opposite result. In fact the record of EEC negotiations over the last decades demonstrates one feature as standing out above all else: deals can be struck in favour of specific agreements on strictly capitalist lines or they can't be struck at all. This does not mean that any country pulling out of the EEC to push 'reformism in one country' would solve any of the big problems alluded to above. It is simply that 1992 will provide very little in the way of gains for ordinary working people in Western Europe.

Even if we assume—and the *if* is truly big—that 1992 does produce a formula for a single West European state, what problems would it actually solve? There would certainly be some stimulus to economic growth in the region, but of a very limited sort. The central banking mechanism and finance ministries would be under minimal influence from the labour movement. The giant corporations would have far easier access to decision-making than ever before. As to the military-welfare trade off, the position for any Left party would be worse rather than better. If Western Europe remained allied to the United States it would rationalise and strengthen its military machine to ease the US load and would almost certainly operate militarily alongside the US in the third world. If it is in conflict with the United States, it would be a nuclear state in its own right with an even larger military sector sold to the electorate on an *anti-American* as well as anti-Soviet basis.

The effect of such a West European super-state would be to exacerbate tensions with the USSR in Europe whatever the character of the Soviet government. And if, as seems likely, the West German Right was powerful in such an arrangement, it would pose a threat of pulling the hinterland states of East Central Europe into relations of dependence on the West, raising the spectre of their incorporation within the new state, or at least their removal from COMECON. This prospect, far from stabilising Eastern Europe would engender uncontrollable tensions within and between these states, turning the region into a cockpit seething with belligerence. Some of the signs of this are already visible.

The real point about the creation of a West European super-state is that its birth would reflect the disintegration of the supposedly open, liberal, international economic order that is supposed to exist, and its replacement by increasingly antagonistic relations between large economic zones: it is this threat which is driving big capital in Western Europe to take protective action against the United States. Given this background, any idea that the long-term future for the world economy is bright, that economic growth will soon be back on the agenda to end the misery of unemployment, the erosion of welfare, predatory activity in the third world, militarism and so on, amounts to little more than whistling in the dark. And anybody with even a slight knowledge of the last eighty years of European history knows full well that the capitalist states of Western and West Central Europe are perfectly capable of behaving in a far more barbaric fashion than the United States.

3. *Towards a Pan-European Strategy*

If a West European super-state were to come into existence then, of course, all political parties of the Left would have to deal with it within its framework. But it is easy to forget, especially if one reads the more utopian literature on the Left, that no such 'Western Europe' actually exists as a hard, political entity today. In political terms Western Europe lacks all the attributes of a professional actor in world politics: neither a centralised taxing bureaucracy to bring in money, nor a large military force on call nor a unified judicial and police system to enforce the new rules, and certainly not a centralised political leadership to mobilise political and economic resources for policy goals. *None* of this exists, and the Left gains nothing by imagining that simply talking about them will conjure them into existence. What is even more pathetic is to hear socialists talk about 'Europe' doing this or achieving that when, in reality, they are referring to the Balkanised rag-bag of countries (and half-countries) inside the EEC zones of Western Europe.

Despite the problems posed by the models already discussed, it is obvious that there is everything to gain from a genuinely European programme and strategy which does *begin* to offer some real soltuions to basic problems and transform the way in which economic, social, civil liberties, ecological, military and third world issues are resolved. The possibilities are enormous if there is a political will which pushes through a change in orientation. This is what could be achieved:

1. *A Programme for Pan-European Recovery*

Currently Western Europe remains a rump excluded from vital supplies of energy while West European industries remain under the shadow of over-capacity: capital, desperate for new investment outlets is busy pumping money into property speculation and the like. But an economic framework which embraced the USSR could lead to a great leap in the productive forces throughout the continent. In Siberia there is a vast new field for productive investment, offering unlimited supplies of raw materials, minerals and energy required by industry in the West. The Soviet market contains 250 million economically active people only too ready to absorb the products of West German, French, Italian or even British industry. The complementaries of the West German and Soviet economies are so obvious that they have been giving periodical nightmares to the US and British ruling classes for the last fifty years. Of course there are large obstacles which would prevent exploitation of the enormous advantages of a unified European framework for economic growth, but surely it is necessary to overcome these roadblocks rather than remain trapped in a Cold War framework which blinds those within it to the historic and progressive opportunities that are now opening up?

2. *Differing Social Systems*

A major obstacle to Pan-European unity supposedly is the obvious split between the differing social systems. The only aspect of the split which is relevant concerns the ability of the state in a planned economy to take strategic decisions about how much and where to invest. The fact is that this is hardly a problem in the USSR. It is in the West that such decisions are taken on the stock market, the global financial markets or in the big West German banks. It is a system which has been aptly characterised as 'casino capitalism'.

The Socialist Parties in the West could push through measures to curb the grip of financial speculators on investment decisions while simultaneously establishing state investment bodies of the sort that Labour leaderships in Britain have been toying with for years. This would facilitate the planned growth of investment and trade between the two Europes, leading to deals which are ten times larger than the giant gas venture between Western Europe and the USSR in the early Eighties. Nor is there any real obstacle, provided there is mass political support, to the West European state trading and investment bodies offering very long term credits at minimal rates of interest for planned economic growth across the continent. The entire package of measures and plans could be foreseen by an all-European council (including government representatives) not only from the EEC and COMECON, but from EFTA and the neutral states in Europe as well. This was the formula used (and abused) by the United States in their drive to integrate Western Europe into the new American-led world economy after the Second World War, through what became the OECD.

Moreover in order to get the European economy fully moving again, Western governments could easily write off the huge foreign debts of states like Poland and Yugoslavia. This would be nothing more than a traditional method of the Western economies. If the British Trade Secretary, Lord Young, can write off £600 million to help a single military corporation, British Aerospace, the example surely could be followed more creatively on a European scale?

3. *A Charter Of Social Rights*
The insipid fare which is offered on the present menu as a 'social EEC' is totally unconvincing, but a pan-European approach to the social rights of the majority of a country's citizens could prove to be enormously beneficial. The Soviet constitution enshrines the statutory right to work. Why should not the Left in Western Europe argue for a similar right? The states of Eastern Europe are committed to providing state nursery facilities for all. Are the states of the West really so poor that they could not match such a commitment and, in fact, provide far better facilities? Why should women in Western Europe have to put up with the limited maternity rights enjoyed by, for instance, Swedish women when women in East Germany enjoy a far better deal? Why should the children of working class families in Britain have less than a tenth of the chance than Soviet working class kids have of going to univeristy? In which European country can an ordinary working person afford to take the powerful to court? Certainly not in Britain. Could it really be the case that the Soviet judicial system (shock, horror, shock!) offers far greater access to judicial redress for its citizens?

4. *Civil Liberties and Democratic Rights*
A Pan-European approach on this front, too, would greatly benefit the citizens of Europe. Rights to freedom of association, of speech and of assembly would be a big step forward for the peoples of Eastern Europe. The right to strike would aid the workers in Eastern Europe and the USSR and such a right, without legal restraints,

could help clarify the position in Western Europe as well. Add to this the civil liberties for gay people and ethnic minorities. In Britain a citizen can be held by the police for 96 hours without charge; in Czechoslovakia the period is 48 hours. Why such a disparity? In Holland and Sweden, political pluralism in the media is the norm: in Britain and East Germany it is virtually excluded. Could it be that glasnost embodies a principle that could be extended across Europe?

5. *A Common Approach to Ecology*
If Chernobyl proved one thing it was that it was not simply a problem for the Soviet Union. The acid rain that followed, the threat to sea life in the Baltic, the effects on livestock throughout Northern Europe make it clear that ecology can only be tackled on a pan-European scale.

6. *Peace and Disarmament*
A genuine disarmament process could move forward rapidly within a pan-European framework and take the continent out of the frontline between the two super-powers. The peace movements have already developed a set of objectives for denuclearisation, demilitarised zones and reductions in conventional forces. The call of certain pseudo-European demilitarisation schemes for a combined Soviet-American pull back from 'Europe', while the West European states seek to merge into a European super-power and drag Eastern Europe into its orbit, would not strengthen reciprocal security. It should not be forgotten that the troop strength of the Bundeswehr today stands at a ratio of one to three to the troop strength of the Soviet Army—the same ratio that existed in 1941! If the military capacity of France, Britain and Italy is added to that—as well as the planned expansion of nuclear capacity and an EEC share of the world GDP which is considerably larger than that of the USSR—it is foolish to imagine that a Western European militarised state could contribute to a stable peace in Europe.

7. *Solidarity and Co-operation With The Third World*
Despite the noisy rhetoric which emanates from Brussels, the record of the major West European states in relation to the countries of the third world is not better than that of the United States. It is true that Western Europe has let Washington monopolise the martial aspects of the dirty work in the third world. But neither Britian nor West Germany has ever provided practical military assistance to a genuine liberation struggle, either in Southern Africa or in Central

America. The attitude of the big EEC states on trade and debt issues is exactly the same as the United States. Most Western aid agencies, are, to be blunt, little more than policy instruments for the manouevres of various Western European chanceries. Despite the cynical operations of the Soviet Union in parts of the third world their support to Cuba, Nicaragua, Angola has been significant. Gorbachev's telegram to Nelson Mandela on his seventieth birthday stood in marked contrast to the appeasers of apartheid in Bonn, Washington and London.

8. *The Balance of Power In Europe*

The programme we have outlined would lead to European co-operation on a scale that has never been seriously discussed, except behind closed doors. If such moves were to be made another question would arise: if the existing military divisions begin to dissolve what would be the new configuration of power in the continent? Here the answer is obvious. Two large nations would dwarf all else in terms of all the traditional indices of state power: the Germans and the Soviet Union. One inescapable dimension of European history in the twentieth century has been the ultimate futility of any European scheme which hinges on either one or the other of these two states. Those European powers who wanted to keep revolutionary Russia out at any cost found themselves unlocking the door to German domination in the Thirties. Stalin's efforts to create a closed system of dependent East European states has, over the last decades, proved largely counter-productive. It is true that for a period, during the boom years, tacit Soviet-US understanding on a joint management of Europe via a divided Germany did provide stability from 1948 to the late Sixties. But one crisis has followed another during the Eighties. We are approaching the end of the post-war world. The politico-military dominance of the United States is now being deployed to undermine the welfare states of Western Europe. The Left has few real options, but to work for a new political balance in Europe which downgrades the role of US power and which embraces both the Soviet Union and the Germans. Such a balance would permit the smaller nations of both Eastern and Western Europe to breathe.

9. *Means and Ends*

The old slogan of European socialism used to be a call for the United Socialist Republics of Europe. That was the goal but it soon began to appear as a utopian ideal. Wars, fascism and Stalinism, mass unemployment did not prove to be harbingers of European unity. It is not that conditions today automatically favour such a transition, but the time is right to seize the initiative. If a programme of the sort we have outlined here were to become the basis for a united effort by Socialist and Communist parties and trade union federations throughout Western Europe, its appeal could be powerful both in the East and the West. The only serious social force capable of mounting such a movement is the labour movement, flanked, needless to add, by the peace, ecology and women's movements. It may surprise some to realise that much of the framework required for such a political offensive already exists: the Helsinki Process. The Helsinki accords of the early Seventies were designed not simply to monitor violations of human rights in the USSR, but to engage in economic, technological and scientific co-operation. These other aspects are usually ignored by the Western media and totally flouted by the COCOM system of economic warfare against the USSR, which was revived in the Eighties after becoming moribund in the late Sixties. Members of the European Parliament belonging to the parties of the Left could easily utilise the Helsinki accords and challenge *all* violations of this. At the same time it would be perfectly possible for the European Socialist Parties to open a line of direct communications with the parties in power in the USSR and Eastern Europe. Willy Brandt took one such initiative which resulted in both Germanies banning chemical weapons. East-West diplomacy is not dependent on being in office. The ground could be well-prepared even before. We can return to the effects of the changes in the Soviet Union on the left. The first and most obvious fact is that the political democratisation in the Soviet Union is a joyous antidote to the poisonous anti-communism of the cold warriors which has crippled the possibility of any real initiatives towards peace and economic co-operation. The New Soviet policy has already dramatically transformed the atmosphere in West Germany and is causing panic amongst the New Right politicians and ideologues. The Thatcherite notion that things are moving 'her way' in the USSR is a pure fantasy. If this were indeed the case then the West would have offered major concessions at the Moscow Summit. Yet, as we know, very little was achieved. And if one uncovers the reality which underlay the rhetoric, the leaders of the West were essentially parroting the same formula: Yes, Gorbachev is a good guy. Yes, the Soviet Union is changing. But he will fail and because we know that he can't succeed we can't make any real concessions. This is simply another way of destabilising Gorbachev in the Soviet Union while shedding crocodile tears in Washington and London. The fact is that the cold warriors and their friends on the right-wing of social democracy and the Western European trades unions in Europe are under an ideological seige because of Gorbachev. The Left in Europe needs to overcome its fear of being labelled as apologists for the gulag or Soviet stooges and establish direct contacts with official bodies in the Soviet Union and Eastern Europe. The Right from Reagan, Thatcher and Strauss downwards has been busy seeking friends and influencing people in the Warsaw Pact for years, secure in the knowledge that they could discredit any leftwing MP or trade-union leader for doing the same. The Greens in West Germany have shown very clearly that it is possible to engage in open, straight-forward discussions with Eastern Europe without attempting to conceal disagreements. Fellow-travelling does not have too many friends in the Soviet Union today because everyone knows what this particular breed did in the West.* Instead of isolating the Stalinist criminals, they justified and apologised on their behalf to anyone who was prepared to listen; and, alas, many were and fell for the deceit. The reality of Soviet communism today is a thousand times more pluralistic than the cold warriors on either side would like to admit and the Left needs to develop its own links through its own organisations. The change of perception amongst ordinary people throughout the world as far as the USSR is concerned is one of the most positive consequences of the policies of the new leaders in Moscow.

There are other options as well. The changes in the USSR make far more possible than ever before coordinated joint actions between Socialists and Communists. Why? Because the reformers in the Kremlin are destroying the myth of Communism as the Scientific Church of the Proletariat. Moscow no longer sees itself as the Third Rome. The absurd fiction that the Politburos of the Communist Parties have a monopoly on the truth or 'scientific thought' and everybody else is a 'class enemy' was always a nonsense, but is now recognised as such. And on the side of the Socialist Parties there has been a weakening of the cold war Right, though it has to be stressed that the German SDP and the British Labour Party remain strongly committed to NATO.

*Fellow-travellers in the Thirties were well known writers and artists who were sympathetic to the Russian Revolution but whose gullibility made them easy tools for the Stalinist bureaucracy.

Ultimately, of course, the transformations will only be secured when pluralism is firmly anchored within the CPSU and the Soviet Union itself as we have discussed in Chapter 6. In Czechoslovakia in 1968 such a pluralism was developing rapidly. The co-operation between the Czech Communists and the Czech Socialist Party, instituted in 1968 by the Czech communist leader, Jaroslav Sabata, in the town of Brno was expressed in the publication of the 'Little Action Programme'. Such a joint programme offers a model to Communists and Socialists throughout Eastern Europe.

Would the sort of programme we have outlined here meet with an enthusiastic response from the Soviet leadership? Some aspects would obviously be appealing: disarmament, ecology, civil and social rights, removal of trade restrictions, but there could be two issues which would not be universally popular. The first is that the entire notion of linking up with the socialist parties on the basis of an international united front of the workers parties of Europe would undoubtedly antagonise the leaders of capitalism in Western Europe. While sections of West European capitalism would gain a great deal *economically* from a pan-European recovery programme, the American and British Right would see this as a *political* blow to their global fantasies. For despite the talk of Washington pulling out of Europe, the fact is that the US dominance in Western Europe is the fulcrum of its world political strategy. Western Europe is the *political* base of the United States for confronting the USSR, and operating in the Middle East. But should this worry the Soviet leadership? Some might answer yes; that this is because the Soviet leaders are emotionally and psychologically committed to dealing with the American state rather than political parties of the Left. This was certainly the case for the ultra-conservatives in the Brezhnev regime: these people loathed any mass political movement. But this is certainly not the case with the leaders of reform communism in the Soviet Union today. The real reason is far more mundane. Gorbachev does not see himself as the Lenin of the world proletariat in the 1990s. He is preoccupied with the reform and modernisation of his own country. The people who can offer the Soviet Union something tangible—ie implement the Helsinki Accords—are quite simply the Right, and especially the United States. Given the economic crisis in the Soviet Union and the real balance of forces between the Soviet Union and the rest of the world, surely one can expect Gorbachev to adhere ruthlessly to a set of policies geared to immediate Soviet recovery rather than any other long-term aims. In this respect there is nothing new about Soviet foreign policy: the continuity extends from 1927 to 1988. But there is one difference. Gorbachev is not going to pretend that he is doing something which he clearly is not doing, and perhaps can not achieve. So the rhetoric will be scaled down and some positive changes will take place, such as a realistic assessment inside the Soviet academies of various regimes in the third world and the real balance of forces inside Western Europe and North America.

The following 'dialectic' can therefore be envisaged: the more the Left parties in Europe advance against the Right and utilise the new openings made possible by Gorbachev in the Soviet Union, the greater will be the pressure on the Americans to strike favourable deals with Moscow while pressuring the latter to keep its distance from the Left in Western Europe. This would give rise to the sort of problems that are posed by success, but these 'problems' only exist on the level of dreams today. One further point needs to be stressed: If the Soviet political structure is changed and there is a real separation of powers between party and state, then, paradoxically, the CPSU might be in a far stronger position to develop links with parties and movements abroad and in a far more open fashion. Gorbachev's success inside his country would also create the basis for a new form of internationalism, whether the Soviet leaders like it or not: the new model would, sooner or later, attract emulators elsewhere. And then what? Would Gorbachev and Yakovlev be able to stay aloof?

The other central issue on which the Soviet leadership would resist a Pan-European programme is the German question. They would be very reluctant to abandon the formula that has worked reasonably well on the basis of a divided Germany. Despite the myths and paranoia of the Anglo-American Right about the USSR wanting to split Western Europe from America, this has never been Soviet policy except for a brief period between 1948 and 1952: Stalin was prepared to offer a united Germany because he was convinced that the United States were preparing a direct strike against the USSR. The Soviet preference for the present arrangement derives from two factors. First, they do not wish to initiate a total break with the United States unless they are left with no other option. American strategists realised this and instructed the Great Communicator to dump his hysterical jargon—the 'evil empire', and so forth. Secondly, there is a genuine fear that German revanchism could come alive and demand chunks of Eastern Europe. The United

States, despite the beliefs of naïve rightwing dissidents in Poland, have no particular interest in Eastern Europe. For them it has always provided a set of very small pawns in their big head to head confrontation with the Kremlin. And the Americans are quite enthusiastic about a divided Germany. It is not completely cynical to state that they are also firm supporters of the Berlin Wall, which both strengthened East Germany and provided successive incumbents of the White House with wonderful photo-call opportunities.

The fact is that the Soviet leadership can not decide—leave alone determine—the evolution of the relationship between growing sections of West European social-democracy and the United States. What the Soviet Union can do is to change the very basis of its *political* relations with Eastern Europe. The fact that Mikhail Gorbachev is extremely popular in most of Eastern Europe is no longer in doubt. In Prague, Belgrade and East Berlin the ordinary people are looking towards this particular reformer at this particular time to deliver the goods. Even in Poland, in July 1988, the reception was warm and it would have been warmer had Gorbachev not maintained an uncharacteristic reserve. He obviously did not wish to destabilise the regime. There is a very simple way in which trust could be rebuilt and that would be to organise an election throughout Eastern Europe and the USSR to the COMECON equivalent of a European Assembly. There is absolutely no real reason why inter-East European relations could not be openly discussed. This would provide the first democratic forum in this part of Europe and, apart from everything else, it could show the Western European Assembly up for it was: a toothless body dominated by a bureaucracy, and with no real powers. A COMECON political assembly could discuss economic relations as well as the problems confronting ethnic minorities in Rumania, Yugoslavia and, of course, the USSR. The fact is that a plurality of candidates in elections to such a body coupled with a proper campaign and television time for all contestants would do a great deal to clear the air of both genuine suspicions and concerns, as well as acute forms of nationalist paranoia.

A cardinal feature of Stalinism was its unremitting drive to crush anything that looked like becoming an alternative model of socialism. That was a fundamental feature of the Brezhnev-Ulbricht drive against Dubcek's Prague in 1968. If this remains a feature of Soviet politics then we will have to forget about any serious possibilities for united action with the USSR for a new relationship in Europe. But the entire thrust of events in the USSR today is a denunciation of the most ferocious kind against the Stalinist model. On this front Gorbachev has gone way beyond Imre Nagy, Khrushchev and Dubcek. There is every reason to hope that the new turn implies a genuine recognition that the struggle for socialism is an open-ended and experimental business. The socialisation of economic life and the democratisation of social and political life need no longer involve the crippling imposition of Stalinist authoritarianism. The entire basis of Stalinist hostility to other models of socialism lay in its morbid suspicion of its own population. Under a regime of socialist democracy, that source of monolithism would have no reason for existence.

Nothing that the Left in the West can do to encourage the development of popular soviet democracy is more important than abandoning its traditional fear of a frank, open and vigorous engagement with Soviet socialists (and the overwhelming majority of these are members of the CPSU). The beginnings of such a dialogue could help educate many socialists in the West. For they will be surprised by what they learn in the Soviet Union. Of course if the Left—whether they be social-democrats or peaceniks or members of Trotskyist sects or whatever—try and engage believing that they are superior and that they know it all, then they will be treated with contempt and rightly so. Soviet communists do not need to be lectured on the evils of Stalinism. They know better than most what it has cost their country. They are, however, greatly interested in other models and in constructive ideas to move forward together.

Many Third World communist parties are in a state of confusion and despair. They had already been worried by the Twentieth Party Congress, but were relieved at the ideological 'stability' offered by Brezhnev. Now they are deeply worried again. The Communist Party of India (Marxist) which is in power in the two large states of West Bengal and Kerala, recently sent a high-powered delegation to plead with the Russians not to denounce Stalin too harshly. For them, Stalin is still a guru. The popular history of the CPSU taught at CPI(M) cadre schools is that well-known bundle of lies ghosted for Stalin by the Red Professors. The gerontocrats from the CPI(M) got short shrift from officialdom in Moscow, but nobody prevented them from laying an official wreath on the tomb of the 'Peoples' Friend' at the foot of the Kremlin wall. One would have thought that

Indian communists, in particular, would have welcomed the birth of socialist democracy in the Soviet Union. After all it had been Brezhnev who on a state visit to India had wondered aloud as to why the country needed any opposition parties in the first place. This had been intended as a gibe against Indian communism. Yet in the medium term, I am sure, we will see the effects of glasnost in the Third World itself. The one-party state syndrome was often presented by rulers in Africa and Asia as a 'progressive model'. What will they say now? Some, like the former Afghan leader, Babrak Karmal will whisper to his followers that Gorbachev is a revisionist and that Marxism-Leninism has been abandoned by the Soviet Union. Gorbachev's assault on the old ideological certainties of Third World Stalinists can only have a positive outcome. In that sense the interdependence of domestic and foreign affairs is very clear.

Soviet foreign policy is also being debated at great length by the unofficial groups throughout the USSR. They have been influenced by the Greens, European Nuclear Disarmament and similar currents of thought. Take, for example, Victor Alexandrovich Gershfeld. His grandfather was a founder-member of the Bolshevik Party, and his father was a General serving under Trotsky and Tukachevsky during the Civil War. Gershfeld himself, at the age of sixteen, become a volunteer and defended Moscow against the Nazis. Having joined the Red Army in 1944, he served as a colonel until 1959. When Khruschev was encouraging military reductions, Gershfeld went to Moscow University to study history. Later he joined the Institute of World Economy, but much of his knowledge of world politics was gained during his army years when he travelled abroad to Germany and France. Gershfeld's intransigent inter-nationalism got him into trouble at the Institute, as he told me in April 1988:

My first clash with the bosses at the Institute was on Sino-Soviet relations. I had written a number of monographs on this subject. I had initially been fired from the Institute for my views in 1968 and was restored only after a year. Well my opinion was that though Maoism smelt too much like Stalinism and was detrimental for China, nonetheless it was the Soviet Union which was responsible for the deterioration of relations. Despite my very great respect for Khruschev—his denunciation of Stalin and releasing the prisoners—I believe that the rift with China was his most serious blunder. I would even call it a crime. It was a continuation of some of our domestic policies. Here was a case of lack of respect towards human beings and constituent republics within the Soviet Union being extended to fraternal countries. Of course Khruschev should have gone to Camp David to meet the American President, but he should have done so via Beijing.

My second big confrontation was on the invasion of Czechoslovakia. Quite frankly I regarded that as an act of counter-revolution. It objectively merged with the counter-revolution being carried out by the rulers of the West during those years. The Conservatives in Western Europe were trying to submerge what the Austrian communist Ernst Fischer called the 'revolution of dreams' and we were doing it in Eastern Europe. Thus we helped to suspend the revolutionary process in Europe. If we had supported Czechoslovakia in 1968 I am sure European history could have been different.

Gershfeld is active in the Communist Party as well as being a major spokesperson for the Popular Front for perestroika. He speaks affectionately of 'this Misha Gorbachev who has offered us hope once again', but he is critical of the leadership's failure to understand the importance of contacts with movements and parties not in governmental positions:

It should always be remembered that it was the Left and democratic movements which helped to save us in 1918–19 by the Hands Off Revolutionary Russia campaigns. In the Second World War we needed an alliance to defeat the fascists. In the postwar period our isolation was broken by the revolutions in the third world, principally China, and then the war in Vietnam showed up the futility of US military power and enabled us to achieve military parity. Listen, I'm all for Gorbachev, but there is still a strong tendency to underestimate the left democratic forces and movements in our world. Too much emphasis is given to relations between Tsars and monarchs and too little attention is paid to improving our relations with democratic and socialist groups. I understand that Franz Josef Strauss is an important interlocuter, but the Green Party, the British Labour Party, the Communists and Le Fontaine as well as the great diversity of progressive forces are a much more important factor.

Gershfeld's friction with the Institute of World Economy increased further when he wrote a text entitled *Peaceful Offensive*. He proposed a global peace offensive around the borders of the Soviet Union. He wanted the USSR to publicly pledge that it would not impose its will on countries by force, and this created a real furore in the Institute.

Gorbachev's speeches in Murmansk and in Belgrade indicate that he is coming round to my positions. When we first started to contemplate the idea of invading Afghanistan my shouts could be heard on all the several storeys of the building. Not because I am a pacifist. I am an officer, a military man and if I had been a young captain I would have participated in the Afghan war. My objections were that it was morally wrong, a stupid and unproductive act.... Any kind of assistance, scientific, economic, military was, of course, essential, but the invasion was a dreadful mistake.

We are supposed to be a super-power, but the Brezhnevite rubbish and many of them are still in power don't realise this fact. What sort of a superpower were we to be frightened by a demonstration of refuseniks in Red Square? In any case I am convinced that with Gorbachev and Shevernadze at the helm we can take some real initiatives. I think it is perfectly possible to unilaterally reduce our armed forces by fifty percent by the year 2000. Restore friendly relations with China: liquidate the frontline on the Sino-Soviet borders, excepting the sea coast. Yugoslavia and Rumania are reducing their military budgets. So is China. There are good developments in the Balkans though they are hushed up in the press. There are moves towards a Balkan Federation. They don't use the word. They say 'union' so as not to frighten too many bureaucrats, but I am optimistic.

But what about the key question in Europe: German unification. I asked Gershfeld about this, not at all sure of how he would reply. As a Red Army man who fought in World War Two he could have frozen at this point, but, in fact, he melted even further:

Look here. Mischenka Gorbachev, who I like very much, and Shevernadze are saying now that the German issue could be solved in a hundred years. I don't agree with the 'hundred years'. I think the left democratic movement must change their vision on the unification of Germany and not let the issue be monopolised by the German Right. This question stands in the way of all East-West problems.... the vision of a neutral and unified German scares NATO and the Warsaw Pact. It won't happen overnight, but the left democratic movements must raise this issue for consideration right now! We must work out our stand on it and introduce this issue into the work of the peace movement. A neutral Scandinavia, a neutral Balkans and a neutral Austria and Germany will help to greatly reduce the chances of World War Three.

Gershfeld had told me that he regarded himself as a modern Bolshevik, but he was very sympathetic to the German Greens. 'A Green Bolshevik?' I inquired. 'Why not?' he riposted. 'Who has anything against the colour green ... I suppose the functionaries in the Foreign Ministries of Europe, but I am for it!' As I was leaving his apartment Gershfeld explained his motto which should be emblazoned on the new emblems of the USSR: 'From the Dictatorship of Weakness to a Democracy of Strength.'

Federation of Soviet Clubs, Leningrad, 1988.

8. WHERE IS THE SOVIET UNION GOING?

'What has happened to the Russians?' I remember the Chegems used to wonder sometimes, with a kind of bewilderment and sorrow.

I believe this question was asked first when the Chegems learned that Lenin had not been buried, but put on display in a coffin in a special place called 'Amausoleum'.

The burial of the dead was so crucial an act to the Chegems that their moral sensibility could never accept the fact that for years the dead Lenin lay in a place above the ground, instead of lying in the earth and merging with the earth.

In general the Chegem attitude to Lenin was one of mysterious tenderness. In part the reason for this feeling may have been that they only really learned anything about the great man's life when they heard about his death and about this iniquitous refusal to commit his remains to the earth. Until then, except for Uncle Sandro and maybe two or three other Chegems, they knew little about Lenin's existence.

I believe this is how the Chegem myth about Lenin arose. The Chegems said of him that he wanted the good, but couldn't manage it. Precisely what good, they didn't specify. Sometimes, ashamed at hearing his name taken in vain and in a way encoding it against the evil curiosity of the forces of nature, they didn't name him but said: He who Desired the Good but did not succeed.

Fazil Iskander, *Kharlampo and Despina, Yunost* magazine, 1988

The entire theme of *Revolution From Above* has been that what is happening in the Soviet Union today is merely the beginnings of a process.

Since the state of dual power that exists within the apparatus was not resolved at the Nineteenth Party Conference, it is impossible to state with certainty the exact course that this political revolution from above will take. It is, of course, extremely tempting to say or, at least, think that there can be no going back. In a partial sense this is true. The evolution of Soviet society since the death of Stalin has been characterised by ups and downs—Khrushchevs and Brezhnevs, Andropovs and Chernenkos—but neither Brezhnev, leave alone Chernenko, were able to turn the clock back full circle. In that sense one can say that a number of the gains would not be reversed even if Gorbachev and Yakovlev were replaced by Razumovsky and Zaikov. The political and economic problems confronting Soviet society, however, are so deep rooted that halting the process now and standing still would create an enormous backlash.

The answer given by most people to a question often asked inside the USSR, namely, what would be the consequences if Gorbachev were to be defeated, is usually very blunt. The Soviet Union would, in the event of the reformers being effectively defeated, confront a social and political Chernobyl. A disaster not even worth contemplating, I was told, but this did not stop the person saying this from contemplating it in great detail! Nor is the process confined to Moscow and its environs. The political stirrings in Siberia, in the Urals, in Armenia, in the Kuriles during the pre-conference period are a very clear sign that what has already happened has encouraged growing mass participation in social and political life. The factories have not been immune to this process nor has the KGB. A point often forgotten in the West is that the most politically advanced workers, with rare exceptions, tend to be members of the Communist Party.

This was brought home to me during a conversation in Moscow in July 1988 with Piotr Siuda, a leader of the Novocherkask strike of 1962 against an increase in food prices. There was a general strike in the town and several workers were shot dead. Siuda, the son of an old Bolshevik executed by Stalin, but who already had been rehabilitated in 1939 (Beria stated that it was one of Yezhov's crimes!), was sent to a prison camp for his leadership of the strike and spent several years in the North. He was excited by the changes, but disappointed that the Party conference had not taken the necessary decisions. When I asked why he was not in the Party he argued forcefully that he did not regard it as a crucial arena of struggle. We argued backwards and forwards on this particular topic. Given that the Gorbachev leadership had revived mass politics and given the level of resistance by the bureaucracy was it not, I suggested, despite everything, still the main arena of political debate, discussion and struggle. He was not convinced. I then asked him what type of workers joined the Communist Party in the Soviet Union. 'Oh well,' he said energetically, 'it's very different in the plants than in the intellectual professions. I would say that many intellectuals join the Party for careerist reasons. It's not like that for workers. The most idealistic workers join the party.' I thought that this tended somewhat to prove my point, but he was still not convinced.

The fact is that some of the strongest pleas for democratisation have been penned by workers; some of the most concrete demands for destroying the bureaucratic powers of party secretaries and instituting a strict system of rank-and-file control through regular elections, has come from workers. So any idea that the only thing Soviet workers are interested in is their wages or low food prices is simply wrong. They are interested in those things too—and a lot more besides—but they know perfectly well that one way they will get them is through a greater democratisation. They are also the victims of the past and know full well the price that has been paid for the crimes and mistakes of the Thirties people. 'Suppose,' I asked an active member of the CPSU, 'they tried to remove Gorbachev?' 'Civil War!' was her reply. Now I do not think she meant this literally, in the sense of the other Civil War, but what she was saying is that there would be a massive resistance from below. The reformers are simply not prepared for another round of servile integration in a corrupt and uncontrollable apparatus.

The leaders of the Bolshevik Party had been in the habit of evoking the French Revolution as a permanent lesson. The spectre of Thermidor* haunted them during the early years. When the Kronstradt uprising took place, Lenin saw it as a 'Thermidor' and wanted it suppressed at all costs. In 1926–27, Trotsky saw 'Thermidor' in the figure of Stalin to whom he said at a meeting of the Politburo: 'You are the gravedigger of the Revolution.' Analogies from 1793 were not totally inapposite, but Lenin and Trotsky both underestimated the persistence of the old society in Russia itself. The civil war, it is true, had been a brutal and vicious affair. It had brought to the surface much of the ugliness which the Revolutions of 1917 had appeared to transcend. It was not only the White armies who unleashed pogroms against the Jews. Undisciplined Red Army commanders often treated the Jews in the same way and the situation got so serious that a Politburo discussion initiated by Trotsky in 1919 considered the problem in great detail. It is true that anti-Semitism was criminalised by the Bolsheviks, but obscurantism and irrationality can not be done away with by legislation or good intentions. Anti-semitism ran very, very deep in Tsarist Russia. It should not be a total surprise, then, to find it in the factories or in the Bolshevik Party. Stalin's blatant anti-semitism *after* the Second World War and the holocaust shocked communists of Jewish origin throughout the world. Was this the last sign of senile

---

*Thermidor was the month according to the French revolutionary calendar of 1789 in which the radical Jacobins led by Robespierre were overthrown in July 1794. The old Bolsheviks were haunted by this and Trotsky later used this term as a historical analogy to designate Stalin's seizure of power.

decay enveloping a desperate despot? The theory is tempting, but sadly false. At the Fifth Party Congress in 1907, when the factional war against the Mensheviks was at its height a Bolshevik delegate, Alexinsky, had made the point that Jews tended to be more Menshevik than Bolshevik. This genetic default was further stressed by Stalin in the following remarks:

> No less interesting is the national composition of the congress. The figures showed that the majority of the Menshevik group were Jews (not counting the Bundists of course), then came Georgians and then Russians. On the other hand, the overwhelming majority of the Bolshevik group were Russians, then came Jews (not counting Poles and Letts, of course), then Georgians, etc. In this connection one of the Bolsheviks (I think it was comrade Alexinsky) observed in jest that the Mensheviks constituted a Jewish group while the Bolsheviks constituted a true-Russian group and, therefore, it wouldn't be a bad idea for us Bolsheviks to organise a pogrom in the Party.

The fact the Bolsheviks of Jewish origin were strongly represented in the leadership of the Moscow and Petrograd parties during the Revolution was often used by the fascist Black Hundreds in their propaganda. 'The Jews have killed out Tsar' was a common theme of the period. It is true that a large section of the Jewish intelligentsia was sympathetic to Russian Social-Democracy. How could it have been otherwise in an absolutist state, but after 1917 the Jewish communities, like the rest of society, were divided. Mikhail Agursky, in his book on National Bolshevism, recounts the case of two brothers of Jewish origin: one of them, Sverdlov became a major leader of the Bolshevik Party and the first President of the infant Soviet Republic. He was the person Lenin trusted completely as the organiser of the party and, if typhus had not claimed his life in 1920, he was the person considered most likely to have run the party apparatus. Stalin stepped into his shoes. As young students, both brothers had been close to Maxim Gorky. Zinovy Sverdlov was adopted by Gorky as a son and baptised. He took Gorky's real name, Peshkov, and during the civil war he fought with the Whites, ultimately leaving Russia with General Wrangel and settling in France. Here he became a close friend of De Gaulle and remained prominent in rightwing French politics till his death in 1966. There were lesser known but numerous other cases of this sort.

Another interesting feature of that period was that popular perceptions were often coloured by somewhat bizarre notions of seeing the 'Bolsheviks' as Russians, but the 'Communists' as aliens and, needless to add, Jews.

The Russian Right was, of course, deeply hostile to October 1917, but the more intelligent figures in the Cadet Party were obsessed with one question: would the central priority of the Bolsheviks be the world revolution (ie. a European outlook) or reinvigorating Russia (ie. socialism in one Country)? Nikolai Ustrialov, a Moscow Professor, whose writings were carefully read by Lenin and Trotsky, was an active member and ideologue of the Cadets. On 24 December 1917, Ulstrialov wrote an interesting article in which he highlighted the nationalist aspect of the Bolshevik seizure of power and tried to claim October for the Slavophiles:

> The events we go through are organically linked with all the history of our liberation movement. They are authentic, they are national. They are part and parcel of our flesh, of our blood. All the Russian intelligentsia and all the Russian people are directly responsible for the current revolution. There is nothing accidental in what happened. *Even if there is not now any Great Russia, it will revive, it will be resurrected.* The sickness is undoubtedly very deep, but it is a sickness of a great organism. It is the greatest event of world history in spite of its nightmarish qualities (my italics—TA).

Here was the authentic voice of Great-Russian chauvinism. On 21 February 1918, Ustrialov announced that German domination was a bigger evil than the Bolsheviks: 'One can hate a red banner, but it is impossible to betray a national banner . . . We would like to bless the slaying of the Bolsheviks, but only by Russian hands . . .' He then did attempt to do precisely that after 1918, but soon his friends had fled to the West. By 1920 the far-Right was trying to accommodate the new regime. Vasily Shulgin wrote a remarkable book which was published in Sofia and republished in Leningrad in 1926 under the title *1920.* Here Shulgin wrote: 'Under the shell of the Soviet state there is a process which has nothing to do with Bolshevism.' Shulgin argued that the old ideas and methods would find their instrument inside the ranks of Bolshevism and that a future leader would emerge who would be a 'Bolshevik in the extent of energy and a nationalist by persuasion.' Shulgin insisted that neither Lenin nor Trotsky could fulfil such a role. They were too deeply immersed in a European culture. Anti-semitism was not confined to politicians. The poet Yesenin introduced a Jewish commissar, Tchekistov, who was portrayed as despising the backwardness of Russians. In fact, as Agursky points out, the words put in the mouth of the Jewish Commissar were 'a carbon copy of what was said of the Russians, not by the Jews, but by Lenin and Gorky'. The poem in itself was not distinguished by its literary brilliance:

TCHEKISTOV: Your people sit like loafers
                   and don't want to help themselves.
                   Nobody is as mediocre and hypocritical
                   as your Russian muzhik-plainsman.
                   If he lives in Riazan province
                   he doesn't care about Tula province.
                   How much better is Europe!
                   You won't find such huts there
                   which, like silly hens, need
                   their heads cut off with an ax.

ZAMARASHKIN: Listen, Tchestov
                   Since when
                   have you become a foreigner?
                   I know that you're a Jew,
                   your name is Liebman,
                   the hell with you, you lived abroad...
                   Only your house in Mogilev.

TCHEKISTOV: Ha, ha!
                   No, Zamarashkin,
                   I am a Weimar citizen
                   and came here, not as a Jew,
                   but, as someone with a talent
                   for taming fools and animals.
                   I scold and will persistently
                   curse you for even a thousand years.
                   Since....
                   Since I'd like to go to the lavatory
                   and there are no lavatories in Russia!
                   You are a strange and ridiculous people
                   you lived all your life in poverty
                   and built divine temples
                   and I want to rebuild them
                   for a long time as latrines.

Yesenin was continuing the tradition of Dostoevsky, a great
novelist, but a pan-Slavic nationalist and a staunch antisemite. This
tradition is far from dead in the Soviet intelligentsia today. The
merger of Great Russian chauvinism and declining political
consciousness in the working class helped the birth of Stalinism. The
consolidation of this system required the elimination of cosmopoli-
tanism (in the real sense of the word and not as a euphemism for
communists of Jewish origin). Ustrialov and his followers gave
Stalin full backing against the Left Opposition and the national

minorities. Ustrialov wrote in October 1926:

> ... it must be recognised that a number of actual concessions recently
> made by the party to the Opposition cannot fail to inspire serious
> misapprehension. All hail to the Political Bureau if the declaration of
> repentance on the part of the leaders of the Opposition is the result of a
> one-sided and unconditional capitulation. But woe to it, if it is the fruit
> of a compromise with them.... The victorious Central Executive
> Committee must acquire an inner immunity against the decomposing
> poison of the Opposition.... Otherwise it will be a calamity for our
> country... That is why we are now definitely in favour of Stalin.

The fact is that the nationalists, like their counterparts elsewhere
in Europe, deliberately ignored or falsified the history of their
country. Stalinism, in that aspect, took Russian nationalism to the
extreme. Pokrovsky, a leading Soviet historian, criticised Trotsky's
historical writings on Russia as deviations because they stressed the
'backwardness' of Russia and insisted that Russia could not go it
alone! In reality Russia has been as good an adaptor and utiliser of
skills, methods, theories, technology and art forms from the rest of
the world as any other European nation.

The Russian language, which is an Indo-European tongue,
derives its contemporary script through Cyril and Methodicus, who
used the Greek alphabet as a prototype.

Christianity arrived in Old Russia via Byzantium. Ivan assumed
the title of Tsar which is a derivative of Caesar. Prior to this the rulers
had used the title 'Knyaz', borrowed from the Scandinavian
'Koning'. Opera derived from art forms brought in from Italy and
France. This was also the case with ballet. The beginnings of Russian
classical music lie partly in church chorals and folk music, but are, in
the main, borrowed from the Western classical tradition. Glinka,
Borodin, Rimsky-Korsakov, Tchaikovsky and other great com-
posers travelled widely and drew on Western traditions and systems
of music. In these examples we see that local traditions existed, but
were enriched (music), transformed (ballet) or surpassed (shift to
Cyrillic, discarding of older faiths in favour of Orthodoxy). The
synthesis helped in the modernisation of Russian culture. In the
Tsar's battle with Napoleon, the majority of Tsarist Generals were
Germans, Frenchmen or Austrians! In the field of technology the
gains were even more important. Thus the somewhat striking
fashion in which the Soviet state adopted a philosophy described by
its founding father as a synthesis of French socialism, English
classical Political Economy and German classical Philosophy, was

nothing more or less but the continuation of an ever present tradition by revolutionary means.

None of this should be taken to mean that the political-cultural winds from elsewhere automatically transformed Russian consiousness. A permanent struggle was necessary. In Central Asia the fight for Soviet power after 1917 took on the flavour of Russian imperialism. Many of the disbanded Black Hundreds and other wasted individuals realised that the Empire could only be preserved by new methods and a new ideology. A significant number of these individuals joined the Bolsheviks in Central Asia and helped to destroy cities and punish the locals. Removing the Emirs and feudal/tribal chiefs was one thing, but punitive military measures and vandalism put the integration of Central Asia in a different light. Bolshevism was very weak. Local backwardness was dominant and it was defeated by Russian nationalist methods. The three Republics of the Caucasus represented a different problem. Here the workers movement was strong. The Bolsheviks had a strong base in Baku; the Mensheviks were strong in Tbilisi; both factions were weak in Yerevan. As we have already pointed out Menshevik Georgia was invaded by force in 1921 and occupied by the Red Army under its political commissar, the Georgian Bolshevik Orzhonokidze.

Lenin had put forward the idea of a Caucasian Federation which united the three Republics economically, politically and administratively. The Central Committee of the Georgian Bolsheviks opposed the project outright. They argued, not without reason, that the population had already been insulted by the method of removing the Menshevik government, that national feelings were strong and that they preferred a system of independence within the Soviet system. They also disliked intensely the proconsular behaviour of Orzhonokidze. One of the opponents of the plan was the veteran Georgian Bolshevik, Makharadze. Nobody could accuse him of a nationalist deviation. He had opposed Lenin's principle of self-determination for nations on a Luxemburgist basis. The Georgian Congress of Soviets declared its opposition to the federation plan and re-asserted Georgian independence within the new Soviet federation. Lenin, from his sick-bed, read all the papers and began to investigate the whole question. He met both sides and it became clear over a period of several months that the majority of Georgia was with Makharadze and not with the Commisar of Nationalities (Stalin) or Orzhonikidze. Lenin, characteristically, retreated and prepared the basis for the existence of a Soviet Union, which was conceived of as a voluntary federation. In his 'Testament' to the party he apologised for his mistake: 'I suppose I have been very remiss with respect to the workers of Russia for not having intervened energetically and decisively enough on the notorious question of autonomisation which, it appears, is officially called the question of the Union of Soviet Socialist Republics.... What a mess we've got ourselves into.' He denounced 'that really Russian man, the Great Russian chauvinist, in substance a rascal and a tyrant, such as the typical Russian Bureaucrat is' and he stated bluntly that this problem existed in the Soviet regime. He denounced the behaviour of Orzhonikidze in using physical violence against a Georgian comrade while Dzerzhinsky watched passively. He demanded that both men be removed from the Party!

Stalin's revenge was, characteristically, brutal. In the years that followed all the Georgian Bolsheviks who had opposed him and made common cause with Lenin were dragged out of their homes and executed. In fact the Georgian Communist Party was totally decimated. Stalinism preserved the Union by sheer physical force. Little Stalins emerged in the Republics who modelled everything on Moscow. All feelings, and not only nationalist ones, were either repressed or suppressed. At the Twelfth Party Congress in 1923, Stalin was criticised on the nationalities policy. Christian Rakovsky defended Lenin's position in a sharp way, though Trotsky on whom Lenin had relied to take the fight to the Conference remained silent. Akmal Ikramov, a Bolshevik leader from Uzbekistan, reproached the Central Committee for its total failure to undertake educational and ideological work in the national republics. He too would later be punished by Stalin and lose his life.

In 1987–88 as the scandal of the mafiocracy in Uzbekistan erupted and key leaders were arrested, Ikramov's son wrote an article entitled 'The Zone of Silence' and despatched it to the *Literaturnaya Gazetta*. The editor, a veteran Stalinist, Chaikovsky, although one who usually permits the younger journalists on his staff to publish what they want, was extremely disturbed by this particular text, as was his deputy Yezumov, a former crony of the disgraced leader of the Moscow mafiocracy, Victor Grishin. Chaikovsky told the journalist that the article was *sub judice* since the trial of the arch-criminal Adilov had not taken place. The journalists did not believe this was the real reason, but they rang Ikramov junior who revised the article and had it delivered to the paper the next day. Chaikovsky was annoyed, and refused to let it be printed. It appeared the following week in *Pravda,* but it indicated that the death agony of Stalinism was somewhat protracted.*

Re-reading Lenin's initial proposal to unify the Caucasian Republics one can't help wondering whether the old man had some premonition of what might happen several decades later. If the Federation had been pushed through would the question have been solved? It is, of course, possible that the small region of Nagorno-Karabakh would not have existed, but it would be foolish to think that an administrative order would have simply dissolved the national question.

The national question was considered 'solved' by Stalin. Khrushschev had no occasion to comment on or deal with the national aspects of politics in the Soviet Union. Brezhnevism laid the basis for permitting the bureaucracies in the national republics to run their regions without too much interference from Moscow. All the vices of the Moscow mafiocracy were repeated in most of the Republics. Witness the following scene in Uzbekistan in the late Seventies: there is a big reception for Leonid Brezhnev in Taskent. All the local notables are present. During the celebration a diffident comrade Adilov arrives and presents comrade Rashidov (the First Secretary of the Uzbek Party) with a gold bust of himself. Brezhnev looks at the solid gold and mutters appreciatively as he is intended to do since the whole charade has been elaborately planned. Rashidov asks Brezhnev whether he would like a similar bust of himself. Brezhnev nods and roars with appreciative laughter. Adilov is instructed to have one prepared. The instruction is carried out. Rashidov will later die in odd circumstances. Adilov is currently in prison for large-scale corruption, torture and murder. The autonomy enjoyed by the local élites under Brezhnevism took regressively nationalist forms. There is popular national sentiment which takes the form of a pride in language, culture and historical traditions. This is common throughout the Soviet Union and deserves protection. Stalin's mass deportations of the Crimean Tatars and the Volga Germans, amongst others, was a crime on a

---

* 'The Zone of Silence' was a searing indictment of the effects of Stalin and Brezhnev's policies in Soviet Central Asia which brought to light many new atrocities. Chaikovsky and Yezumov have a habit of writing on the margin of articles such as these the phrase: 'What about our lofty ideals?' a phrase which is treated somewhat cynically by the staff. Both men were in fact appointed by the Central Committee secretariat. If it was up to the journalists and writers who regularly contribute to the newspaper they would be voted out immediately.

big scale, but nothing like that has ever been repeated. Instead the local leaderships have sought to win a legitimacy for themselves by using the more ugly aspects of nationalism: theories of racial/cultural superiority, etc. These are designed to distract attention from the feudal methods used by the bureaucracy and to cover up a whole host of crimes.

Lenin may have been wrong in the timing of his proposal for a Caucasian Federation, but the idea as such is a useful one. Moscow, however, rejected any notion of inter-republic solidarity. It emerged in the Soviet press that the leaderships of Armenia and Azerbaijan had not met for fifteen years; the leaders of Uzbekistan and Tadjikistan had not met for twenty years. They spoke to each other via Moscow. That is one part of the explanation for the uprising in Nagorno-Karabakh, a region which is administered by Azerbaijan, but a majority of whose population is Armenian. The main demand was for the region to be handed back to Armenia. This was rejected by Moscow. A compromise solution was proposed: direct rule from Moscow pending a full settlement. This was turned down by the Supreme Soviet after a long and frank discussion, much of which was broadcast live on Soviet TV. The fact is that thought the Nagorno-Karabakh explosion in 1988 took a national form, an extremely powerful Soviet TV documentary which lasted two hours and was shown on prime time in April 1988 told a different story. The national resentment was the cover to complain about appalling living conditions (the slums in the capital of Nagorno-Karabakh reminded me of shanty-towns in Mexico); shortage of basic food supplies and an aloof and distant bureaucracy, which was Azarbaijani and thus seen as totally oblivious to the needs of the majority of the population.

A speaker during the Supreme Soviet debate referred to the crisis in the Caucasus as a 'landmine under perestroika' and Gorbachev himself acknowledged that unless a solution was found it could have 'far-reaching consequences for all perestroika.' Now it is useful to ask why this should be the case. The crisis has revealed the weakness of the Communist Party in Armenia and Nagorno-Karabakh. The giant strikes and demonstrations have revealed the masses totally out of the control of the party apparatus. This is the real 'problem' for the leadership. If the situation is not brought under control it is feared that the supporters of the status quo will demand a stop to the entire process. For those who look upon every nationalist manifestation as something positive (and the Left has a fair share of people who give a progressive gloss to the same events which the Right gleefully paints as the beginning of the end of the Soviet Union) there are problems. Hundreds of thousands of people have demonstrated in Azerbaijan as well. The Armenians, especially in the early demonstration carried the portrait of Gorbachev and supported the slogan of perestroika. The Azerbaijain masses chanted the slogan; 'Ligachev for First Secretary' and clearly favoured a halt and a return to the *status quo ante*. The criteria for evaluating a struggle with nationalist overtones has to be within the context of an overall political judgement of what is happening in the USSR. Jonathan Steele voiced a perceptive criticism of the authorities in a despatch from Moscow which was published in the *Guardian* in London on 27 July 1988:

> Perhaps the greatest weakness is the inability to see people's behaviour in any complexity. The system still tends to treat society as a set of wooden categories—youth, women, the intelligentsia, the working class, and so on. 'Why are the strikes being allowed to continue?' an extraordinary article in *Izvestia* asked the other day... 'The working class has not yet had its say. It is high time it did.' One hesitated to point out to the *Izvestia* man that the 'working class' was having its say, even as he wrote. Many, perhaps most, of its members were on strike.

The debate in the Supreme Soviet in July 1988 revealed a tense and nervous First Secretary. At the Nineteenth Party Conference he had been in an ebullient mood and his interruptions of speakers were generally regarded as benign and encouraging. The discussion on the Nagorno-Karabakh crisis revealed a somewhat distant Russian chieftain. Gorbachev's rudeness and constant heckling of a distinguished Armenian academic was not a very pleasant sight. Here was a political leader who had stubbornly refused to visit Nagorno-Karabakh, Armenia or Azerbaijan during the height of the crisis, and who was now reprimanding the Armenians for making their voice heard. Fortunately the Armenian Professor did not get intimidated but fought his ground well. The decision of the Supreme Soviet, approved in advance by the Politburo was nothing short of scandalous. It essentially backed the Azerbaijani case instead of preserving an essential neutrality. In fact the proposal of E. Primakov, Head of the Institute of World Economy, was a sensible compromise. He argued that Nagorno-Karabakh be given either the status of an autonomous republic or be ruled directly from Moscow for the next period, to permit a cooling of tensions. Both these ideas were rejected. It is obvious that the Politburo had taken a very hard line. In that case one could ask why there should not be reports of the Politburo meeting published in the press. It would be useful for the population as a whole to know who says what on the body which still determines all. Gorbachev may genuinely believe that he did the right thing, or he may have been a prisoner of the Politburo. Whatever the truth the consequences have not been good. If the removal of Boris Yeltsin marked the first real defeat for the new leadership, it has to be said that the decisions on Nagorno-Karabakh and the conduct of the First Secretary represents a second grave error, whose consequences can not be underestimated.

The future of the Soviet Union will be decided on three levels: the transformations in the economy: the full democratisation of Soviet society and, an important corallary of the latter, a correct evaluation of the national question. Neither the collectivisations, not the bureaucratic methods of planning, nor Brezhnevite corruption have succeeded in finding a solution to the latter. An economy more responsive to mass needs, a democracy which permits the birth of new organisations would go a long way to erasing the fears of the national minorities. They are all three interrelated in the Soviet Union today. This feeling was clear at the Nineteenth Party Conference in June 1988. The fear of the apparatus is that opening up politically could lead to the formation of nationalist parties. Perhaps. The antidote, however, does not lie in bureaucratic repression, but in refounding the CPSU by changing its functions. This, in its turn, is tied to the democratisation of the Soviets and a rigid separation of party and state institutions. Now many of the ideas on this level have been initiated from above. Their implentation, however, will depend on a movement from below. It is only when the soviets are multi-party bodies that a real separation between the CPSU and the state can take place. A single party can guarantee many things, but *not* democracy. For pointing this out, L. I. Abalkin, a delegate to the Conference was strongly criticised, but surely he was one hundred per cent correct. His view is shared by countless rank-and-file reformers inside the CPSU, for they, too, are deprived of their rights as members of a political party. They are only waiting to be permitted to turn all their political energies towards a movement from below that implements perestroika.

For over six decades socialists outside the Soviet Union have sat and watched in despair. I naturally exclude from this category those who have blindly supported every twist and turn of Soviet domestic and foreign policy, because that has much more to do with religion than any tradition within classical Marxism. The world is observing the opening shots of what might be a long battle, but the very fact that Soviet society is on the move again is a cause for celebration and joy. And this brings us back to Fazil Iskander's Chegems at the beginning of this chapter. What about the 'One who Desired the Good but did not Succeed'? Stalin's revenge against Lenin was to commit the crimes against socialism in his name. For that purpose Lenin was drained of all content and transformed into an icon: his thoughts were distorted and misused as religious incantations; his writings became a dreary catechism for the faithful. Whatever his mistakes and shortcomings—and they undoubtedly existed—the burden of Stalinism can not be laid on his shoulders.

The decision to pump Lenin's body full of chemicals and display his mummified remains was an affront to the entire Marxist tradition. His widow's cries of outrage were cruelly ignored. The time has come to bury Lenin's body once and for all. It will be a cathartic process for many but it is the only way.

I

Boris Yeltsin's Speech at
Nineteenth Party Conference, June 1988

Speech of comrade B.N. Yeltsin, (First deputy chairman of Gosstroi USSR—minister of the USSR), *Pravda*, 2 July 1988. Translated by Judith Shapiro.

Comrade delegates! First of all I must answer a series of questions as demanded by Comrade Zagainov who spoke here.

The first question. Why did I give an interview to foreign television, and not to the Soviet press? I'll answer. First of all APN approached me, and I gave them an interview, a long time before the television companies. But that interview wasn't printed in *Moscow News*.

Later APN approached me a second time, but, as they say, also without a guarantee that the interview would be printed. The editorial office of *Ogonyok* approached me for an interview before that. I gave a two-hour interview, but this interview hasn't been published, although a month and a half has passed. According to comrade Korotich's statement, you see, it wasn't permitted.

The next question. Why did I speak so 'inarticulately' at the organisational plenum of the Moscow City Party Committee [gorkom]? I'll answer. I was seriously ill, chained to the bed, without the right, without the possibility to get up from that bed. An hour and a half before the plenum they called me to the plenum and so the doctors pumped me full of medicine. And I sat at that plenum, but I couldn't feel anything, and effectively could speak even less.

Further, I received a letter from USSR Gostelradio [State Committee for Television and Radio Broadcasting] with an explanation and request that in connection with the conference they have been assigned to co-ordinate interviews given to foreign television companies by our leaders, and they asked me to give them a series of them.

Up to that time fifteen such requests had accumulated. I said to the first deputy chairman of Gostelradio USSR, comrade Kravchenko, because of time I could give only two to three, not more. After that there followed from the Committee a Telephonegram which fixed three television companies, BBC, CBS, ABC. So I named a time and gave an interview in my office to the three companies. Questions and answers were immediate. I decisively rebuffed improper questions which could be detrimental in any way to our state, party, or their prestige.

Then there were questions in relation to comrade Ligachev. I said that we had a single point of view on the strategic level, on the decisions of the Congress, on the tasks of perestroika etc. But we had some differing points of view on the tactics of perestroika, on questions of social justice, on the style of his work. I didn't go into details. There was this question: Do you consider that if there was someone else in place of comrade Ligachev perestroika would go faster? I answered 'Yes'. Because of the distortion of what I said the US television company CBS carried my refutation and gave me a written apology for the mistake with the signature of the Vice-President of the company.

Then Comrade Solomentsev summoned me, demanded an explanation. I expressed my indignation at the fact of a summons on such a question and answered verbally to each question about the interview. The attempt to find an offence on my part against the [Party] Rules didn't work out. I consider myself completely innocent in this. The tape with the full recording was handed over to comrade Solomentsev by our interpreter. What will be done further with me I don't know, but this is highly reminiscent of the shadow of the recent, not too distant past.

I'll go on to my speech.

Comrade delegates! The main question of the conference as it was conceived is democratisation in the party, bearing in mind that with time it has been seriously deformed. And, of course, discussion of today's burning questions of perestroika as a whole and the revolutionary renewal of society. The period of conference preparation itself called forth unusual interest and hopes among communists and all Soviet people. The perestroika is shaking up the people. And, evidently, the perestroika should have begun with the party itself. Then it would have led eveyone else with it as always. But the party, right from the point of view of the perestroika, lagged behind. That is, it turns out that today's conference should have been held considerably earlier. This is my personal point of view.

But even now the preparations have been somehow hasty. The theses were published late, put together by the CC apparat. They didn't include the main point about the political system which appeared in the report. Even the majority of CC members weren't widely involved in working out the Theses. To take into account in the decisions of our conference all the proposals put forward, all this popular mine of wisdom, of course can't be done.

The election of delegates, despite comrade Razumovsky's attempt in *Pravda* to convince everyone that they were democratic, were nonetheless carried out in a number of organisations according to the old pattern and showed again that the top echelon apparat isn't being restructured.

But discussion at the conference itself is interesting. And now the most important thing, what will be the decisions taken? Will they satisfy the communists of the country, society as a whole? Judging by the first day, the impression was very guarded I would say, even grave. But with each day the incandescence is growing and it is becoming more and more interesting to listen to the delegates, and, obviously, this will be reflected in the decisions taken.

I would like to make some remarks and proposals concerning the CC Theses, taking into account the report of comrade Gorbachev.

On the political system. Here I consider the main thing is that there be a mechanism acting in the party and in society which would preclude errors even closely resembling those of the past, which put our country back decades, wouldn't make for 'vozhds' and 'vozhidism' [great leaders and leadership cults], and would create authentic popular power and give that a firm guarantee.

The proposal of the report on the combining of functions of the first secretary of the party committee and the Soviet organs turned out to be so unexpected for the delegates that a worker here said in his speech that 'he still cannot understand it.' I as a minister say: me too. Time is needed for comprehension. This is too complex a question. And thus I, for instance, propose the holding of a national referendum on this question. [*Applause*]

Some proposals on elections: They should be universal, direct and secret, and that includes secretaries [of party committees] and the General Secretary of the CC, from top to bottom, from among the staff of the oblast bureaus or the Politburo, which should also be elected in the same way by all communists (making two rounds of elections). This should also apply to the Supreme Soviet, the trade unions and Komsomol.

Tenure in an elected post to be limited to two terms, without all sorts of exceptions, especially for the top echelon. Election to a second term only on the basis of real results of work in the previous period. Strict age limits of sixty-five to be introduced in these organs, including the Politburo. The reckoning of terms to begin with the previous elections and the age from this year. Our party and society as a whole have matured sufficiently to trust them to decide such questions independently and perestroika can only gain from this.

All that has been said, and not the proposals by some of a two-party system, will in my opinion be a definite guarantee against a cult of the personality, which will set in not in ten/fifteen years, but will be born right away if it has the soil. I think we already need to beware of it because of the disdain for Leninist principles over the years gone by and the many misfortunes which have befallen the people. There should be strict barriers, established by the Rules or law.

In a number of the country there is an established order: the leader goes, the leadership goes. We are accustomed to blaming the dead for everything. Especially since you won't get any comeback. Now it turns out: only Brezhnev was to blame for the stagnation. And where were those who were in the Politburo for ten, fifteen, twenty years, and are still there now? Each time they voted for the varying programmes. Why were they silent when one man was deciding, on the say-so of the CC apparat, the fate of the party, the country, socialism? They kept on voting until one man had five stars and society as a whole was in crisis. Why was the ill Chernenko put forward? Why was the Party Control Commission, while punishing relatively smallish deviations from the norms of party life, afraid and is still afraid, to undertake proceedings against the major leaders of the republics and oblasts for their bribe-taking, their millions in losses to the state and other things? While certainly knowing something about them. It is necessary to say that this liberalism on the part of comrade Solementsev toward the millionaire-bribetakers causes some unease.

I consider that some members of the Politburo, guilty as members of a collective organ, invested with the confidence of the CC and the Party, should answer: why has the country and the party been reduced to such a state? And after that conclusions should be drawn—to remove them from the Politburo. [*Applause*] This is a more humane step than criticising them posthumously, then moving them to a different grave! The following procedure is proposed for the future: if the general secretary changes, the Politburo is renewed except for those who have recently arrived; in general the CC apparat is also renovated. Then people won't be caught in a permanent administrative trap. Then people won't criticise others only after their death, because they'll know that everyone including all elected organs, has to answer to the party.

And another thing. While the General Secretary has clearly stated there are no zones and leaders above criticism, including him, in fact it doesn't turn out like that. Zones, lines exist, beyond which on the first attempt at criticism is followed by the instant warning 'Don't touch!' And so it turns out that even members of the CC are afraid to express their personal opinion, if they differ from the report, to speak out against the leadership.

This does the greatest damage, deforms the party conscience and personality, trains everyone, with each sentence—'the opinion is'—to immediately raise their hands: all for. The present conference is, very likely, the first exception to this, which has already become the rule. It still happens that a policy pursued by the leading bodies basically remains indisputable, remains above criticism, remains beyond control of the popular masses even today.

One has to agree with the proposal in the report about the creation of commissions on specific spheres, made up of members of the CC, without whose scrutiny and consent no major party CC resolution would be adopted. At present resolutions basically come not from the CC but from its apparatus, and many of them immediately become stillborn. Major drafts should be discussed by the whole party and country, and referenda should be the practice. As a rule joint resolutions of the CC and the Council of Ministers of the USSR should be abolished.

Yes, we are proud of socialism and proud of what has been done, but we must not strut about it. After all, after seventy years we haven't solved the main questions—to feed and clothe people, to take care of the service sector, to solve the social questions. The perestroika of society is directed to this, but it proceeds with a great deal of delay. Which means that each of us is not working hard enough, not fighting enough for it. But also one of the main reasons for the difficulty of the perestroika is its declarative character. It was declared without sufficient analysis of the reasons for the stagnation which has arisen, analysis of the contemporary situation of society, without deep analysis, in the historical context, of the errors and omissions of the party. And as a result of the perestroika, in three years no sort of tangible real problem has been resolved for people, still less have we achieved any sort of revolutionary re-organisation.

In implementing perestroika we should not only set targets for the year 2000 (many are not interested now in what they may or may not happen to be getting then) but we should set one or two tasks to be achieved for the people's benefit every two or three years. Rather than trying to do everything at once, at the expense of other spheres, we should concentrate everything there—resources, science, people's energy etc. Then with a sharply increased faith that the perestroika of society is going forward, that it is producing results, and that it is irreversible, people will decide other problems considerably more rapidly. Right now people's faith could be rocked at any moment. Until now everyone has been hypnotised by words—that has saved us. In the future there is a risk of losing the helm of management and political stability.

And about openness in the Party. In the Party the existence of varied opinions must be a normal phenomenon (after all, it is not a question of standardisation). And the existence of a difference of opinion of a minority will not destroy, but strengthen, the unity of the Party. The Party is for the people and the people should know all that it does. This, unfortunately, is not the case. There should be detailed reports from the Politburo and the Secretariat (apart from questions concerning state secrets) and knowledge of the life and biography of the leaders, what they do, how much they earn and what results there have been from each leader in the top higher echelon in his area. And regular television appearance, the results of admissions to the Party, the summaries of working people's letters to the CC and so on. In general, there should be a whole party sociology about the moral health of the leaders of the Party and the state. It must be open to all, and not secret.

There are 'forbidden' 'secret' topics such as, for example, questions of party budget finances. In the Rules it says 'How the finances are spent is determined by the CC of the CPSU', that is, not the apparatus but the CC. But such questions aren't discussed at Plenums. I propose that in future this should be done without fail since where the party money is spent (and this is hundreds of millions of rubles) isn't known to members of the CC nor, of course, to other communists. The Auditing Commission at the Congress doesn't report on this at the Congress and even they, apparently, don't have access to the till.

I know, for instance, how many millions of rubles are sent to the CC from Moscow and Sverdlovsk oblast party organisations. But where it is spent—I don't know. Only I see that apart from rational expenditures luxurious residences and dachas are built and sanitoria on such a scale that it becomes embarrassing when representatives of other parties go there. Yet that money should be used to support the primary party organisations including their leaders' pay. And then we're surprised that some major party leaders dirty themselves in corruption, bribes, distortions of reports, and have lost their decency, moral purity, modesty, and sense of party comradeship.

The degeneration of the upper strata in the Brezhnev period gripped many regions, and it mustn't be underestimated, simplified. The rot, evidently, is deeper than some suppose, and a mafia, I know from Moscow, definitely exists.

Questions of social justice. Of course, in broad terms, on socialist principles they have been resolved in our country. But there remain some issues which haven't been resolved, and this arouses popular indignation, lowering the authority of the party, and also has pernicious effect on the tempo of perestroika.

My opinion is that this is what should happen: if something is in insufficient supply here, in a socialist society, then the shortage should be felt evenly by all without exception. [Applause] But different contributions of work to society should be regulated by different wages. We should, at last, abolish the food 'rations' for the, so to say, 'starving nomenklatura', eradicate elitism in society, eradicate the substance and the form of the word 'spets' from our lexicon, as we don't have any special communists.

I think that this will very much help party workers in working with people. It will help perestroika.

The structure and reduction of the party apparatus. The Leninist call 'All power to the Soviets!' will not be put into practice with such a mighty party apparatus. I propose to cut the oblast committee apparat to half or a third, the CC to one sixth or one tenth, with the elimination of separate departments.

I would like to say something about youth. There is virtually nothing about them in the theses. The report says a great deal, and I would support the proposal to adopt a separate resolution on youth. It is not we but they who are and will be assigned the main role in the renewal of our socialist society. We must boldly train them to lead the processes at all levels, we must boldly hand over whole layers of leadership at absolutely every level to the youth.

Comrade delegates! The tricky question. I only wanted to turn to the question of the political rehabilitation of me, personally. After the October plenum of the CC. [*Noise in auditorium*] If you consider that time doesn't permit this, then that's all.

M. S. Gorbachev. Boris Nikolaevich, speak, they're asking. [*Applause*] I think we should take the mystery away from the Eltsin affair. Let Boris Nikolaevich say all that he considered necessary to say. And if something occurs to us it can also be said. Please, Boris Nikolaevich.

B. N. Yeltsin. Comrade delegates. Rehabilitation after fifty years has now become customary, and has had a good effect in making society healthier. But I personally ask political rehabilitation in my own lifetime. I consider this question one of principle, in place in the light of the socialist pluralism of opinions, freedom of criticism, tolerance toward opponent proclaimed in the report and in the speeches.

You know that my speech at the October CC plenum of the CPSU was called 'politically mistaken' by a resolution of the Plenum. But questions raised then, at the Plenum, have been repeatedly raised by the press and posed by communists. During these days all these questions have sounded out from this tribune in the report and in the speeches. I consider that my single mistake in my speech was that I came forward at the wrong time—before the seventieth anniversary of the October Revolution.

Evidently all of us need to master the rules of political discussion, to tolerate the opinion of opponents, as V. I. Lenin did, not pinning labels on people right away, considering them heretics.

Comrade delegates! The speeches at the conference and my own speech have fully reflected the issues raised by me at the October [1987] Plenum of the CC of the CPSU. I feel keenly what happened and I ask the conference to revoke the decision of the Plenum on this question. If you consider it possible to revoke it, you will thus rehabilitate me in the eyes of communists. And that is not only personal matter, that will be in the spirit of perestroika, that will be democratic, and, it seems to me, it will help restructuring, having increased people's confidence.

Yes, the renewal of society is difficult. But progress, even though not great, is being made and life itself obliges us to follow only this path. [*Applause*]

II

Complete text of interview with Yuri Afanasiev, April 1988

Could I start by asking you for your impressions of the nineteenth Party Conference and what you think has been achieved?

YA: Answering this question on its own could occupy the best part of today. The subject is very vast. However I'll try and summarise what I think impressed me the most, but please don't regard this as an exhaustive answer to your question. This is the first time since the Twenties that all the vital problems facing the country were actually discussed by the representatives of the Party. Of course previous conferences did discuss certain problems, but never really got down to a proper discussion of the real issues at stake. This time it happened and its importance should not be underestimated. The result was that the situation in the country was seen in all its complexities.

Many problems were posed, but, and this has to be said, there was no clarity as to the solutions. And this too was stated at the Conference. The Conference itself was a continuation of the surge of activity to continue the search for a solution to the outstanding problems which confront our society today. The Conference itself offered a model. If all party forums confronted problems in this way then we could say that this is the major result of the Conference because this is what we need. Secondly, there was the unusual form of the Conference. There were heated debates, explosions of emotion, sincerity, spontaneous speeches, genuine applause and slow handclaps for those who the delegates felt had nothing to say. The audience participation was amazing. The feel of the Conference was of something alive rather than boredom and pomposity, which was usually the case in recent decades.

TA: What you describe sounds just like the Twenties.

YA: Yes, of course. But one has to look further and see what the problems were. We could start with the problem which is the essence of our lives, the economy. There were very different approaches on this front. For instance in Abalkin's speech and in other interventions that it was difficult, if not impossible, to see any major changes in this field since the beginning of perestroika three years ago. He emphasised the fact that the eleventh Five Year Plan period was during the years of stagnation, but it still showed better results than the twelfth Five Year Plan. He explained why by sharing his thoughts with us. The reaction was varied. Some supported him, while others opposed him very strongly. This diversion of views is a positive phenomenon. However I believe that the reaction of many of the party executives from the districts to Abalkin's speech manifested either an inability or a desire to avoid looking truth in the face. So much hostility towards an independent thinking scientist. So I would say that the Conference both alarmed and delighted me.

TA: For those of us watching the pre-Conference preparation from afar the most disturbing aspect was the way that the delegates were elected or rather selected. What was positive, of course, was that the party masses did not simply accept the *fait accompli*. There were protest meetings and demonstrations in Sakhalin, in some towns in the Ukraine and Siberia and your own students at this Institute protested very sharply at the decision by Moscow Executive to reject the overwhelming nominations in your favour. This is healthy, but can not detract from the fundamental problem. The old principle was that delegates are elected by the party rank-and-file members. How do you view all this?

YA: I understand what you're saying, but the formal procedure is that delegates are elected by the regional and district plenums of the executive committees and not by the rank-and-file members. You can of course criticise this aspect of the party constitution, but formally speaking the elections were conducted according to this constitution. Moreover I don't think that you can have only one judgement on the outcome of the elections. Of course you're quite right to stress the efforts of party and non-party members to influence the procedure of nominating delegates at the early stage. This was not just restricted to Moscow, but was a universal phenomenon and I think this was a very positive development. The whole demand by party and non-party members for free elections is a concrete result of perestroika. There open disagreements were expressed with some undemocratic decisions, but alongside all this there was a traditional bureaucratic approach. There were undemocratic elections and there was throughout the entire pre-conference period what we might call the pressure of the apparatus, which has to be sharply criticised. The self-promotion of the functionaries of this apparatus was one of the most negative phenomena of this Conference. But these were the lessons of democracy. The very first and elementary lessons of democracy for the broad masses as well as for members of the party. We could say that these democratic lessons are the equivalent of the entrance exams to junior school.

TA: If we could now move on to the subject of history with which you are directly concerned in your capacity as a Rector of this institute and as someone who speaks often against any forbidden zones in this important discipline. Just to start, could you explain why the history exams have been cancelled throughout the Soviet Union?

YA: I think the answer is very simple, although the problem we confront is itself quite complex. The fact is that history textbooks in our country, especially those concerned with Soviet history are completely falsified. These are not falsifications in some aspects or minor details of one sort or another, but total falsifications. And to make teenagers repeat all these lies in the course of their exams is, quite frankly, immoral. Therefore we had no other option. Naturally this is only a temporary measure, but I think it was necessary.

TA: And are new textbooks being written?

YA: Yes, some steps have been taken. Some people have been entrusted with this task and special teams of authors have been entrusted with this task. But you know here again there is something which I simply cannot accept and I have expressed my disagreement on more than one occasion. I just think that it is unfair, incorrect and counter-productive if the whole country has to simply follow one textbook. This is a continuation of an authoritarian and monolithic approach in the field of pedagogy. This is based on the principle that you should know and learn only what you are given. Nothing more. Such an approach is totally negative and needs to be rejected. There must be a wide selection of texts available and not just that but a wide range of books, which may contradict each other. This is the only way to develop the critical faculties of our students. Both the teacher and the student must have a choice.

TA: Of all the people involved in the debate on history you have been the most forthright in demanding justice for all the old Bolsheviks without exception. So far the process of glasnost has rehabilated almost everyone: Bukharin, Zinoviev, Kamenev, Rykov, Rakovsky, etc. Some have even been posthumously returned their party cards. The question of Trotsky, however still remains unresolved. Why?

YA: The question of Trotsky is a very special one in many respects, at least, this is my opinion. First, none of the Bolshevik old guard around Lenin played such a major role in both the Revolution or the civil war that followed as Trotsky. Secondly, Trotsky is the only one of Lenin's old guard who for many years openly criticised Stalin and Stalinism. Thirdly, Trotsky is part and parcel of the history of the International, especially concerning a study and appraisal of Stalin's regime as nobody else from the old guard. That is why getting rid of the stereotypes of Trotsky in the Soviet Union is a measure of getting rid of the last vestiges of Stalinism in our society. This is why it is a special question.

I am not a Trotskyist sympathiser, but I am in favour of an objective assessment of his role in our history. We should report comprehensively on his work and activities and have an open mind on the question. It is impossible to get rid of the Stalinist legacy without getting rid of the Stalinist stereotype of Trotsky. That is why I insist on objectivity on the question of Trotsky and attach special importance to this issue. And that is why I call for Trotsky's rehabilitation.

TA: Have you actually read Trotsky's *History of the Russian Revolution?*

YA: Yes, I have read it. Not in Russian, but in French. All his major works were available to me in French. I think the History is also available in Russian, but it wasn't published here.

TA: As a historian, what is your estimate of it as a history?

YA: It is a noteworthy work and must be available along with other writings on the Revolution: Plekhanov, Sukhanov, Lenin, Martov, etc. All these writings need to be read and evaluated. There are the histories by the proponents and architects of the revolution and also others by its opponents. There are histories which defend the October Revolution and Trotsky's takes its place amongst them. Martov and Sukhanov are in a slightly different category. And then there are the outright opponents of October like Kerensky and Miliukov. These are all different lines. All these books should be made available and judged on the basis of whether or not they correspond to logic and facts.

TA: Before his death in 1967, Isaac Deutscher had expressed the hope on a number of occasions that his books would one day be published in the Soviet Union. With the advent of glasnost surely it is time that his books are published in the Soviet Union. We read in the papers that Stephen Cohen's biography of Bukharin is going to be published any day. This is very good news, but surely the list should be extended.

YA: You see it is not me who makes the decisions so it is very difficult for me to answer these questions. Personally I think it is quite possible that Deutscher will be published one of these days. I know Deutscher's works and I must say that I think they are ideologically oriented. It is easier to publish non-Marxist historians because they aim at objectivity. Deutscher is ideologically and party oriented. I don't see anything unnatural in this and I think these books should be published. His Trotskyist sympathies are very clear, but this could be made clear in a publisher's statement...

TA: He has, incidentally, been published in China!

YA: Yes, well I think his books are very interesting. They abound in facts and their interpretation. They are very worthy books. There have been quite a lot of derogatory remarks about his work in the Soviet Union and there was a time when we used to shape our thoughts on the basis of these remarks.

TA: The one book which I think is totally objective is *The Unfinished Revolution*. It is translated in Russian and is in the library of the Central Committee. I met a friend who had actually read it in that library while engaged on some other research for the Central Committee apparatus. These are lectures he gave in the fiftieth anniversary year of the Revolution at Cambridge University.

YA: Yes, yes. I know this book. I read it a long time ago.

TA: Well then you will remember that he predicts in this book the emergence of a reform current inside the Soviet Communist Party.

YA: I do not remember everything in the book, but I do recall that it produced a favourable impression on me. I must thank you for reminding me of it again.

TA: Lastly, I would like to ask you about the debate on pluralism. It is a very interesting debate because for those of us who are socialists in the West know that is quite possible to have three large parties who can disagree about the pace of change, but never on the nature of change in capitalist society. So having more than one party doesn't *necessarily* mean a pluralism of ideas. This is especially true of the United States where there are important tactical differences between the Republican and Democratic Parties, but nothing fundamental or strategic divides each from the other. I have followed very closely the debates inside the Soviet Union. The question is this: if you have a pluralism of ideas you can't legislate that it should stop there. Suppose things reach a stage that people who believe in certain ideas wish to organise around these ideas with like-minded people. Ideas rarely exist in isolation for ever. In 1918–19, because of the civil war, all Soviet parties were effectively banned, except for the ruling Bolshevik Party.

At the time of the Tenth Party Conference in 1921 all the leaders of the Bolshevik Party stressed that the banning of tendencies and factions inside the party—in other words the outlawing of dissent within the ranks of Bolshevism—was a temporary measure. Stalin was to utilise this ban to institutionalise authoritarianism in the country. As I see it, it was the banning of other Soviet parties such as the Left Mensheviks and the Left SRs which paved the way for barring pluralism inside the party itself. Now we can see the film being reversed. If pluralism within the party leads to the emergence of other parties surely the heavens will not fall? Don't you think that it is perfectly possible to accommodate other parties within the soviet system? I would have thought that it was perfectly possible to move towards a form of soviet democracy which was much more real in terms of mass participation than any existing capitalist democracy?

YA: Well I must say in the first place that I agree with you. For me what you've just said is perfectly acceptable. I have the same assessment as you of the Tenth Party Conference. It was meant to be a temporary measure. This was indeed the spirit in which that resolution was passed. This 'temporary measure' has lasted from 1921 until 1988. It is impossible to regard this situation as normal. The party must not represent a monolith, because a monolith is like a boulder. It is something totally inanimate. Of course differences of opinion are perfectly normal in a political party. I think that at the present stage there is very great scope for the development of a pluralism of ideas even within the framework of a one-party system. Of course only if the Party itself is radically transformed. What does this mean? It means the Party must abandon the commandist and administrative methods of rule and instead offer guidance through persuasion and participation. In other words a party should lead not by the authority of its physical force, but rather through the force of its moral authority. This is what we are moving towards and that is why this whole subject was much debated at the Nineteenth Party Conference. Secondly, I believe that tendencies and factions should exist inside the Party, which should represent a community of independent ideas. We should have differing platforms articulating differing political positions and that's what will happen soon. I think the existence of tendencies and factions is a positive phenomenon. It's healthy provided that the factions do not behave organisationally in a way that is contrary to the constitution. As for the presence of other organisations it is already a fact. In Estonia there is the Popular Front for Perestroika which is legally registered. There are over 1000 unofficial groups in our country. They are part of the new political realities. On the eve of the Nineteenth Party Conference I was present at a conference of the independent, unofficial groups in Moscow. They had studied and discussed the Theses of the Central Committee which were presented to the Conference and worked out their positions on them. I must say I was impressed by their seriousness. The Party has to see this as part of the growing process of democratisation which has to be taken into account. It must not be ignored and nor should the Party treat these groups in a condescending fashion. I think our life is beginning to manifest what you said but perhaps not in such a clearcut and succinct fashion as you. There are still problems. There remains a hostile attitude to the mass movement and its leaders, but things are moving in the right direction.

TA: There is a fear sometimes expressed both inside and outside the Soviet Union that in this critical time, given the balance of forces within the apparatus, they might remove Gorbachev and Yakovlev in much the same way as they dispensed with Khruschev in 1964. Is this a possibility?

YA: In my opinion, as of today, we do not have any guarantees. We can only have such guarantees if we have social and political institutions which can provide the necessary safeguards. The democratisation process both in the party and the society has a long way to go. At the moment we have just drawn a sketch of the road that needs to be followed. Of course we have done many real things. Glasnost is a reality today and represents a tremendous gain for the whole country. But we still have to revive the soviets because till now they have been inanimate. Public and social organisations have to break from the old mould and begin to correspond to the needs of the democratic society. We have a great deal to do in order to build up the institutions which can guarantee soviet democracy. We must not get hung up on the personal qualities of the leadership. Of course we must rejoice that both Gorbachev and Yakovlev do possess such qualities, but these qualities alone are not enough to make the process of perestroika and democratisation irreversible.

TA: Many of us who remain socialists in the West are beginning to regard the Soviet Union once again as a country of hope. Because if you succeed it could help in the rebirth of mass socialism elsewhere in the world. In that sense the fight for a socialist democracy is not just important for you, but for the whole world.

YA: I think very many of us are well aware of this fact. For me it is obvious that Stalin and Stalinism has damaged the socialist project more than all the bourgeois ideologies in the world added together. Stalinism has discredited the idea of socialism. What will change things is not the quality of all our publications and our debates. It is the change in life itself inside the USSR that will help socialism elsewhere in the world. Don't think we underestimate the difficulties confronted by socialist and workers' parties in the West having to fight for socialism when the model they had before them over the last two decades, for instance, was Brezhnev, Kunaev, etc. I am aware of how much we discredited socialism.

III

A brief Comment on the Debate in *Pravda* on 26 July 1988

Yuri Afanasiev, as readers can judge for themselves in both my interview with him and the polemic in *Pravda*, is one of the most vigorous defenders of perestroika. In the interview Afanasiev goes some way beyond current party orthodoxy on history as well as the question of Trotsky. In this regard it is worth comparing his comments with those of Otto Latsis in the main text of the book.

The *Pravda* debate reveals Afanasiev in a ironical and angry mood. Yet there are two substantial points raised by the editors of *Pravda*, which, it is worth remembering, is the voice of the Politburo. One can therefore assume that the response to Afanasiev reflects the current thinking of that body. The interesting question is whether both Ligachev and Yakovlev would agree with the tone and content of the newspaper's response to the historian. The central issue which preoccupies the daily organ of the Central Committee is whether or not there was another road to the one followed by the Party in the late Twenties and Thirties. Afanasiev, Shatrov and countless others insist that there was an alternative to Stalinism. *Pravda*'s editors note ominously that there was no other alternative, despite the crimes, mistakes, repression, etc. In his critique of this view Afanasiev is on very strong ground, though in the heat of this battle of ideas he leaves his flank unguarded on occasions. He does not consider 'the society in our country socialist, however "deformed" '. *Pravda* seizes this point and asks whether the absence of exploiting classes, unemployment and the 'social ownership of the means of production' constitute a socialist system or not? I doubt whether Afanasiev would deny for a minute that capitalism does not exist in the USSR and was definitely destroyed in October 1917. However it is perfectly possible to argue that the Soviet Union is a society in transition (and seventy years is not a very long period in history) from capitalism, but this does not mean that it *is* already socialist. The material conditions are today present for a rapid transition to socialist democracy, but there is one major obstacle: the bureaucracy. The Soviet élite or nomenklatura is a gigantic roadblock on the road to a fundamental social and political transformation of the country. This is a point which has been made by many supporters of perestroika. When Boris Yeltsin talks of 'social justice' he means ending the privileges of the party bureaucracy. It is the apparatus which stands between socialism and the Soviet Union. Moreover the only force which could get rid of the bureaucracy with very little pain is the party rank-and-file backed by workers in the factories and sections of the intelligentsia. On this debate Afanasiev is one hundred per cent correct and *Pravda* is awkwardly attempting to straddle two positions which are at the moment contradictory. The big danger at the moment is felt by many to lie in the amoeba-like ability of the apparatus to integrate and smother the leaders of the reform programme.

The debate in the pages of *Pravda*, however, does reveal the extent to which politics in the Soviet Union has already changed since 1985. Discussion of this sort has been absent from the political journals in the Soviet Union since the late Twenties. The translation is by Judith Shapiro.

TA

Answers of an Historian

'Questions to a historian' was the name of an item published in Pravda *for 25 June this year. These questions were addressed to Professor Yu. N. Afanas'yev on his article* 'Perestroika and historical knowledge' *in* Literaturnaya Rossiya. *Following this Yu. N. Afanasiev sent Pravda a letter. We print it without abridgement or editing.*

I read with great attention P. Kuznetsov's article in *Pravda* for 25 June with the 'perplexed questions' to myself and his accusations of 'doubtful hypotheses and in places even simply untruths'. In this article and the author's personal views one encounters the political and historical position P. Kuznetsov opposes to that which he considers dubious and false. For me—and for every reader of the newspaper—it is a superb occasion to become pensive.

First of all: I warned that an integral, systematic approach to Soviet history was essential, rather than the helpless evaluation based on the principle of 'on the one hand ... on the other hand'. That is 'on the one hand mass repression and crimes, and on the other daily joy and records'. My opponent answers that 'in actual life tragic repression and the enthusiasm of people building socialism were interwoven'. Enthusiasm, P. Kuznetsov writes, existed (but I in no way intend to simply deny this) however ... 'combined with mass repression'. If 'interwoven' and 'combined' are only other words for the expression of the self-same schema of the 'two hands,' practically borrowed from Saltykov-Shchedrin's 'History of Stupid City'—then I understand at least what logic, in a manner of speaking, the author likes and the sort of 'thoughtful readers' whose sympathies he is counting on. But no! ... Straight out it's said 'For the thoughtful reader it is evident that the division of history into bad and good or into the history of the great leader and the masses diverges from an analysis of real processes ...' Splendid! This means that, if only on this point, it would seem P. Kuznetsov agrees with me—and, consequently, doesn't agree with himself. 'Repression and enthusiasm' it turns out, didn't simply exist side by side, 'combined'—but grew from the same roots and comprised an *inseparable*, the author confesses, historical reality. We'll remember this.

And we turn in this case to the second and main 'perplexing question', which actually consists of two questions: (a) is it possible to consider that under Stalin and his successors some sort of socialist society was successfully built, however insufficiently socialist? (b) was there an historic alternative to 'Stalinist socialism', or was Lenin, with his NEP, reckoned on 'seriously and for a long time', tragically mistaken—and was the inevitable outcome of October a bloody dictatorial regime? My 'subjective hypothesis'—and mine alone among the readers of *Pravda*?—is that (a) 'despite the immense sacrifices we haven't achieved socialism in the form in which it was imagined by Lenin and the Leninist guard in the twenties'—hence the necessity of a revolutionary perestroika, (b) the counter-revolutionary path of Stalin and his gigantic apparatus was not historically necessary and thus justified— hence the chance in the course of perestroika to utilise the unrealised, mutilated alternative economic, political, legal, social-psychological possibilities of our country, to regenerate the Leninist principles in new conditions, in part more auspicious than at the end of the twenties and in the thirties, in part much more grave. The issue is not the threat of the formation of an inhuman barracks 'socialism' but the consequences of the long domination of this system, whose underlying causes haven't been eliminated to this day, and which is not hurrying to give way voluntarily to genuine, that is democratic, socialism.

How does my opponent, who heatedly rejected all sorts of 'untruth and half-truth,' object to this position, which I hope is sufficiently clear? That 'having at our disposal the Leninist orientation of building socialism' 'we couldn't, we weren't able to be completely consistent successors, the external circumstances didn't give us such a chance ... and as a result we got a deformed socialist society'. 'Us', 'we' ... well isn't that fascinating? 'We' the millions of *zeks* [slang for prisoners] under the leadership of Yagoda, Yezhov, Beria. 'Us', this unfortunate enslaved and robbed peasantry, annihilated as a class under the leadership of Stalin and the Stalinist 'cohort'. 'Us', that is a thoroughly great revolution betrayed and flouted in its enthusiasm, in its unreasoning faith, with sixty years of unbelief, spiritual devastation and demoralisation of the suffering Soviet people grafted on—*together with* those who gave the orders! Oh, comrade P. Kuznetsov! Thank you so much for this far from doubtful and incorrect elucidation.

It is necessary to bear in mind that Stalin replaced NEP, converted (no, not alone, but at the head of a whole social layer) the Bolshevik party into an 'order of sword-carriers', dismantled the union with the peasantry, placed the workers under barracks discipline, crushed or annihilated the intelligentsia, set up foundations of a state of blood and fear—for he 'didn't succeed in being a consistent successor' in relation to the 'Leninist guide lines' ... and in fact this 'inconsistent' transformation of social guide lines into totalitarian and terrorist ones was, we are told, 'historically necessary'.

If this 'inconsistency' 'departure' was, moreover, justified by the 'circumstances', if 'we,' even being imprisoned, like you, my optimistic opponent, in a camp, 'did not turn from the path opened by October' then, my God, what conceptions about this path, about October, about Lenin, are there in such formulas and incantations, widely disseminated by us?

What use are the phrases which refer to 'bitter mistakes and tragic crimes of the past', phrases no one can manage to do without today—if 'we' (and P. Kuznetsov) can't manage to think anything at all through to the end?

And I—not at all wishing 'this question to be consciously left without an answer'—say, and let this opinion be shared by a great many without fright: I don't consider the society created in our country socialist, however 'deformed'. 'Deformation' touches its vital foundations, political system, relations of productions and decidedly everything else. This is not a disarming conclusion, in so far as coming to it, however bitter and frightening it may sound, is only unsatisfactory to the propagandists of the 'half-truths'. We, not all the inhabitants of the country, but the conscious fighters for perestroika, and with time, one must hope, the vast majority of the population, will find in ourselves the strength, theoretical approaches and adequate political tactics, to roll out anew on the socialist road. Only then will our understanding and determination on the really revolutionary reconstruction become sober, real and therefore hope-inspiring. I am convinced that otherwise—through lullabying or self-interested half-truths we will come only to half measures, and thus to the downfall of our last historical attempt to get out of the terrible cul-de-sac.

And the pain, anxiety and hope in me, and in my fellow citizens, is too great to spend the rest of the space in the article on a trivial polemic with P. Kuznetsov about the numerous logical sleights-of-hand in his 'Letter to an Historian'. Well, Lenin himself said in 1923 that 'we are compelled to acknowledge a *radical change* in our entire view of socialism' (my italics—Yu. A.), but P. Kuznetsov prefers to call this 'correction by practice' and 'reinterpretation' of the previous, that is war-communist, conceptions. In that connection the sick Lenin had only begun to consider the political side (the guarantee) of this 'radical change' and Vladimir Ilich couldn't possibly even dream of the post-Stalin and post-Brezhnev situation. So a *contemporary* theory of socialism (I consider, as before, despite P. Kuzentsov) must be created *anew* with the help of Lenin, and not simply sought in his works.

Take, for example, such a joyous cry by P. Kuznetsov: 'In our literature there is already sufficiently detailed research which shows on what wave Stalinism and the cult of the personality arose, what role the character of Stalin played and what role objective circumstances.' Some two months ago party historical science, in the person of V.I. Kasyanenko, came to the conclusion that 'historians still have few documents, few conceptions, ideas and evaluations of the periods and events to truthfully and fully reveal the condition of society and the party'. I regret that I remain in ignorance about what 'detailed research' rectified this position.

But, I repeat, let's abandon this bookish wordplay. There are after all not only 'questions to an historian' but 'perplexed questions' to, as we customarily express it, 'someone' of our leading ideologues and politicians. With great respect I would like to understand the following assertion heard 'somewhere' not long ago. Has the direct strength called forth by the resistance of anti-perestroika forces increased recently, as determined in the

Pravda leader of 5 April—or is this idea 'tossed out' to us? And are there divergences on basic principles [within the Politburo—TA]? If this is denied, if one declares that there is no divergence, and that a real and growing threat to perestroika isn't strength (a threat *not* from the direction of Nina Andreeva but from those who stood with the modest chemistry lecturer and turned her letter into an instruction, which was used there and then by more than thirty regional [oblast] committees of the CPSU)—then is it necessary to look for a more eloquent confirmation that a divergence does *exist*, and a threat: so far as the direct challenge of the *Pravda* article referred to.*

Furthermore, if the idea of the strengthening of the resistance to perestroika is analogous to the Stalinist 'conception' of growing class struggle under socialism let someone (not necessarily P. Kuznetsov, although it's about precisely this, and not Yuri N. Afanas'yev's article, that he should appropriately be disturbed), let someone dispel my other perplexing question: Stalin advanced his 'theory' one and a half decades *after* the victory of October; maybe perestroika triumphed fifteen years ago? And we have in mind now the resistance which spilled over in the beginning of the Seventies to civil servants' pensions? Or does the resistance growing as before really represent forces in relation to the state power, beginning to take the threat of a revolutionary transformation seriously?

And another thing: if 'someone' now has to retire on a personal pension, would this be a return to the terror against the party's Leninist cadres? Or is retirement—as opposed to hard labour or the firing squad—somehow compatible with popular power and normal political struggle?

And another thing: is the idea of market socialism one which we achieved ourselves through suffering through all our history—or is it, as before, a diversionary idea of the enemies of the USSR?

And another thing: if some purported improvements in the economy may be proved to be a certain percentage increase, fulfillment and other things, and the like, then after all they informed us of a not bad percentage five or ten years ago. And had the structural reform begun? Let's answer simply: has the food and industrial goods situation become better, even by 'a little'; do people live more easily, than three years ago? From the 'percentage increase in the productivity of labour' about which domestic statistics inform us, you can't cook borscht and feet aren't shod, otherwise we would long ago have had social prosperity. Urgent and sharp measures are essential, so that people will actually experience the results of perestroika in that and in much else—for example, in the explosive sphere of national relations.

As you please, P. Kuznetsov, but I, seeing that after seventy years movement toward socialism (and not from it) by 'Leninist guidelines' (in

*(This figure rests on the author's conscience. We didn't find confirmation of these facts. *Editors*)

these cases it's usually explained among people: 'it would be curious to
listen to what a stunned Lenin would say, if he were to be resurrected
now (... and how would he be called to order by, let's say, P. Kuznetsov?)),
seeing a ration system in 1988 and the dreams of Russians in the multi-
millioned backwoods for a stick of adulterated limp sausage; seeing that
thirty-five years after the death of Stalin we are only just 'learning
democracy', resembling fifteen-year old adolescents in beginning classes,
and so far getting a barely passing grade ['three'], I would be ashamed to
explain the 'forced inconsistency' and 'deformations' on an unchanging
glorious path. Much has changed over the last three years—and we no
longer have the power to give up hope. Hope for socialism. For free labour,
for prosperity, for democracy.

There are so many questions to historians, and questions to politicians.
And the answers are diverse and disputed. However I think there is
something indisputable. It's this: either socialism was 'barracks socialism'
(that is 'on the one hand', half a jar of honey, 'on the other hand', half
tar)—and here we'll have a look at the answer in ten years, or five years ...
Or we'll become a completely different country, an unrecognisably
different and prosperous society ... or we'll continue our deep reasoning
about the well known 'inconsistency' of socialism without freedom and
without bread without butter. Only is there much time left to us historians
for such intoxicating casuistry?

If the idea of socialism after all that's been endured is still taken to heart,
let's, dear comrade Pobisk Kuznetsov and sympathising comrades, clean it
off and put it aside for a better future. Maybe it will prove useful.

Reply to Yuri Afanasiev

From the editors of *Pravda*

So then, questions posed, answers received. It's possible to put a full stop
there and leave it to the readers to judge about the rightness or wrongness of
the points of view presented. However a newspaper can't keep silent
concerning some of Professor Yuri Afanasiev's judgments.

To the question contained in P. Kuznetsov's article, whether the society
created in our country is (or was) socialist Professor Afanasiev quite
definitely and categorically declares: 'I don't consider the society created
socialist, even if "deformed". Has Yuri Afanasiev really 'forgotten' about
such defined features of our social order as the socialist system of economy,
based on social ownership of the means of production, the absence of
exploiting classes and unemployment, about how such characteristics as
the absence of exploitation of man by man and fundamentally new
economic and social goals were confirmed with the very first steps of
socialism in the USSR and remain unchanged? It's doubtful that the matter
here is one of forgetfulness.

There is probably no need to recall one more time that the 'cancelling out
of reality' is by no means the best method of scientific discussion, that such
an approach doesn't answer to the goals and tasks of perestroika, the

revolutionary renewal of socialism, begun by the initiative of, and under the leadership of, the party. It's generally known that this process isn't progressing simply, that there are still not tangible improvements everywhere, that the revolutionary transformation has still not been made irreversible. There are many things in store to be done, in order to overcome the deep inhibiting processes, to link up and in some ways to work out the renewal mechanisms. But perestroika progresses, millions of Soviet people take part in it, striving to add their effort, their knowledge, experience, and energy to this historic concern. The party directs and spurs a genuine creative search in all directions, including a serious scientific analysis of the past from a Marxist-Leninist position, its lessons and the tasks flowing out of this for today. It is only in this way that profound results answering to the demands of perestroika can be achieved.

From Yuri Afanasiev's statement, and it is necessary for readers to pay attention to this, flows his special views on perestroika, his claim to a special place in interpreting its tasks. It turns out that only if you agree with his assertions and evaluations, 'Only then will our attention and resoluteness about a really revolutionary perestroika become sober, real and therefore reassuring.' He appeals to us to relate to his statement 'without fright', for, however bitter and frightening this conclusion may sound, only those not satisfied by propagandistic 'half-truths', 'we,—not all the inhabitants of the country, but the conscious fighters for perestroika, and, with time, one must hope, the immense majority of the population—will find in ourselves the strength to roll out again on the socialist road'. It's not difficult to see that his 'platform' is strikingly different from one worked out collectively, with a sense of historical responsibility and on the basis of historical truth, party evaluations and conclusions, from an objective, dialectical picture of our achievements and failures, heavy ordeals and undoubted feats on the road of socialist construction, its heroism and drama. And the main thing is that in this and other Afanasiev articles, in his numerous speeches and interviews, where the author isn't reticent in expressing similar positions, which are even intentionally given a sharp provocative character by him, it is difficult, if it is at all possible to find a constructive approach, a serious scientific analysis of concrete facts and documents. But it's agreed that without this there isn't and can't be real science, real participation in a scientific search in the interests of perestroika.

In his answers Yuri Afanasiev touches upon interpretations of alternatives in the country's development, on the choice implemented by the Party at the end of the Twenties. Analysing past history in connection with the seventieth anniversary of the October Revolution the leadership of the Party gave an answer to the question whether it was possible in those conditions, taking into account the totality of internal and international realities, to choose another course than that which was proposed by the party: if we want to keep to historical method, life's truth, there can only be one answer: no, it wasn't possible. It was on precisely this road that it was possible to save the homeland from mortal danger, to save socialism for the future. Together with this there were enormous losses along our path, grievous mistakes and miscalculations, mass repressions, crimes. Hence perestroika is understood as the overcoming of phenomena alien to socialism, as the renewal of socialist society, as the restoration on the theoretical and practical level of the Leninist conception of socialism.

Such an interpretation of the historical choice, about which he speaks with such definiteness, doesn't satisfy Professor Afanasiev. He doesn't evidently grasp first of all in the history of the country that immense conscious activity which the people carried out under the leadership of the party, and the repression and crimes are regarded as the main determining feature of development. With such an approach it isn't possible to see the real content of the historical process in all its fullness and contradictions. And it's not accidental that the leadership of the Party, revealing the full weight of the Stalinist crimes, along with this indicated the historical significance of the conscious socialist activity of the people, the vitality of the plans put forward by the party, understood and grasped by the masses, the slogans, in which the revolutionary spirit of October was expressed.

Reading the article it's impossible not to notice that it was written by a very angry person, that the author is ready to register his opponent as a supporter of Nina Andreeva, and to ascribe to him things he did not say. What is Yuri Afanasiev so angry at? If the questions put showed him, as he writes, unmasked, then after all he hasn't hid his views before, and doesn't in the present article. Evidently, the conception of perestroika as the restoration of the Leninist conception of socialism, the cleansing of the socialism which has been constructed of alien deposits, the elimination of the alienation of the working person from ownership and power, etc., etc. for some reason or other doesn't suit the author. Trying to prove that it's necessary to begin everything all over again, to create anew a contemporary theory of socialism 'with the help of Lenin', Yuri Afanasiev at the same time repudiates him in the availability of a conception of socialism. One can't, he says, 'simply seek' in Lenin's works. But whoever today considers that the Leninist inheritance may be studied 'simply', mechanically, not in a dialectical interaction with contemporaneity?

With all his claims to objectivity and directness the author allows some evident distortion of some positions in his opponent's article. Thus he declares that he accuses him of doubtful hypotheses and even in places untruth. In reality the article affirms in the most general form, not in relation to Yuri Afanasiev, that complicated, debatable questions must be decided on the basis of a study of the facts, arguments and practical experience. Flights of fantasy, extremely doubtful hypotheses, and even in places untruth and half-truth don't aid the issue. Isn't that really so?

And finally, on the sufficiently caustic rejoinder by Yuri Afanasiev, who writes as if the author of the article in *Pravda* speaks of the possibility of 'interweaving' and 'combining' enthusiasm and repression. The question is posed, to put it mildly, incorrectly, for in the article the issue was on different terms. And it's necessary to look for the answer in history itself, in how 'it was on earth'. It's possible to adduce a multitude of facts, attested to by contemporaries, which convincingly show that millions of people joined with real enthusiasm in the construction of Soviet industry, in the realisation of the socialist transformation, conscious that they were joining in a great historic matter. And they completed this, overcoming enormous difficulties, including the creation of an atmosphere of repression and lawlessness, the centralised administrative command system, various sorts of deformations and deviations from socialism, which brought the people harsh losses. Can one speak ironically about the feat of a people, achieved in these hard circumstances, can you forget about it? History is irreversible, you can't correct it, you can't do it over—it's necessary to deeply, responsibly comprehend it, and to extract the lessons, as the party and people are doing today.

As regards the 'perplexing' questions posed by Yuri Afanasiev, there are answers to them. Yes anti-perestroika forces are still alive, and it's necessary to fight energetically against them. And commodity-money relations are inherent in socialism, it's necessary to use them skilfully in the framework of planned production. And structural reforms of the economy, the political system, the laws are being implemented. Whether successfully is another question, which *Pravda* seeks to answer in its publications.

Pravda, 26 July 1988

IV

A Note on Trotsky and Bukharin

In retrospect it is easy to see that one of the great tragedies of the Soviet Twenties was the failure of Stalin's opponents to understand that their first task was to form a united bloc against him and to end the tyranny of the apparatus over the party masses, as a crucial first step to revive political life in the country as a whole. The two letters from Trotsky to Bukharin that are contained in the following appendix are thus interesting on both a political and a psychological level. From the first letter it is abundantly clear that the basis for the Stalinisation of the party was established during Lenin's lifetime. The bureaucratic counter-revolution from above, in other words, was helped by the way in which the Leningrad and Moscow parties were operating in the mid-Twenties. It is true that to succeed the Stalinist counter-revolution had to destroy millions of people and this entailed destroying the old Bolsheviks, thus erasing the historic memory of the Party and the Revolution. There are lessons in this for the reformers. Stalin killed millions in order to establish his rule. The present leaders need to restore the political life of the people and encourage mass mobilisations so that the remnants of Stalinism can be finally laid to rest!

The stereotypes of Trotsky are so deeply embedded in the minds of many party intellectuals that it will take a very long time for the prejudices to disappear. This was the case with many Stalinist intellectuals in the West during the Thirties, Forties and Fifties and they believed what they did without a gun pointing at their heads or the threat of the gulag. Trotsky, for instance, is regarded as a 'super-industrialiser' 'an opponent of the peasants', 'a wild adventurer', etc. All these were Stalin's phrases. The differences between Trotsky and Bukharin were indeed very profound on some questions, but these were often not those which were commonly touted by Stalinism. Thus today many of the reformers believe that Trotsky was implacably hostile to any form of market socialism. This is quite simply false. Trotsky was, contrary to popular belief in both the USSR and the West, an amazing realist. Take, for instance, his speech at the Twelfth Party Conference in 1923:

> The first conclusion which should be made from this is the *concentration of industry*, concentrating industry in the next few years on the very best equipped, the very best located geographically in a trade sense, enterprises. This work is being carried out, but slowly, it flags. It does, it is true, come up against the greatest difficulty of a material, as well as political and moral character. We are confronting the necessity to sack workers, [male and female]. This is a hard, very hard nut, for our party to crack in the course of

the next few years. It mustn't, however, be evaded, for it would be the greatest cowardice on the part of the working class as a whole and its party if they were to conceal unemployment, that is to keep in the plants an excess number of workers [male and female], barely working, half-working, a third working, only so as not to doom them to open unemployment. There can be no doubt that hidden unemployment is the worst, the least effective, the most expensive form of social security. First of all, this false form of social security corrupts our economic apparatus, which can't calculate correctly in these conditions. We say completely openly to the workers on this: that only a workers' state can help the unemployed, it will help them, through the trade unions and through the local Soviets, and other ways. But in the given condition of our economy we haven't the strength to run at the present all the industrial apparatus at full strength. . . . It's better, more correct and healthier to directly and openly support the unemployed than by the concealed route. You can't lead the economy with an extinguished torch.*

Or take Trotsky's position on the relationship between the market and the plan, which he stood by till he died:

If there existed a universal brain, registering simultaneously all the processes of nature in society, measuring their dynamics, forecasting the results of their interactions, then such a brain would no doubt concoct a faultless and complete state plan. True the bureaucracy sometimes considers that it has just such a brain. That is why it so easily frees itself from the supervision of the market and of Soviet democracy. The innumerable live participants in the economy, state collective and private, must make known their needs and their relative intensity not only through statistical compilations of planning commissions but directly to the pressure of demand and supply. The plan is checked and to a considerable extent realized through the market. The regulation of the market itself must base itself on the tendencies showing themselves in it. The drafts made in offices must prove their economic rationality through commercial calculation. The economy of the transition period is unthinkable without control by the rouble. Only through the interaction of three elements: state planning, the market, and Soviet democracy, can the economy be correctly controlled in the transition epoch.†

This statement could easily be emblazoned on the banners of perestroika and would receive near-universal support, provided the name of the man who penned these lines was not mentioned! Would Bukharin have disagreed with either of these statements? I think not.

The two letters are clearly designed as an appeal and an olive branch. Trotsky, whose arrogance was well-known, is in these letters appealing to Bukharin for support against the apparatus. Bukharin was tempted to

*Pages 324–5 of Twelfth Congress Stenographic Report, Moscow, 1968 edition. No one disagreed with Trotsky on this. In his summing up he added that Smidovich [who is listed as heading the women worker's department], asked him to bear in mind the need to preserve some female proletarian cadres in the event of redundancies, which he supported [page 414].

†*Bulletin of the Opposition*, 1932, No 31, p. 8.

accept Trotsky's request in the second letter and visit the factory in question, but Stalin persuaded him against the venture. Trotsky's strength lay in his clear understanding that Stalin's strength derived from the apparatus. Why then did he not propose a united front in the party on this single question of party democracy. Factional battles of all sorts, whether they are in political parties or the boardrooms, tend to develop an autonomous logic. Bukharin was viewed by the Left Opposition as the brain behind Stalin. This was not false, but a strategy should have been devised to detach Bukharin from Stalin. These letters indicate that Trotsky was alive to the problem in 1926. In later years the whole question became academic as Bukharin led the Stalinist assault on the party dissidents and thus tragically paved the way for his own liquidation. The failure of these two old Bolsheviks to unite against Stalin was both tragic and fateful. A settling of accounts with the Stalinist legacy requires a just appreciation of the necessity for drawing on all that is positive in both Trotsky and Bukharin's legacy. It is sectarian and dangerous to suppose that either a purely Leninist or a purely Trotskyist or a purely Bukharinite tradition supplies all the answers. Glasnost and perestroika would receive a great deal of nourishment by making available to the Soviet reading public the vast corpus of socialist and Marxist thought that exists without totems or taboos.

I have often wondered what these two old Bolsheviks thought to themselves after they had been politically destroyed by Stalin. Trotsky's life in exile has been covered in great detail and includes a revealing memoir by his wife. There is an image of Bukharin in Vienna in 1913 by Rosa Meyer-Levine which is very striking:

> I first saw Bukharin in Vienna in the winter of 1913-14, at one of those arrangements common in the Russian colonies abroad, literary and political lectures, discussions, occasionally even dances. There used to be quite a few striking faces in the audience, even Trotsky was sometimes present at those gatherings. But Bukharin stood out among them through a quality of his own. There was in his appearance something of a saint, rather than a rebel or a thinker. The image of Count Myshikin of Dostoyevsky's 'Idiot' involuntarily sprang to mind, at least the way the Russian actors tried to portray him. Perhaps this made me detect at once the mainly humanitarian aspect of that unusual man. He was slightly built and looked even younger than his real age, only twenty-six at the time. His open face with the huge forehead and clear shining eyes was in its quieter sincerity sometimes almost ageless.*

For an inner glimpse of Bukharin after the Revolution, we await the forthcoming *Memoirs* by his widow, Anna Larina, due for publication in 1989.

*Quoted in Ken Tarbuck's introduction to Bukharin's *Imperialism and the Accumulation of Capital*, Allen Lane, 1972.

Two Letters from Trotsky to Bukharin

8 January, 1926.

Nikolai Ivanovich:

You will perhaps recall that two years ago during a session of the Politburo at my home I said that the mass of the Leningrad party* was muzzled more than was the case elsewhere. This expression (I confess, a very strong one) was used by me in an intimate circle, just as you used in your personal note the words: 'unconscionable demagogy'.

To be sure, this did not prevent my remark concerning the muzzling of the party mass by the Leningrad party apparatus from being broadcast through meetings and through the press. But this is a special item and—I hope—not a precedent... But doesn't this mean that I did see the actual state of things? However in contrast to certain comrades, I saw it a year and a half, and two and three years ago. At that time, during the same session I remarked that everything in Leningrad goes splendidly (100%) five minutes before things get very bad. This is possible only under a super-apparatus regime. Why then do you say that I did not see the actual state of things? True, I did not consider that Leningrad was separated from the rest of the country by an impenetrable barrier. The theory of a 'sick Leningrad' and a 'healthy country' which was held in high respect under Kerensky was never my theory. I said and I repeat now that the traits of apparatus bureaucratism, peculiar to the whole party, have been brought to their extreme expression in the regime of the Leningrad party. I must however add that in these two and a half years (i.e., since the autumn of 1923) the apparatus-bureaucratic tendencies have grown in the extreme not only in Leningrad but throughout the entire party.

Consider for a moment this fact: Moscow** and Leningrad† two main proletarian centres, adopt *simultaneously* and furthermore *unanimously* (think of it: *unanimously!*) at their district party conferences two resolutions aimed against each other. And consider also this, that our official party mind, represented by the press, does not even dwell on this truly shocking fact.

What are those special (?) social (?!) conditions in Leningrad and Moscow which permit such a drastic and 'unanimous' polar opposition? No one seeks for them, no one asks himself about them. What then is the explanation. Simply this, that everybody silently says to himself: *the 100 per cent opposition of Leningrad to Moscow is the work of the apparatus*. This, N.I., is the gist of the 'genuine state of things.'

---

*Controlled by Zinoviev-Kamenev allied in 1924 with Stalin.
**Controlled at the time (1926) by Bukharin-Rykov-Uglanov (generally regarded as the Right-wing of the Party) in a bloc with Stalin.
†Controlled at the time (1926) by Zinoviev and Kamenev who had broken with Stalin and entered into a bloc with the Left Opposition.

Byt Leningrad does not stand alone as regards 'day-to-day routine.' In the past year we had on the one hand, the Chita business, and on the other, that in Kherson. Naturally you and I understand that the Chita and Kherson abominations* are exceptions precisely because of their excesses. But these exceptions are *symptomatic*. Could the things that happened in Chita have occurred had there not been among the Chita summits a special, binding, mutual amnesty, with independence from the rank and file as its basis? Did you read the report of Schlichter's investigating committee on Khersonovism? The document is instructive to the highest degree – not only because it characterizes some of the Khersonovist personnel, but also because it characterizes certain aspects of the party regime as a whole. To the question why all the local communists, who had known of the crimes of the responsible workers, kept quiet, apparently for a period of two-three years, Schlichter received the answer: 'Just try to speak up – you will lose your job, you'll get kicked into a village, etc., etc.' I quote, of course, from memory, but that is the gist of it. And Schlichter exclaims apropos of this: 'What! Up to now only oppositionists have told us that for this or that opinion they have been *allegedly* (?!) removed from posts, kicked into a village, etc., etc. But now we hear from party members that they do not protest against criminal actions of leading comrades for fear of being removed, thrown into a village, expelled from the party, etc.' I cite again from memory.

I know that certain comrades, possibly you among them, have been carrying out until recent times a plan somewhat as follows: give the workers in the nuclei the possibility and at the same time, crack down resolutely on every 'opposition' emanating from the upper ranks of the party. In this way, the apparatus-regime as a whole was to be preserved by providing it with a broader base. *But this experiment was not at all successful.* The methods and habits of the apparatus-regime inevitably seep down from the top. If every criticism of the Central Committee and even criticism inside the Central Committee is equated, under all conditions, to a factional struggle for power, with all the ensuing consequences, then the Leningrad Committee will carry out the self-same policy in relation to those who criticize it in the sphere of its plenipotentiary powers, and under the Leningrad Committee there are districts and sub-districts.

When in 1923 the opposition arose in Moscow (without the aid of the local apparatus, and against its resistance) the central and local apparatus brought the bludgeon down on Moscow's skull under the slogan: 'Shut up! You do not recognize the peasantry.' In the same apparatus-way you are now bludgeoning the Leningrad organization, and crying, 'Shut up! You don't recognize the middle peasant.' You are thus terrorizing in two main

---

*In 1925–26 numerous cases were laid bare of criminal abuse of power by ranking provincial bureaucrats. The Chita and Kherson affairs were the most notorious instances at the time of corruption, grafting, terrorization of the party membership and of the populace, and other crimes. A comparison with the Uzbek–Moscow mafia scandal of today would be extremely revealing.

centres of proletarian dictatorship the best proletarian elements, re-educating them from expressing aloud not only their views, correct or erroneous alike, but also their alarm concerning the general questions of the revolution and socialism. And meanwhile, the democratic rights granted to the rural areas are entrenched.

Can't you see all the dangers that flow from this?

4 March, 1926
Personal

N(ikolai) Ivanovich,

I write this letter in longhand (although I have grown unaccustomed to it) inasmuch as it is embarrassing to dictate to a stenographer what I have to say.

You are of course aware that in accordance with the Uglanov* line there is being conducted against me in Moscow a half-concealed struggle with all sorts of sallies and insinuations which I refrain from characterizing here as they deserve.

By all sorts of machinations—in part and wholly unworthy of and degrading to our organization—I am not permitted to speak at workers' meetings. At the same time rumours are being spread systemically through the workers' nuclei that I give lectures 'for the bourgeoisie' and refuse to speak to workers. Now just listen to what luxuriates on this soil, and this, once again, not at all accidentally. I cite verbatim from a letter of a worker party member.

'In our nucleus the question has been posed why you arrange to give paid reports. The prices of admission to these reports are very high and the workers cannot afford them. Consequently only the bourgeoisie attends. The secretary of our nucleus explains to us in his talks that for these reports you charge fees, percentages for your own benefit. He tells us that for every one of your articles and for your by-line you also take a fee, that you have a big family and, says he, you run shy of funds. Does a member of the Polit-buro really have to sell his by-line? etc., etc. You will ask; isn't this silly nonsense? No, to our sorrow, it is not nonsense. I have verified it. At first it was decided to write a letter to the Central Control Commission (or Central Committee), signed by several members of the nucleus, but then they decided not to, saying: 'They will drive us out of the factory, and we have families'.

In this way a fear has seized the worker-party member that if he tries to verify the mot infamous slander against a member of the Politburo he, a party member, can be driven from the factory for following party

*Uglanov was one of the Right-wing leaders of the inquisitions and purges against the Left Opposition during the period of the Right-Centre Bloc (1925–1929). He openly gave the green light for anti-semitic propaganda to be used against the Left opposition, many of whose leaders and supporters were of Jewish origin as indeed was the case with the party as a whole!

procedure. And you know, were he to ask me, I could not in all sincerity say that this would not happen. The same secretary of the same nucleus says—and again not at all accidentally: 'In the Politburo the sheenies are running wild.' And again no one dared to say anything about it to anyone—for the selfsame openly formulated reason: they will drive us out of the factory.

Another item. The author of the letter which I cited above is a Jewish worker. He, too, did not dare to write about the 'sheenies who agitate against Leninism.' The motive is as follows: 'If the others, the non-Jews, keep quiet it would be awkward for me . . .' And this worker—who wrote me to ask whether it is true that I sell my speeches and my by-line to the bourgeoisie—is now also expecting that he will be driven any hour from the factory. This is a fact. Another fact is that I am not at all sure that this won't happen—if not immediately, then a month from now; there are plenty of pretexts. And everybody in the nucleus knows 'that's how it was, that's how it will be'—and they hang their heads.

In other words: members of the communist party are afraid to report to the party organs about Black-Hundred agitation, thinking that it is they who will be driven out and not the Black-Hundred gangster.

You will say: Exaggeration! I, too, would like to think so. Therefore I have a proposal to make: Let us both take a trip to the nucleus and check up on it. I think that you and I—two members of the Politburo—have after all a few things in common, enough to calmly and conscientiously verify: whether it is true, whether it is possible that in our party, in Moscow, in a workers' nucleus, propaganda is being conducted with impunity which is vile and slanderous, on the one hand, and antisemitic, on the other; and that honest workers are afraid to question or to verify or try to refute any stupidity, lest they be driven into the street with their families. Of course you can refer me to the 'proper bodies.' But this would signify only closing the vicious circle.

I want to hope that you will not do this; and it is precisely this hope which prompts this letter.

INDEX